SENTIMENTAL JOURNEY

Books by Martin W. Bowman include:

Fields of Little America
Castles In The Air
Home By Christmas?
The Bedford Triangle
The Men Who Flew The Mosquito
Confounding the Reich (with Tom Cushing)
Wild Blue Yonder – Glory Days of the 8th AF In England
Remembering D-Day: Personal Histories of Everyday Heroes

Sentimental Journey
Reminiscences of War

Martin W. Bowman

THE ERSKINE PRESS
2005

SENTIMENTAL JOURNEY

First published in 2005 by
The Erskine Press, The White House, Eccles, Quidenham,
Norfolk NR16 2PB

ISBN 1 85297 089 8

British Library Cataloguing-in-Publication Data
A catalogue record of this book is available
from the British Library

Typeset by Waveney Typesetters, Wymondham, Norfolk
Printed in Great Britain at
the University Press, Cambridge

Contents

HRH Princess Elizabeth and HM Queen Elizabeth during a visit to an American base in 1944

Acknowledgements

I am extremely grateful to the following individuals, living and deceased, for their immense help in preparing this volume. I have met and made lasting friendships with several of these fine people including Yorkshireman Jim Moore, for many years a Norfolk resident, and Larry Goldstein, once of New York City now living in California where he was recently elected President of the 8th Air Force Historical Society. I will never forget the great times 'Goldie' and I had when he showed me around the city that never sleeps. I am also greatly indebted to Mike Bailey, the well known Norwich aviation artist for the kind loan of photographs and for advice and permission to use his painting of *Lady Jane* on p. 181 and my Dutch friend and fellow author, Theo Boiten. I must also single out Forrest S. Clark of Florida who once flew from Shipdham, Norfolk. Forrest has been a fund of stories for several years. I am proud to know him and to be able to include his wonderful anecdotes here. I am equally appreciate of the efforts of all the following:

Ben Alexander; Mel Bourne; Don Bruce; Dick Butler; Bob Collis; Nora Norgate Canfield; Harry Castledine; Richard Clements; Derrick Coleman; Derek Daniels; Harry H. Darrah; William Donald; Ralph H. Elliott; Bill Gibbons; Graham and Anne Simons of GMS Enterprises; Larry Goldstein; Jackson W. Granholm; Leo Hawel; Russ D. Hayes; Gerhard Heilig; Lawrence Jenkins; Loren E. Jackson; Myron Keilman; Beirne Lay Jr.; General Andy S. Low; John B. 'Buff' Maguire; George Makin; Newton L. McLaughlin; Jim 'Dinty' Moore DFC; Bill Odell; Richard Olsen; Simon Parry; Sheila Peal; Jack Peppiatt; Russell Reeve; Connie and Gordon Richards; Keith Roberts; Ann K. Spredbury; Max Stout; William van Dijik; Hank Wentland; Alfred Plank von Bachselten; Peter and Lisa Worby; Joe Wroblewski.

1

BLENHEIM BOYS

Jim 'Dinty' Moore, DFC

On Monday 28 August 1939, having been advised to report to the Recruiting Depot at Bradford, Yorkshire, Jim 'Dinty' Moore caught the train from his home in Hawes at the head of Wensleydale and set off on the first leg of a journey that would last six years and five months. He was nineteen. During the summer of 1939 the nineteen-year-old had been accepted as a wireless operator. AC2 Moore's feelings were a mixture of excitement and apprehension, and he certainly had no idea that within twelve months he would be flying over Western Europe as a member of the crew of a Bristol Blenheim.

'I was at Padgate, a training establishment on the outskirts of Warrington, when on Sunday morning, 3 September, the radio in my hut was switched on and instead of the normal programmes serious music was being played. It was then solemnly announced that the nation was to be addressed by the Prime Minister, Neville Chamberlain. His address began, "This morning the British Ambassador to Berlin handed the German Government a final note saying that unless we hear from them by 11 o'clock that they were prepared, at once, to withdraw their troops from Poland, a state of war would exist between us. I have to tell you that no such undertaking has been received and that, consequently, this country is at war with Germany."

'The remainder of his speech was drowned by cheers and excited conversation for, it must be remembered, we were all youngsters who were actually excited at the prospect of being at war with our old enemy. Considering that the last war, the war to end all wars, had ended only twenty years earlier with an appalling loss of life, we should have had a clearer idea of the reality of war.'

The Advanced Air Striking Force and 70 Wing RAF went to France to support the British Expeditionary Force (BEF) but, generally speaking, Germany was content to carry on preparing and planning for their forthcoming *Blitzkrieg*. The allies, on the other hand, would not allow themselves to believe that the war would ever really start in earnest. Leaders like Chamberlain seemed to believe that his appeals to the German people for peace would be accepted. The period became known as the 'Phoney War', when little aggressive action was taken by either side in the conflict. Chamberlain claimed that 'Hitler has missed the bus' but on 9 April 1940 Norway was invaded by the Germans and on 10 May the 'Phoney War' ended with the German western offensive and the invasion of Holland, Belgium and Luxembourg. Chamberlain resigned that same day and Winston Churchill took over as British Prime Minister. German armour penetrated the French line near Sedan and began its thrust to the coast. Holland capitulated on 15 May in the face of the onslaught and on 28 May Belgium surrendered. On 26 May, two days before, it was decided to evacuate as many British troops as possible from Dunkirk. By 4 June 338,226 troops had been rescued.

During his training as a wireless operator/air gunner at No. 5 Bombing and Gunnery School at Jurby near Ramsay on the Isle of Man AC2 Jim Moore had heard glowing reports on the wireless about the exploits of the RAF and the 'Miracle of Dunkirk'. After a brief sojourn at home in Hawes Jim Moore entrained for 17 OTU Upwood, proudly wearing his wireless-operator and air gunner badges on his uniform. However, when he entered the carriage some soldiers who had just returned from Dunkirk belligerently enquired, 'Where the blazes were you lot?' or words to that effect.

   'We had also been told of the magnificent efforts of the RAF in covering the withdrawal. It was therefore a sobering experience when, on the train to Upwood, I met some of the survivors from the Dunkirk beaches who made some very uncomplimentary remarks about the lack of air support they had received. Neither they nor I had any idea how few operational aircraft were available to the RAF at that time.'[1]

After brushing up his gunnery skills at Squires Gate aerodrome near Blackpool, Jim Moore, now a Sergeant, was posted with his crew, on 12 August 1940, to 18 Squadron flying Blenheims at RAF West Raynham in Norfolk.

   'Sergeant Roger Speedy was a very competent pilot who came from Worcester. Sergeant Bob Weston, from Coventry, was an extremely good navigator. Squadron Leader Deacon, a rather reserved, fatherly figure was in charge of A Flight to which we were allocated.'

   18 Squadron, like every other unit in the AASF, had been badly mauled in France, losing nine aircraft and their crews during the month of May. Personnel had arrived in England in just the clothes they stood up in and, with only three

---

[1] On 22 June 1940 France concluded an Armistice with Germany and in Britain the threat of invasion became very real. Hitler had to have air supremacy over Britain before any invasion could be attempted. The British Army withdrew from the Continent and Winston Churchill declared *…the Battle of France is over; the Battle of Britain is about to begin.*

'A' flight, 18 Squadron, West Raynham, September 1940
Sgt R. Weston, back row 4th from right; Sgt R. Speedy, middle row, 4th from right, Sgt J. Moore, front row, 4th from right.

Blenheims left, they had finally decamped to West Raynham where the painful task of rebuilding the squadron was taking place. Jim Moore and his crew were unaware of the dreadful losses suffered by the Blenheim squadrons. 2 Group had lost 31 aircraft in July with three written off because of battle damage and four in accidents. Three wing commanders, 15 other officers and 40 sergeants had also been killed. They also had no idea that the 'powers that be' had decided that most of the squadrons in 2 Group were to go over to night operations. Jim Moore was '…acutely aware that I had just 56 hours by day and just 3 hours 50 minutes at night under my belt.'

In the summer of 1940, people expected Hitler's army to arrive at any time but the *Nazi* invasion never came. Churchill refused to consider peace on German terms and Hitler realized that he might have to invade Britain. He code-named his invasion *Seelowe* (Sea Lion). If the *Luftwaffe* failed to win control of the skies, an invasion would be impossible because German invaders would be under constant air attack. *Reichsmarschall* Hermann Göring believed that the *Luftwaffe* would easily defeat the Royal Air Force, and so the German army and navy prepared to invade. By 6 September, a huge German invasion fleet appeared to be ready to sail. British forces were put on 'Alert No. 2', meaning that an attack was probable in the next three days.

As the *Luftwaffe* attacks started in July 1940 many worked to defend Britain, to prevent a German invasion and to support The Few – the pilots of RAF Fighter Command. Despite 16 tense weeks of fighting and bombing, the *Luftwaffe* failed to defeat Fighter Command. By October, Hitler accepted that the invasion was impossible, and he postponed the operation.

Throughout the Battle of Britain the Blenheim crews were among the little publicised units which also stood ready to defeat the German invasion should it come. On 16 August 1940 Jim Moore in 18 Squadron at West Raynham looked at the Battle Order.

'There were our names at the top of the list of six crews detailed to fly on operations that night. I don't know about Roger Speedy and Bob Weston but I do know my feelings were a strange mixture of excitement and apprehension. This was it, this was what we had been preparing for and above all there was a feeling of expectancy. Time almost seemed to stand still though eventually we were called to the Operations Room where there was a buzz of conversation as we awaited our briefing. Behind a raised dais was a curtain which was unveiled, after the CO took his place, to reveal, not surprisingly, a map of Western Europe. He indicated that our target was the *Luftwaffe* aerodrome at De Kooy in Holland. After the CO's opening address, the Met Officer gave us his weather forecast including details of the winds we could expect. It was then the turn of the Intelligence Officer to advise us about known anti-aircraft concentrations and so on. The actual course to and from the target was left to the individual crew as we shared the skies over Western Europe throughout that winter with a limited number of Wellingtons, Whitleys and Hampdens, which represented the heavy bombers of the RAF. Those of us who had the privilege of flying in the Blenheim developed a real affection for these machines.

'This was the first time the squadron had operated at night so it was a new experience for all concerned. We were due to take off at 2100. During the evening we got our flying gear together, emptied our pockets of any item which might be of interest to the enemy, and, as we would be flying at heights of up to 10,000ft, put on sufficient clothing to keep warm. The minutes ticked slowly by until the flight truck was ready to take us out to the dispersal point where our aircraft *L-Leather* was waiting. She was still painted with daylight camouflage although later the underside of the wings were painted a non-reflective black. The ground crew fussed around, making sure everything was in order whilst we climbed in. Bob and I stowed our parachutes, settled into our positions and I switched on the radio and we conversed over the intercom to make sure it was working.

'Roger started up the engines in turn, revving them up to a healthy roar, to make sure they were in order. At a signal from him, one of the ground crew removed the chocks from the front of the landing wheels. We then taxied out to the boundary fence, turning into wind to await our signal to take off. On seeing the signal from our flight controller Roger revved up the engines again before releasing the brakes, and we started to move, gaining speed as we headed across the field until we lifted off over the far hedge. Roger flew back over the aerodrome before turning on to the first course Bob had given him, gaining height as we flew towards the coast. It was still daylight and looking down at the fields, houses and villages, they seemed to assume a special significance. I still felt the thrill of flying but this was something new, an adventure which for us was into the unknown. What exactly was waiting for us on the other side of the North Sea? As I looked back at the coast of Norfolk I couldn't help wondering if I would ever see it again.

'We droned on over the sea, gradually losing height on the course dictated by Bob, as the daylight faded. My responsibilities were to search the sky for enemy night fighters and to listen out on the radio in case there were any messages for us.

I had, after checking with Roger, fired a short burst from my machine gun, once we were over the sea, to make sure it was working satisfactorily. In due course I heard Bob say we could see the Dutch coast and we were making our correct landfall. Turning the turret around to look ahead I could clearly see the coastline in the moonlight just as if I was looking at a large map.

'Our arrival had not gone unnoticed and soon we could see the beams of search-lights, accompanied by bursts of inaccurate flak, probing the sky looking for us. The light flak was multi-coloured, rather like some of the rockets on bonfire night, whereas the heavy flak bursts left ominous-looking small black clouds.

'Bob had given Roger a new course in crossing the coast so we were now heading for the target where we hoped to dish out treatment to the *Luftwaffe*, in the same way they had been bombing our aerodromes in East Anglia. On the final run up to the target Roger kept the aircraft in a straight run responding to Bob's instructions: "Steady-steady-left-steady" and so forth, until I heard him say, "Bombs Gone!" Our aircraft lifted, relieved of the weight of our four 250lb bombs. It had been, as it always would be, an uncomfortable few minutes on the bombing run, as there was no question of taking evasive action to avoid the flak and we were at our most vulnerable. Having delivered our bombs, feeling very relieved, we turned on to another course for home.

'We had turned on to this course when, to my surprise, I saw the silhouette of a single-engined fighter in the moonlight behind and slightly above us. It was the accepted policy to avoid combat with fighters if possible so, resisting the natural temptation to open fire, I gave Roger directions to take evasive action and we soon lost him. This brief encounter made me appreciate how absolutely vital it was for me never to relax and to keep searching the sky.

'We crossed the Dutch coast, heading for home, when Bob asked me to get a radio fix. I contacted the wireless station at Bircham Newton, near Hunstanton, requesting a fix. On receiving an acknowledgement, I was required to press my Morse key for a few seconds, during which time two ground stations took bearings on our position. Where these two bearings crossed fixed our position on the map and the operator sitting comfortably on the ground supplied these details to me. I passed on this information to Bob who could then check if we were on course or whether we needed to make any correction. Soon I heard Bob say he could see the coast of Norfolk and shortly afterwards he asked me to contact the operator at West Raynham to get a bearing to take us home. I felt rather pleased with myself for getting the necessary information on this, our first operational flight.

'Finally, we could see our aerodrome identification letters being flashed in Morse code from the beacon near the field and, on the ground, the lights of the kerosene lamps which had been lit on the edge of the runway to guide us in. Roger made a perfect landing, taxi-ing to our dispersal point where our ground crew were anxiously waiting to greet us. It was a marvellous feeling to climb out of the kite, feeling stiff, after a flight of three hours and 15 minutes but we had really made it. We were now an operational crew. No sooner had we left the aircraft than the ground crew were refuelling and 'bombing it up' again, a practice which was to continue until the threat of invasion faded. We were looking forward eagerly to our first operational breakfast of bacon and eggs in the Sergeant's Mess, which no doubt would be accompanied by a great deal of excited conversation going on over the events of the night, but first we had to attend de-briefing. We gave the Intelligence Officer details of the operation. He was particularly interested in the fighter I had seen. We then discovered that we were the only aircraft which had been on operations as the trip for the other five crews on the Battle Order had been cancelled after we became airborne!

'During August the squadron dispatched 62 aircraft on operations, losing four and their crews, none of whom we had the opportunity to really get to know. During the latter part of the month we moved our squadron's aircraft to a temporary aerodrome at Great Massingham, some 3 miles from West Raynham. The object of the exercise was to spread our aircraft to minimize the damage that could be caused by attacks from enemy bombers. Apart from the landing field, there were none of the buildings one found on a permanent 'drome, only a few Nissen huts. It was necessary, therefore, to find accommodation for us in the lovely little villages of Great Massingham and Little Massingham which adjoined the airfield. They were so close, in fact, that the roofs of one row of cottages were damaged, from time to time, by the trailing aerials of Blenheims when the WOP/AG had forgotten to wind them in as, of course, he should have done before coming in to land.

'On 1 September 1940, on attending our briefing, we were informed that we were to make our first visit to the Ruhr, the industrial heart of Germany. The Met Officer advised us that the weather would be clear all the way to and from the target. At 2130 hours we took off as planned, climbing steadily to our operational height of between 10,000 and 12,000ft, droning steadily along the North Sea. On arrival over the Dutch coast we found we were flying over a solid bank of cloud which rendered the enemy searchlights useless, although some bursts of flak lit up the sky. Roger flew on in the faint hope of finding a gap in the cloud through which Bob could identify our target. We stooged around for ages, without any luck, before turning for home. Finally, in the region of Schiphol in Holland, we at last found a gap in the cloud through which a bunch of searchlights did their best to latch on to us. Not wishing to take our bombs home Bob lined up the aircraft onto the source of this nuisance and dropped our full load on them.

'By this time our true position had, due to cloud over which we were again flying, become a matter of guesswork so the radio fix I was able to obtain from Bircham Newton was particularly helpful. We found our way back over the North Sea. Looking forward to touching down at Massingham I received a signal informing us that due to the weather this was not practicable. We were directed to Honington, not far from Massingham, the home of a Wellington squadron where we were very thankful to land. We were made very welcome and managed to get a little sleep before flying home.

'A few days after the fall of France, the Germans started moving hundreds of barges, each 300ft long, along the canals of Western Europe towards the North Sea and the Channel ports. These enormous barges were essential to the German invasion force, which they intended to land on the shores of our embattled island. These concentrations of barges were to be the focus of the attention of all the squadrons in Bomber Command during September. We were briefed as to the type of attacks we would be required to make on German naval vessels and troop carrying craft. We were also advised that, should the invasion take place, we would be moving to an aerodrome near Exeter.

'The Germans had either installed or seized from the French some heavy naval guns at Cap Gris Nez on the French coast, which had formed the unpleasant habit of shelling shipping passing through the Straits of Dover and the town of Dover itself. We made three trips in August-September to bomb these guns and followed with attacks on barge concentrations in the ports of Dunkirk, which we visited three times, Flushing, Boulogne, Ostend and Calais. On these trips, which took approximately three hours, the defences were very alert with large concentrations of searchlights and pretty spectacular displays of anti-aircraft fire. We hoped we were doing the maximum amount of damage to these barges, which represented such a threat to our island.

'On one of these trips it was still daylight when we clambered into our aircraft to prepare for take off. Roger hadn't started the engines when the anti-aircraft gunners on the 'drome opened fire at some low flying Junkers 88 medium bombers who were paying us a visit. Roger and Bob shot out of their hatch like corks out of a bottle whilst I, hampered by heavy clothing, followed a poor third to take refuge under a heavy log. Not very heroic, although, with the engines switched off, my turret couldn't be operated, so I was unable to fire at the intruders who flew on to

West Raynham where they dropped their bombs but with little damage. During the month the squadron flew 127 sorties with the loss of only one aircraft and crew.

'At the beginning of October the weather was less kind to us and a number of operations had to be cancelled. In fact, the squadron was only able to fly 51 sorties. Roger, Bob and I did, however, make another visit to Cap Gris Nez on 8/9 October, following this with an attack on the docks at Boulogne on 12/13 October. By now the Battle of Britain was over and the immediate threat of invasion had receded, at least for the winter, so the efforts of Bomber Command could be directed at targets of industrial importance in Germany.

'We now had more spare time and while Fakenham and King's Lynn were within easy reach, the most popular venue was the beautiful city of Norwich, some 30 miles away. A number of us would share a taxi there to spend the evening doing what came naturally. Norwich had already been the subject of attacks by German bombers though at that time it was still relatively undamaged. After one low-level attack carried out in daylight, Lord Haw-Haw, in his English broadcast from Berlin, informed us that the crews involved in this raid had reported that the clock on the city hall was slow.

'At 2240 hours on 24 October, in accordance with the Command's new policy, we took off for an attack on the railway yards at Haltern in the heart of the Ruhr where we found that the Germans had been very busy improving their defences. The concentration of flak was not only heavy over the target area but at intervals all the way from the Dutch coast. Nevertheless we were able to deliver our bomb load – everything, including the weather report, going according to schedule. We had been warned that German intruders were attacking our bombers as they were coming into land after operations. It was evident that the WOP/AG could not afford to relax from searching the sky at any time during an operation. The only time I wasn't doing so was when it was imperative to use the radio to get a fix or a bearing.[1]

'Our next operation was on 29 October. Our target was another railway yard, this time at Krefeld, in the Ruhr or, as it was popularly known, the 'Happy Valley'. It was identical to our attack on Haltern and we returned 'in one piece' after a flight of almost four hours. Sometimes, aircrew returning from operations over Western Europe were forced to ditch in the North Sea. The more fortunate ones

---

[1] Three days later, on 27 October, Massingham (and West Raynham) was indeed raided by German intruders. Three aircraft thought to be Ju 88s attacked three times, dropping ten bombs which destroyed one Blenheim and damaged eleven others, although these were soon repaired. Four personnel were killed and seven injured, three seriously.

were able to get out and climb into their inflatable dinghies. On the 31st we were briefed to fly at low-level over the North Sea, in daylight, searching for any aircrew who had managed to survive in this way and were awaiting rescue. We took off at 1055, flying to within sight of the Dutch coast, feeling very much alone, searching the area which had been allocated to us. It seemed strange to be operating in daylight over a sea which looked both cold and cruel without, sadly, having any success. We landed disappointed, back at Massingham. It was at least comforting to know should the same fate befall us we would not be forgotten and there was a chance of being rescued. There are no figures to say how many aircraft and their crews were lost due to faulty weather forecasts but there must have been quite a few.

'The first three operations in November took place in weather which, much to our surprise, was as predicted by our Met officer and we were able to identify and bomb the targets allocated to us. On 5/6 November our target was the oil works at Antwerp, 7/8 November the Krupps armament factory at Essen and on 10/11 November, the docks at Le Havre. As the weather became colder the 'boffins' came up with a variety of bright ideas to make life easier for us aircrew. One, which applied to all of us, was what we would call "Wakey-Wakey" tablets. We took one tablet before take off and another in flight and these were supposed to help us stay alert. This was fine, except on occasions when, having taken the first tablet, the operation was cancelled and you were unable to go to sleep. Another idea was a tot of rum on returning from an operation to 'help the circulation.' We were also encouraged to eat plenty of carrots, which were supposed to improve our night vision and to take a variety of capsules for the same reason. We were also issued with flight rations of which barley sugar was the most popular.

'The WOP/AG had the coldest position in the aircraft, with temperatures down to 10 degrees below zero, so they devised a woollen lined leather suit, with electrically heated gloves and boots. They worked very well although they were so cumbersome you felt as if you were dressed for deep sea diving, which made it especially difficult to operate a wireless set. Whenever possible, rather than wear this outfit we wore three pairs of gloves – the first silk, the second wool, and the third leather, thick woollen underwear, flying suit and boots with thick woollen stockings.

'On 13 November we were briefed for another trip to the Ruhr, so at 0210 we took off and headed for the continent following our usual plan in climbing steadily as we crossed the North Sea. On our arrival over the Dutch coast we encountered dense cloud, over which Roger managed to climb, keeping to the course Bob had worked out for us. We flew on and on searching in vain for a gap in the clouds through which we could identify the target. Finally we did find a small gap through which we could see some searchlights and we dropped our bombs, although where exactly is doubtful. We turned for home, flying over mountains of enormous white clouds, passing between some of them as if we were flying through a valley and watching the sunrise, which was truly beautiful. Wandering about over Western Europe in daylight was not to be recommended and we watched the sky anxiously in case any Luftwaffe fighters had managed to find their way up through the cloud. We were beginning to wonder where the cloud would end when, well out over the North Sea, on our way home, we left it behind. Once again I was able to raise the wireless station at Bircham Newton where the operator was able to provide us with a fix for which Bob was more than usually thankful. Arriving over the Norfolk coast I contacted West Raynham and obtained the necessary bearing to get us home.

'By the time we were coming in to land, we had been in the air for 5 hours 45 minutes and Roger would have been so very weary he must have allowed his concentration to lapse as we landed very heavily. The undercarriage collapsed and we skated merrily across the airfield before coming to a stop. There is always a risk of fire in these circumstances so we wasted no time in getting out, feeling more than thankful we had dropped our bombs somewhere over Germany. The fire tender and sundry ground crew were quickly on the scene and seemed rather frustrated to find us all in one piece. Thankfully there was no fire and the aircraft was soon repaired and back in action.

'Sitting in one position, in cramped conditions, subjected to the severe cold, the noise and smell of the engines, never able to relax and ever conscious of the dangers of flak and enemy fighters, made great physical demands of all three of us but this was especially true of the pilot. There was no automatic pilot, so there was no opportunity for him to relax. We managed to get some sleep before spending an hour carrying out some take-offs and landings, which was the usual practice after this kind of incident. Despite this bumpy landing Bob and I had complete faith in Roger and would not have wanted to fly with anyone else.

'In the early afternoon of 14 November we were briefed for a night raid on enemy airfields. This night the *Luftwaffe* devastated the city centre of Coventry. Plans of the large-scale attack were known in advance because of Ultra intelligence but the knowledge had to be kept secret from the Germans so no additional measures were taken to repel the raid. However, squadrons from 2 Group were directed to attack aerodromes from which the enemy bombers were operating to cause as much disruption as possible. At our briefing we were instructed to attack the aerodromes at Flers and Lesquin, spending some time over their airspace to deter them from using their landing lights. At 1910 hours it was our turn to take off. We were soon climbing away from the airstrip and turning onto course. On this occasion the weather was exactly as predicted, so despite the attention of the anti-aircraft gunners and searchlight operators, we were able to find both aerodromes. We stooged around for a while without seeing any signs of activity before dropping our bombs and turning for home. We certainly hoped we had been able to dissuade some of the bombers from taking off.

'In a similar attack during November on the *Luftwaffe* base at Melun, Pilot Officer Reg Buskell made two attacks from a relatively low level causing a great deal of damage. He was awarded the DFC, the first 'gong' to be given to a member of the squadron since our arrival. This attack is another illustration of how the route to and from the target and the manner of attack were, at this stage of the war, generally left to the individual crew.

'The attack on Coventry seemed to me to bring about a change of policy for the bombers of the RAF, who, up to that point, had generally been instructed to aim for targets of industrial or military importance. In our case, at our briefing on 16 November, we were initially instructed to bomb the docks at Hamburg. Later, we were recalled to the briefing room to be directed to drop our bombs on the city itself. War in the air is impersonal but in the case of Bob and others from Coventry, or other English towns which had been bombed, they may well have felt differently as their families and friends were likely to be killed. In their case could you blame them if they felt this was an act of retaliation although, to be fair to Bob, he never spoke about it in this way.

'At 1905 hours we took off on this operation, which was to last 4 hours 25 minutes, against a target which was particularly well defended. The city, being on an estuary, was relatively easy to find, although the reception we received by way of flak and searchlights was pretty impressive. Bob picked up the target, on to which he directed Roger, the seconds ticking away like hours as we flew straight on the bomb run, before the magic words, *Bombs Gone!* and we were able to take some evasive action. After this operation we were granted leave.

'On return to Massingham we were soon in action again, our first operation being on 6 December when we took off at 2325 to attack and disrupt the *Luftwaffe* aerodromes at Harkamp and Rotterdam. After dropping our bombs we loitered around for some time over the 'dromes to prevent their use. Two days later it was back to the 'Happy Valley' with an attack on Düsseldorf, where we found the defences had been greatly improved, as they had at all targets in Germany. At one stage we were caught by the searchlights, which is a terrifying experience, feeling like a fly caught in a spider's web. Roger, by changing height and direction was able to shake them off and we were able to bomb the target. On our way back to Massingham Bob asked me to get the usual fix but when I went to let out the trailing aerial I found it was missing. Thankfully, the weather was being kind to us and Bob was pretty confident of our position so he was able to manage, with the assistance of some bearings I was able to get from the wireless station at West Raynham.

'During our flights to targets in Germany the intelligence boffins at Air Ministry had found us an additional pastime. We were to act as 'litter louts,' scattering propaganda leaflets across the countryside, advising the Germans they ought to make peace. In order to drop these leaflets it was necessary to open the escape hatch and some of my friends hit on the idea of dropping empty beer bottles at the same time. On the night of 11/12 December, as a spot of light relief, we made yet another trip to bomb our old friends, the heavy naval guns at Cap Gris Nez, an operation that went off without incident. On 21 December our target was an oil refinery at Gelsenkirchen. A tour of operations was 30 trips; this was our 27th together, so we were looking forward to a rest. Nevertheless, having got this far one began to feel rather anxious, hoping the good luck would continue. At 0320 hours the following morning, when all good people should be in bed, we took off and headed once again for the Ruhr. We need not have worried, for everything worked perfectly. We dropped our bombs, returned and landed at Massingham at 0730 as it was becoming light.

'On 22 December our target was the railway yard at Wiesbach. We took off at 0315 hours for an operation which was to last five and half-hours. There were the usual searchlights probing the sky and bursts of light and heavy flak along our route, especially over the target, but our luck was in and having bombed the target, we flew back over the Dutch coast unscathed. Returning over the North Sea it was becoming daylight and we felt very exposed although no enemy fighter appeared on the scene.

'On the 28th we were briefed for another operation and I duly put on my flying suit in readiness for take-off, although I was feeling far from well, going alternately hot and cold. Thankfully, the operation was cancelled and the next morning my friends sent for the squadron medical officer. He diagnosed pneumonia and I was despatched by ambulance to the RAF hospital at Ely. I felt terrible and had hardly any recollection of the journey or of my first few days in the hospital. In my absence Roger and Bob, without flying on any further operations, were told that their first tour was over and they were to be posted "on rest". This term was used to describe the periods between operational tours, which, normally, would be duty as an instructor. However, in their case they were to go to Takoradi in West Africa where they were to fly Blenheims, as they were delivered by sea, across the African continent to our forces in Egypt. Apart from being an unpleasant place to fly from, it was a really hazardous duty as it meant flying over wild and uncivilized country where they could ill-afford to force land. During our partnership we had flown nearly 100 hours in completing 28 operations. We had suffered no battle damage, had always dropped our bombs, and found our way back to base. We had no opportunity to say good-bye nor have I met them since but I sincerely hope that they both survived the war. Roger was a truly competent pilot, ideally suited for the type of operations in which we had been engaged, whilst Bob was a first class observer and I was truly sorry we had to part company. However, whilst I hardly enjoyed my period in hospital, someone up there spared me from this distinctly unpleasant duty in Africa.

The 'three Ms', (l–r) Jim Moore, Pilot Officer George W. Milson, Sgt Ron Millar RNZAF outside Blickling Hall, June 1941

'During my absence 18 Squadron suffered from bad weather which had limited them to 29 operational sorties in January and 40 in February (compared with 127 we had flown the previous September). During March 1941 the situation was not much better, 33 sorties having been flown, with, sadly, the loss of one crew. With my return to the Squadron, and not being part of a crew, I felt very much the odd man out, even though there were a number of new faces. Then a WOP/AG in one of the crews for some reason was taken off operational flying and I was elected to take his place. I could not have been more fortunate because the pilot, Sergeant George Milson, who hailed from Coningsby in Lincolnshire, had a natural flair for flying, coupled with courage and the ability to be decisive in combat. His observer, Sergeant Ron Millar, a New Zealander, turned out to be very competent and both of them were easy to get along with. They had joined the squadron shortly before I was admitted to hospital and had, so far, flown six night operational flights. We became known as "The Three Ms" (Milson, Millar and Moore). I was now about to share in what, I believe, was the most exciting period in the life of the aircrews of 2 Group.'

2

THE DAY THE *LUFTWAFFE* STAYED
FOR BREAKFAST

Ostern, 1941. (l–r) Gefreiter Blasius Regnant, observer/bomb aimer; Gefreiter Bruno Kauhardt, radio operator; Leutnant Alfred Plank Bachselten, pilot; Unteroffizier Walter Richter, flight engineer

One Nazi plane which crashed and burst into flames on Sunday morning is believed by residents to be a Heinkel 111. One of the crew was found to be dead. His three companions got away but were soon captured by police officers, who took them to a police station before handing them over to the Military. One of the crew was wearing a decoration…another plane, a Junkers 88, crashed and burst in flames some miles away…

'Eastern Daily Press' Monday 5 May 1941

In the spring of 1941 Britain was forced to endure the *Luftwaffe Blitz* on its towns and cities as almost nightly German bombers blasted residential areas, docks and industrial targets from East Anglia to London, the Midlands to Merseyside. East Anglia had many air raids and Norwich and several Norfolk villages suffered death and devastation by German 'tip and run' raiders in broad daylight. The beautiful broadland village of Horning seems an unlikely target but when war broke out in 1939 the firm of H. C. Banham Ltd started Admiralty work on 27-ft whalers. Then they co-operated for war production with the Percival firm and joined in the construction of motor launches, motor torpedo boats and invasion craft generally until the end of 1944 when the building of the larger ships was drawing to a close. The Fairmile Marine Company delivered 1,500 tons of ships of war fully equipped for action, mainly for the Navy but also for the Royal Air Force. One of the RAF's favourite drinking haunts was the Ferry Inn at Horning, on the banks of the River Bure. Pilots from all the Coltishall squadrons nearby drank in the bar three or four evenings a week.

On a dark moonless night, Saturday 26 April 1941 at a quarter to ten a Junkers Ju 88 flying at 500 ft dropped fifteen bombs in the vicinity of the inn. The bulk of them fell aimlessly on the surrounding marshland. Of the four that fell on the Ferry Inn property one dropped on the pontoon ferry-boat, ten on the Woodbastwick side of the river and one in the river itself. The second of the series of bombs hit the pub killing 21 people and injuring several more. Of six members of the family of Mr. Henry Sutton, a well-known figure in the Yarmouth fishing trade, five were killed including Mr. Sutton himself. The landlord, Albert Stringer and about half a dozen others had been dug out alive, though most of them were seriously injured.[1]

Among the RAF dead was Robinson, 222 Squadron's adjutant, one of their pilots, Flight Lieutenant B. van Mentz and Attwell, the Coltishall Station Medical officer. Squadron Leader Robert Stanford Tuck DSO DFC the CO of 257 'Burma' Squadron at Coltishall and his fiancée, Joyce, whom he had met recently in the upstairs bar of the 'King's Arms' in North Walsham, escaped death or injury by leaving early. Tuck said that all at once, quite unaccountably, he grew feverishly restless. He drained his glass and said: 'Come on, everybody, let's whip into Norwich!' Van Mentz had looked up at the bar clock and shook his head. 'Not worth it. We'd never get there before closing time.' The others murmured in agreement.[2] Tuck, Joyce and his bloodhound 'Shuffles' jumped into his car and sped off. At the next crossroads he turned off for Coltishall. Next morning as he was shaving his great friend Flight Lieutenant Peter 'Cowboy' Blatchford DFC, a popular Canadian from Alberta, told him, 'Drinking will be the death of you, Bobbie.'[3]

'Meaning what?'

'You were at the Ferry last night—that so?' Tuck nodded, watching him in the mirror. 'Well, for once you must have left before closing time, because just as the bell rang for last orders a bloody Hun came over and scored a direct hit with a five hundred pounder. Bloody grim show.'

Did Tuck have a premonition of disaster? Throughout the war 'Tuck's Luck' served him to an almost supernatural degree.[4] On the Monday, the Eastern Daily Press carried a carefully censored half column story of the raid without disclosing the exact locality. It was just another tragedy in East Anglia. A month later a photograph of the ruins was published.

One of the main *Luftwaffe* targets in May 1941 was Liverpool, which was bombed by 43 Heinkel He 111s and Ju 88s on the night of 1/2 May, and by another 79 German bombers on the night of 2/3 May. Beaufighters accounted for two of the

---

[1] Rescue squads came from Aylsham and Sprowston and their efforts were supplemented by troops stationed locally. On the Sunday "Lord Haw-Haw" gloated on the wireless over this triumph for the German war machine, and gleefully announced that an establishment on the Broads for building warships had been successfully raided from the air.

[2] *Fly For Your Life* by Larry Forrester. Frederick Muller Ltd, 1956.

[3] Wing Commander Howard Peter 'Cowboy' Blatchford DFC RCAF, OC Coltishall Wing was KIA on 3 May 1943 leading Spitfires on an escort for medium bombers to the Royal Dutch Steel works at Ijmuiden, Holland. He ditched 40 miles off Mundesley on the Norfolk coast. His body was never found.

[4] On 28 January 1942 Tuck, who had 27 victories, was shot down flying a Spitfire over France and made PoW. He died on 5 May 1987.

Heinkel He111

raiders along the south coast on the first night and on the following night a Beaufighter of 604 Squadron shot down a Ju 88 over Hampshire. Flight Lieutenant Edmiston of 151 Squadron was credited with a Ju 88-A5 of *1./KG30*. Edmiston fired and put both of *Feldwebel* Erwin Geiger's engines out and the German pilot crash-landed in shallow water near the beach at Weybourne, Norfolk. The crew was captured and the Junkers was recovered intact.

At the end of August 1940 151 Squadron had been withdrawn to the Midlands for rest and to begin retraining for night fighting. Like almost every other RAF squadron in 1940 151 Squadron was severely mauled, but its Hurricane Is scored a number of victories over German planes based at Abbeville and Vitry-en-Artois. Now, in May 1941 the *Stukageschwader* of *Jagdfliegerführer 2*, and Heinkel 111Hs of *Kampfgeschwader 53* in *Fliegerkorps I* respectively, were using these very same French airfields in the nightly bombing assault on Britain.

One of the Heinkel pilots at Vitry was 22-year old *Leutnant* Alfred Plank von Bachselten, an Austrian by birth. His German crew comprised *Gefreiter* Blasis Regnat, a 22-year old *Beobachter* (observer, navigator), 20-year old Gefreiter Bruno Kauhardt, the *Bordfunker/Bordschütze* (radio operator/air gunner), and *Unteroffizier* Walter Richter, a 21-year old *Bordmechaniker* (flight engineer).

Heinkel 111s en route to England

On the night of 3/4 May, von Bachselten's crew was one of many engaged in bombing operations over the United Kingdom. In all, 298 *Luftwaffe* bombers set out for Merseyside, 20 to Hartlepool, 24 to Portsmouth, and 99 others to various targets. For the luckless citizens of Liverpool this was the third night in succession that their city had been selected as the target. Ranged against the *Luftwaffe* raiders were RAF Fighter Command squadrons equipped mainly with Havocs, Beaufighters, Spitfires, Hurricanes and Defiants. Despite its shortcomings as a day fighter, the Defiant, with its electrically operated Boulton Paul 'A' Mk.IID turret containing four .303 Browning machine-guns, each with 600 rounds per gun, was a potent weapon at night.

In 12 Group in the West Midlands, Sergeant Henry Bodien and his WOP/AG Sergeant Wrampling, a 151 Squadron Defiant I crew, was on standby at Wittering. Bodien, born in Hackney, East London in 1916, had joined the RAF in September 1933 as an Aircraft Apprentice at Halton and had trained as a fitter. He was later accepted for pilot training and on 28 October 1940 arrived at 6 OTU from 48 (Coastal) Squadron for fighter training as a sergeant. Bodien and Wrampling were something of old hands on 151 Squadron, having shot down a Dornier Do 17Z of *3./KG2* near Corby on the night of 4/5 February. Then, on the night of 9/10 April they shot down a He 111P flown by *Unteroffizier* Rudolf Müller, over Birmingham. Müller and one other of his crew bailed out before the Heinkel hit a balloon cable and crashed on houses in Hale's Lane, Smethwick, killing seven civilians as well as the two remaining crew. One of the airmen who bailed out fell on a roof and was badly beaten by local people before he was taken away by the military authorities.

Bodien and Wrampling took off from Wittering at 2328 hours on a 'Freelance patrol'. 151 Squadron shared Wittering with the Beaufighter I night fighters of 25 Squadron, who, an hour earlier, had sent off on patrol Sergeant M. M. Hill and his gunner, Sergeant B. J. Hollis. They were unable to intercept the enemy bombers raiding Liverpool but elsewhere Fighter Command had some success. Havocs of 85 Squadron patrolling over East Anglia claimed a He 111, damaged near Dunwich. Near Halesworth, Suffolk, another Havoc intercepted a pair of Heinkels and claimed one damaged while the other raider carried out violent evasive action and escaped into the night.

Aboard the Heinkel though, everything was going according to plan. *Leutnant* Alfred Plank von Bachselten had reached Liverpool without incident. Liverpool was near the limit of the Heinkel's range and beyond the limit of German fighter cover. Von Bachselten crossed over the burning dock area and added his bombs to the conflagration before turning for home, hoping that they could evade the fighters and defences.

On the return journey a number of *Luftwaffe* aircraft took a direct course which brought them along the North Norfolk coastline. There they could obtain a visual fix from the Cromer lighthouse high above the town, which remained on throughout the war, and was an acknowledged navigational aid to the *Luftwaffe* prior to crossing the North Sea. Nearby were the tall masts of the West Beckham CH (Chain Home) radar station.

The early night was clear and fine but in the very early hours of Sunday 4 May moonlight silhouetted the inland intrusion of the waters of The Wash over which the Heinkel flew. Defiant Is and Beaufighter Ifs from Wittering were directed by CCI and AI (Airborne Intercept) radar units onto the string of German bombers returning that night. Among the defending fighters in patrol action were the 25

Squadron Beaufighter If crewed by Sergeant M. M. Hill and his gunner, Sergeant B. J. Hollis, and the 151 Squadron Defiant I flown by Sergeant Henry Bodien with Sergeant Wrampling uncomfortably manning the gun turret. Over Norfolk during the early hours of 4 May these two crews attacked an enemy bomber and both laid claim to it.

Boulton Paul Defiant I

Landing back at Wittering Hill and Hollis were debriefed by the Intelligence Officer, and submitted their claim for 'a He 111 destroyed at 0025 hrs near Breedon-on-the-Hill'.

Similarly, Henry Bodien and Sergeant Wrampling gave their report, which was dutifully compiled by Flying Officer A. A. Williams of SHQ Intelligence at Wittering.

While both crews laid claim to the enemy bomber, there is no doubt that the victim was Heinkel He 111H-4, Werk Nr. 3235 A1+LK piloted by *Leutnant* Alfred Plank von Bachselten. The Austrian pilot had dived his Heinkel through 10,000 feet in an attempt to evade his attackers, levelling out over the North Norfolk coastline before turning the stricken bomber through a right-hand turn. With landing and navigational lights switched on, he knew he had to crash land in the first available field. On his final approach he sought to maintain sufficient air speed to 'lift' the Heinkel over some hedges which appeared in front of him, rather than to slide through it. Von Bachselten crash-landed at Sharrington, near Holt, five miles inland from the Norfolk coast, at 0204 hours DBST (Double British Summer Time). After coming to rest three of the crew clambered out and prepared to destroy their aircraft, which, thanks to the skill of the pilot, had survived a 'wheels up' crash landing mostly intact, other than for the propeller blades which were bent around the engine nacelles and damage to the long glass nose sustained when it slid through twin hedgerows each side of a farm service lane. *Gefreiter* Bruno Kauhardt was dead, so the crew carefully removed his body from the aircraft and placed him in a hollow close to the gateway to the field where he would be easily found, and some distance from the aircraft, which they now intended to destroy by using a self-destruct device. When this failed to ignite they pumped aviation fuel up from the main tank and ignited the aircraft by soaking their flight maps in fuel. Equipment such as cameras and film of the night raid together with maps and documents were destroyed. The crew intended to masquerade as 'Dutch' airmen and so they emptied their pockets of German coins and other items in a hedge near the crash site.

Shortly after, Roy Lovell, an Army despatch rider from Brinton Road army camp who lived in Sharrington, having heard the noise of the approaching aircraft, journeyed up the farm lane on his motorcycle to investigate. By the time Lovell arrived the aircraft was on fire with the crew beside the aircraft. He quickly withdrew from the scene to get assistance. Soon, all that would remain of the Heinkel would be a burnt out black shell with the vertical tail-plane, which still carried the swastika insignia and a yellow "L" on the upper wing tip. The RAF later recovered seven light (7.92mm) MG 15 machine guns and the wreckage of large external bomb racks.

Police Constable R. Massingham was on duty at Holt police station.

'The clocks were put forward one hour on this date, and it was questioned whether the crash was at 1 am old time or 2 a.m. new time. I received the call which stated that an aircraft had come down in a field at Sharrington. It was not known whether it was British or German. It was on fire. Having reported that fact I was instructed to go to the scene. On my arrival I found that the plane, which was a Heinkel 111, had pancaked through a lane into a field Holt side of Sharrington "Swan" Public House. PC Bunnett of Binham was already there. The plane was on fire. We found the dead gunner in a ditch nearby. He had been shot through the heart. We pulled him out and he was searched. It was ascertained that a dispatch rider had come along, presumably saw some of the crew near the plane and had gone for help. We thought there were four in the aircraft so a search of the area was made to locate the other three.'

Unbeknown to PC Massingham, the crew, after setting fire to the aircraft, had left the field and had made their way towards the main Fakenham to Holt road. The night was now still and quiet and the crew chatted quietly amongst themselves. Mrs Allison, who still lives in the cottages at the end of the lane, was alone with her two little girls as her husband had been called up. They watched

Kelling Police House

from their bedroom window as the glow in the adjacent fields got larger and then heard the crew talking as they arrived at the main road. Having no contact with local inhabitants the crew elected to walk towards Holt, the nearby market town, and they walked unchallenged through the village of Letheringsett and into Holt. In the early hours of Sunday morning Holt was deserted. Fatigued by the night's events, the crew sought shelter inside a pillbox, which at that time had been constructed on the small square adjacent to the main Holt Post Office. Suitably rested and having failed to find any police officers or military authorities to whom they might give themselves up, the crew walked through Holt and off along the Kelling road via Kelling woods over the heath towards the coast. They finally reached

Charles Barnard – 1 April 1941; wife and two daughters

the coast at Bard Hill, Salthouse Heath, at dawn. There the crew lit a small fire to warm themselves and this brought them to the attention of two servicemen manning a small caravan radio beacon installation.

PC Charles Barnard, a local Kelling police officer, was going about his duty when he cycled over the heath at 6.10 am on Sunday morning and came upon the German aircrew. Barnard did not hesitate and he apprehended the airmen. However, when he took the crew home to his wife and two young children at the Kelling police house where they lived, the 'capture' evolved more into a social event. Mrs. Vera Barnard gave them tea and breakfast and the crew signed their names and addresses in her husband's 1941 diary pocket book, which she still has. The crew was introduced to the Barnard's two little girls, who still vividly recall the time their father brought the German airmen home for breakfast! They recall the crew's appreciation of the English flowers on her kitchen table and them thanking her for her care, saying she had acted to them as a true mother would.

Meanwhile, acting Sergeant George Chapman, a policeman 6ft 3ins tall, had been unsuccessful in his hunt for the German airmen, who were now known to be wandering around Norfolk. Chapman, who because of his height rode a specially constructed police cycle with two crossbars, one below the other (now preserved in a local museum) decided to extend his search by calling on PC Barnard at Kelling Police House. When Chapman arrived he was amazed to see the constable and his family having tea with the Germans and exchanging names and addresses for after the war!

PC Massingham continues:

'I received a message that the three had been picked up at Bard Hill (Salthouse Heath) and taken to Kelling Police House. I escorted them to Holt Police Station and they were later handed over to the Military at Gresham's School, Holt. I spoke to the pilot, who informed me in broken English that he had been to Liverpool that night, and had made plenty of fires. He said he was very shy of our Spitfires. He also informed me that he had taken all minor roads after setting light to his plane, also burning the film they had taken during the raid on Liverpool. This crash happened on the Sunday morning and at 2 pm I was instructed to guard the aircraft until 9.30 pm. A collection was made for the Red Cross and several pounds were collected from people visiting the area that day.'

When the captured crew were finally presented late in the day to the main police station in Holt the senior officer on duty, no doubt in response to the apparent casual surrender by the German crew, was heard to say,

'I suppose you Germans think you are going to win this bloody war'?

Later that day the crew was handed over to the military authorities at the Gresham School Hall, which was then used by the army as the school had been evacuated to Newquay, Cornwall. The crew were transported initially to Newmarket where they were sheltered for the night in a stable, this time under armed guard. During the night they were joined by *Leutnant* Joachim Wreschnik, pilot of a Ju 88A-5 of *3./KG*77, which he had crash-landed at Welney Wash after his starboard engine failed on the return flight from Liverpool. After struggling on for some distance the port engine failed and caught fire. Baling his crew out over March,

Von Bachselten (3rd from left) and his crew passing through London on their way to prison camp. Von Bachselten is trying to conceal his Iron Cross from the cameraman.

[26]

Cambridgeshire, Wreschnik belly-landed in a field after skimming over the top of a wood. He suffered head and facial injuries but jumped to safety. Not satisfied with the progress the engine fire was making towards destroying his aircraft, he proceeded to empty his pistol into the engine nacelle in an attempt to make the fire spread. Unfortunately for him, the Home Guard disarmed him and extinguished the fire before the Ju 88 was too badly damaged – not that it contained any new features or equipment of any consequence.

After a night in the stables the Germans were to be taken to London by train. Still with thoughts towards an escape route Alfred Bachselten sought a corner seat, only to find that on that journey to London all stations were called 'BOVRIL'. They were marched under armed guard from the platform at Liverpool Street railway station and later transferred to a prisoner of war camp.

Gefreiter Bruno Kauhardt was buried in the churchyard at Brinton, nearby, but at the end of the war he was re-interred at the German Military Cemetery at Cannock Chase, Staffordshire. Cannock Chase is 30 miles north of Birmingham. The Chase is a pretty rural area. One of its major attractions is the ancient herd of fallow deer,

which still roam the area as it has done for centuries. Cannock is now twinned with Dattelin Nord Rhein, where it is considered the areas have similar interests and activities.

Although a moonlit night, the Heinkel crew had been unable to identify the attacking aircraft. The AI1(g) intelligence report describes how .303 bullet strikes were found in a section of the starboard wing, entering from below and ahead. Further .303 hits were found in the starboard fuselage and the bomb doors so unless Sergeant Hill carried out an extraordinarily aerobatic head-on night attack with machine guns only, one has to find favour with the Defiant crew of Bodien and Wrampling.

Henry Bodien was promoted to Pilot Officer and was awarded the DFC in March 1942, subsequently being promoted to Flight Lieutenant on 1 May 1943 and finally to Squadron Leader. He was posted to 21 Squadron on 13 February

1944 and flew Mosquito fighter-bombers on *Day Rangers* over Europe. He finished the war with five confirmed victories, two of them while flying Mosquito II night fighters of 151 Squadron with Sergeant G. B. Brooker as his navigator/radio operator, in 1942-43. In September 1944 he was awarded the DSO. During the Korean War Bodien was attached to the USAAF, 1950-51 and he flew B-26 bombers on night interdiction missions, being awarded the US Air Medal. From May 1951 to January 1952 he commanded 29 Squadron, and he left the RAF in April 1953 to take up a position in the RCAF.

4 May 1941 had been a significant day in the lives of the aircrew of Al+LK. They had survived a fighter attack and an aircraft crash in the very early hours. They had walked some 7-8 miles across to the Norfolk coastline before being captured.

Even now crops do not grow well at the site of the crash, which in May 1991, Alfred von Bachselten and his wife Dolly, visited, with ex-Cromer resident and historian, Russell Reeve, and the late Helmut Rix, a former *Luftwaffe* fighter pilot and POW who lived in England after the war. Russell recalls,

'Alfred Bachselten, having read in my report of the distress experienced by Mrs Allison and her family at the time of the crash, felt he would wish to meet her and a new friendship was established with photographs and offers of tea after the delay of a mere fifty years! Alfred Bachselten engaged the present owner of the ex police house in conversation and photographs were taken. By chance a Norfolk Constabulary police car passed slowly on the roadway, no doubt wondering what all the fuss was about.

'Even after the passage of years I find difficulty in adequately expressing my feelings of admiration for the conduct and bravery of the late PC Charles Barnard. At the end of a rather extraordinary day we were to return to Cromer for tea. The assembled company mused on the futility of war and the significance of lasting friendship. We were pleased to walk up Happy Valley and round the lighthouse, which previously had been viewed only from the air. We gazed across the bleak North Sea enshrouded that day in mist. Alfred Bachselten had obtained his *Luftwaffe* logbook and other material. The entry 4 May 1941 merely recorded "Did not return". I am glad they did.'

3

BLENHEIMS, BLICKLING AND THE BIRTH OF LEND-LEASE

In 1432, Sir John Fastolfe, a famous soldier, who Shakespeare altered slightly for his comic hero Falstaff, purchased Blickling Hall in Norfolk. Fastolfe died at Caister Castle in 1459, having sold Blickling to Geoffrey Boleyn. Tradition has it that his daughter, Anne Boleyn (1507-36), second wife of Henry VIII and mother of Elizabeth I of England, was born at Blickling. Beheaded in the Tower of London her ghost is said to haunt the Hall. Sir Henry Hobart had the house rebuilt in 1619, using brick and Ketton dressed stone. The structure was uncompleted at the time of his death in 1625. The Hobarts were followed by the Earls of Buckinghamshire, Lady Suffield and the Lothians, who assumed title in the mid-1800s.

In 1932, fifty year old Philip Henry Kerr, 11th Marquis of Lothian, decided, like several celebrated families before him, to make Blickling Hall his principal English seat. Lothian saw his beautiful mansion as a working house, 'A place from which public or intellectual or artistic activities go forth.'

Lothian had been private secretary to Lloyd George and had drafted the preface to the Treaty of Versailles in 1919 though his reputation as a statesman had been questioned as a result of his association with the Cliveden set and their pro-German influence on British foreign policy in the period just before the war. In 1934, Joachim von Ribbentrop, trusted advisor to the *Führer* and, from 1936 to 1938, German ambassador to Great Britain, stayed at Blickling Hall. When, in March 1936, Hitler's forces reoccupied the Rhineland Lord Lothian assured the British people that Hitler was merely taking over 'his back garden'. Always the idealist, this British aristocrat with boyish good looks and air of self-confidence had only ever supported liberal groups in pre-war Germany. In 1936 Blickling Hall had been lent to Prime Minister Stanley Baldwin. Lord Halifax, the Foreign Secretary 1938-40, (later Britain's wartime ambassador to the US) was another notable visitor. In 1936 Lothian became Britain's ambassador to the USA and he used the position to significantly influence America to side with Britain in her hour of greatest need.

Lothian's appointment as Ambassador to the US had come as something of a surprise, for he had neither diplomatic training nor the experience of high political office. However, as a journalist and as secretary of the Rhodes Trust he had spent much time travelling in the USA and he had met many leading dignitaries. His knowledge of foreign affairs and his familiarity with American life and thought more than compensated and were to prove very valuable after Britain went to war in 1939. Lothian liked Americans and his 'democratic attitude won him admirers throughout the States. He put forward a very good case for Britain's involvement in the war and pointed out her sacrifices and her aims for which her people were dying. He also spelled out the dangers a *Nazi* victory would mean for the USA. Many US politicians, and the American public, wary of the British (especially those with titles), were won over by his tolerant, affable approach.

Lord Lothian worked unceasingly at his task. He made seventeen speeches and a radio broadcast during his all-too-short tenure in the USA. He persuaded Winston Churchill to write the historic letter to President Franklin D. Roosevelt, which revealed Britain's heavily depleted military strength. Lothian then used a daringly timed press conference in Washington to deliver a similar message to the American public and, in so doing, helped establish the political stage for Roosevelt to enact Lend-Lease with its substantial aid to Britain.

On 6 January 1941 Roosevelt outlined the Lend-Lease program and enunciated the 'Four Freedoms' principle. The President asked Congress for approval to extend arms credits 'to those nations which are now in actual war with aggressor nations. Our most useful and immediate role is to act as an arsenal for them as well as ourselves. They do not need manpower, but they do need billions of dollars worth of weapons of defence. The time is near when they will not be able to pay for them all in ready cash'.

In a radio broadcast to the US on 9 February, Churchill pleaded for arms support:

'Give us the tools and we will finish the job.'

The Lend-Lease Act passed Congress on 11 March 1941, when British Commonwealth reserves were almost exhausted. Roosevelt said:

'This decision is the end of any attempt at appeasement in our land; the end of urging us to get along with the dictators; the end of compromise with tyranny and the forces of oppression.'

Lothian last saw Blickling Hall in October 1940, during a day's break in his busy schedule. That same year, he had applied the Lend-Lease principle to his beloved Hall when, after rising costs threatened its future, he bequeathed Blickling to the National Trust. Blickling was the first of almost a hundred great houses to pass to this great institution, whereby, in place of death duties, whole houses and their estates are left to the British nation with their income as an endowment. By then, parts of Blickling had been requisitioned by the RAF for accommodation and messing facilities for personnel at nearby RAF Oulton and the park ploughed up.

Lothian ordered some of the soft furnishings which had been put away for the duration to be brought out to make the officers more comfortable. Lothian returned to Washington in November, and died on 12 December 1940 from uremic poisoning.[1]

On the day before he died, he made his last appeal to the American people:

'If you back us you won't be backing a quitter. The issue now depends largely on what you decide to do. Nobody can share that responsibility with you.'

Lothian had completed his life's most momentous task and it was thanks to the efforts of men such as him that Lend-Lease aircraft like Hudsons and Venturas, Bostons, Fortresses and Liberators were sited at the dispersals at RAF Oulton during WWII. Had he been able to look out from the portals of Blickling Hall Lothian would no doubt have been delighted at what his diplomacy had achieved. As it was, Lothian's death was mourned in both America and Britain.

When the RAF took over part of Blickling Hall they occupied the barns to the east of the west wing and used accommodation in the private rooms (now the conference rooms) at the rear of the hall. High in the attics, where 16th century maids had slept in small rooms, now slept the 'erks', batmen, and flight sergeants. The Harness Room became a guardroom. Lord Lothian's fearsome secretary, Miss O'Sullivan, nicknamed 'Mrs Dandridge' (from Daphne du Maurier's *Rebecca*) or, just simply, 'the Dragon,' ensured that the RAF remained in their allotted area It was reputed that the RAF officers were more frightened of her than they were of their CO!

By spring 1941 Sergeant Jim (Dinty) Moore was wireless operator of a new crew in 18 Squadron of pilot Sergeant George Milson and Sergeant Ron Millar. He continues:

'On 3 April 1941 18 Squadron moved to Oulton, near the market town of Aylsham, which had opened as a satellite airfield to Horsham St. Faith on 31 July 1940. Crews of 114 Squadron were the first to use Oulton and Blickling Hall, flying Bristol Blenheims on daylight strikes. The Squadron had been posted to RAF Leuchars in Scotland to make way for us. Our accommodation could not have been less like that which we had enjoyed at Massingham, for we now found ourselves living in the beautiful Blickling Hall, the home of landed gentry since the time of the Doomsday Book.

[1] It could have been treated but some years earlier, under the influence of Lady Astor, another distinguished guest at Blickling, he had become a Christian Scientist and refused the treatment that would have saved his life.

'We occupied about two-thirds of the house and most of the buildings in the grounds, with access to the acres of grounds and the lake in which we were able to swim despite a large swan who appeared to resent our presence. The estate even had its own church and a small public house. The Wing Commander had a very grand room, which, it was said, had been occupied by Anne Boleyn, overlooking the park and the lake. Many of the estate employees still lived in their cottages and must have found our presence somewhat different from anything to which they had become accustomed. On one memorable occasion one of our colleagues, having spent the evening in Norwich, imbibing more than his share of the local ale, took a fancy to one of those large yellow balls on the top of a pedestrian crossing sign. He purloined this, bringing it back joyfully to the Hall, where he deposited it in the garden. The following morning the head gardener emerged from his cottage and, having heard warnings of explosive devices being dropped by the *Luftwaffe* hurriedly alerted the bomb squad. On their arrival these gentlemen were not impressed and their comments are unprintable!

'During the evenings I was introduced to an Australian drinking session which I will entitle "chug-a-lug". You had to drink a pint of beer breaking off to recite a poem, which began, 'Here's to the health of Cardinal Puff' and had to complete the drink and the poem without any mistake. As the evening wore on this task became increasingly difficult.

'My return to the squadron had coincided with a decision by Bomber Command that 2 Group must adopt a much more aggressive role and there were to be no more night operations. On 11 April 1941 Blenheims of 105 Squadron flew the last 2 Group night operation, bombing targets at Cologne, Bremerhaven and Brest. Instead, we were to operate in daylight on tasks that came roughly under two headings. Attacks at low level were to be made on enemy shipping close to the enemy coast, these shipping lanes from Norway to the Bay of Biscay being split into "beats". We would either be detailed to look exclusively for shipping or, on occasions, when no shipping was sighted, to cross the coast to look for and bomb suitable targets. Secondly, low-level attacks were to be made on industrial or military targets on the Continent, sometimes using cloud for cover. Later (during May) we were allocated a further task, to operate in formation at heights of about 10,000 feet with fighter escort. These operations, known as *Circuses*, were to be flown with the primary objective of persuading the fighters of the *Luftwaffe* to attack us so that they could be engaged and destroyed by our escorting fighters. Similar operations, known as *Ramrods*, were also to be flown where the target, rather than ourselves, acting as the "sacrificial lamb", was the primary objective.

'Having been involved in night operations, our squadron began a period of low-level flying exercises across the East Anglian countryside, preparing to make our contribution to this campaign. Flying low meant literally skimming over hedgerows, with telegraph and electrical wires proving to be quite a hazard, while flocks of birds were the cause of many accidents. Collecting twigs and assorted greenery on the leading edges of the wings was also commonplace. Compared with flying at medium or high level, when you were not conscious of the speed at which you were travelling, flying at low level was truly exciting and exhilarating, requiring total concentration by the pilot who could ill afford even to sneeze. Over the sea it was even more difficult: the sea and sky seeming to merge, especially if it was at all hazy. We also dropped practice bombs on the wreck of a ship lying just off the cliffs at Trimingham.

'One major improvement that had been carried out to the Blenheims during the winter was the removal of the single Vickers Gas Operated Machine Gun in the turret, which was replaced by two Browning .303 machine guns, which were no longer fed by pans of ammunition but by belts. We WOP/AGs now felt we had something worthwhile to fight back with, and we were to be given the opportunity to make full use of them. The black paint had been removed from the underside of the wings and replaced by a light blue to make us more difficult to find. We were declared operational shortly after our move to Oulton and crews were dispatched on the shipping patrols, though "The Three Ms" (Moore, Milson and Millar) had to wait. On 15 April our new CO who had been with the squadron less than a month was shot down whilst attacking one of the first convoys sighted. Flying at 200 mph, skimming the waves, there was little hope of survival if the aircraft or the pilot was hit by flak. The casualties among the senior officers in the Group were to prove to be exorbitantly high.

'On 25 April, a very pleasant spring day, we caught the flight truck up to the airstrip as usual, but this was to be a day different from any that had gone before. We were called to the briefing room where we were briefed for a solo 'fringe beat' off the Dutch coast near Flushing. If we failed to sight any shipping we could fly inland to search for a suitable target on which to unload our four 250-lb bombs, which had been fitted with 11-second delay fuses. There was that same mixture of excitement and apprehension I had experienced on the occasion of my very first operation in August 1940. The minutes seemed to stand still as we waited our time for take-off. But finally it arrived and we taxied out and took off at 1848 hours, climbing to about 1,000 feet before setting course for the Norfolk coast. As soon as we were over the sea, George brought the aircraft down to nought feet, our slipstream making a wake in the sea behind us. We flew on alone until the Dutch coast came into view, then turned north and flew parallel to the coast, searching in vain for any sign of enemy shipping. At the end of our area of search George turned the aircraft and headed for the land, where I felt the aircraft lift as we went over the sea wall like a steeplechaser. The countryside was very flat, not unlike parts of East Anglia, and an old man on his bicycle looked up and gave us a cheery wave. We flew on undisturbed to the outskirts of Flushing. Finding no other suitable target, my colleagues decided to drop our bombs on the docks but just as Ron was pressing the bomb switch, George had to lift a wing to miss a derrick, and the bombs fell on the railway line. This aggressive act was the signal for German anti-aircraft gunners to open fire with great enthusiasm to indicate their disapproval of our disturbing their evening schnapps or whatever. They must have been pretty accurate, as they managed to knock two sizeable holes in our tail unit. George responded by "putting his foot down", still keeping at nought feet, and dropping down over a sea wall into an estuary that led to the sea. At one stage, as we were flying along the estuary, I was actually looking up at a German gun emplacement, which must have been infuriating for the gunners, who couldn't depress their guns sufficiently to fire at us whereas I was able to fire at them.

'We headed out to sea expecting, but not receiving, the attention of the *Luftwaffe*, landing at Oulton after a flight lasting 2 hours 20 minutes, feeling very pleased with ourselves. It had been a fairly exhilarating experience in which thrill had taken the place of fear – certainly an operation I would never forget. Being able to see what we were bombing and to see the face of the enemy gave a whole new meaning to the task in which we were engaged, and it was such a marvellous contrast to the night operations on which we had flown the previous autumn and winter.'

'On the morning of 27 April we flew south to Chivenor in North Devon to re-fuel and to patrol a shipping beat off the French coast. At 1320 hours we took off again with five other Blenheims heading south until we reached a point 30 miles from the enemy coast, where we split up into three pairs to sweep a larger area. We flew on until we were close to the coast, when we saw the telltale smoke of a small convoy of two merchant ships escorted by a patrol boat. There was no hesitation as we headed for our target, each aircraft heading for a different ship, George jinking our kite to present a more difficult target. We remained at nought feet until at the last moment George hauled us up just over the masts of our target while Ron dropped our bombs. As we hurtled over the top of the mast I found that I was looking up at the belly of the other Blenheim that had just bombed, but fortunately we did not collide. We returned to nought feet immediately and I was able to fire several bursts at the unfortunate seamen who, together with the patrol boat, had sent up a terrific concentration of flak, through which we had to pass, without managing to hit us. As we flew away, looking back, I'm afraid I was unable to report any dramatic hits on our targets, though it must be remembered that the fuses on our bombs had an 11-second delay. We called in at Chivenor to re-fuel, after a flight that had taken 3 hours 50 minutes, stopping about an hour before flying back to Oulton.

'During the month one particularly successful shipping strike was carried out by the Commander of 'B' Flight, Squadron Leader Hugh J. N. Lindsaye, who found and attacked a 7,000-ton enemy vessel, gaining a direct hit and leaving it with a 35-degree list. Sadly, a few days later, on the 30th, he was flying a Blenheim locally on a test flight when the aircraft crashed, killing him and Flying Officer Frank Holmes. While we were saddened by the losses on operations, the impact was even greater when they died as the result of an accident.

'On 3 May 18 Squadron moved, temporarily, to a new airstrip at Portreath near Redruth on the north coast of Cornwall. On the 7th we carried out a shipping patrol, within sight of the French coast, without seeing signs of any shipping. However, at the same time, in an attack on an enemy convoy, Squadron Leader Robert Bramston 'Binks' Barker (who had replaced Lindsaye) was shot down and killed. His observer, Sergeant Norman H. Meanwell, was a very good friend of mine. He had taken me to his home at Great Yarmouth to meet his wife Margaret and their baby daughter.

'On 9 May patrolling off Brest we saw smoke on the horizon and as we approached we found a small convoy with the usual escorting patrol boat. We flew straight into the attack, following the same pattern as before; George doing his best to drop our bombs down the funnels of the merchantman. Quickly returning to sea level after the attack, I was again able to machine gun the decks of this ship and the patrol boat. Sadly we were unable to claim any direct hits, though we didn't hang around to find out. The concentration of flak was just as impressive but "lady luck" was with us and we emerged unscathed. On our way back to Portreath we flew over the Scilly Isles, which, as we had climbed to a reasonable height, looked very small indeed. The same afternoon, in attacking another convoy we lost one of the original pilots of the squadron, who had been a member at the outbreak of the war, Flight Lieutenant R. Langebear and his crew, Flight Sergeant A. K. Newberry and Sergeant I. R. Stone. On the 12th those of us who had an aircraft that had not been damaged in the raid by the *Luftwaffe* flew away from sunny Cornwall to the grey skies of Oulton and the comfort of Blickling Hall.

'On the 17th we took off at 1010 hours to fly another shipping "beat", being in the air for 3½ hours, doing our best to find a target, but without success. On each shipping patrol you took off with the desire to find a convoy to attack, which you knew would be defended by a murderous curtain of flak, fighting with your natural desire to stay alive. You would fly alone or in company mile after mile over an empty cruel-looking sea searching continuously for an elusive target. If your search was successful, or unsuccessful, depending on your point of view, the whole action would be over in a matter of moments. I submit that the manner in which this campaign was carried out, in aircraft ill suited for the task, showed a high degree of courage and determination on the part of the crews involved. Later, cannon-firing fighters and Beaufighter strike wings, some carrying torpedoes and others fitted with cannon, made such attacks which were extremely successful.

'On 25 May we were briefed to carry out a low-level attack on a seaplane base on the island of Nordeney in the Frisian Islands off the north-west coast of Germany. The raid was to be carried out by eight Blenheims, five from our squadron and three from another in the Group. The raid was to be led by Squadron Leader Johnny Munro, a man for whom we had the highest regard. On the ground he had a slight speech impediment, whereas in the air he was articulate, decisive and a born leader. The plan was to fly to a point north of Nordeney and to approach the target from that direction with the intention of confusing the defenders. We taxied out and took off at 1355 hours, one behind the other, forming up into three Vic formations with ourselves as No 2 to Munro. We crossed the Norfolk coast before coming down to sea level, settling down on to a course that would take us to the point where we would turn for our run into the island. It was a beautiful sunny day with excellent visibility and one couldn't help wondering what the folk at home would be doing on this Sunday afternoon. We knew it was to be a long flight, during which we would be constantly on the alert, searching for any sign of either ships or enemy aircraft. During operational flights we were required to keep radio silence so as not to give our position away to the enemy. When we changed course to head for Nordeney we could only make frantic signals to our leader to indicate that smoke of a convoy on the horizon had been seen. On this occasion the land target was our main priority so, although there was the risk of an alert wireless operator on the convoy notifying the defenders on Nordeney of our approach, there was little choice but to carry on. Finally the island came into view, with a heavily armoured German patrol boat directly in our path, which we could have avoided. However, as if that wasn't enough, patrolling over the island were five Me 109F fighters who were obviously a welcoming committee we could have done without.

'It is stating the obvious to say that "our cover was blown", so our fears of an alert wireless operator reporting our approach were justified. Whatever Munro might have decided as to whether or not to carry on with the raid, the matter was decided for him as the three aircraft from the other squadron turned inside us and headed west with the rest of us in hot pursuit. We kept close together for our joint protection, jettisoning the bombs, giving the engines full boost and keeping as low as possible. The fighters wasted no time in mounting an attack and the sea bubbled and foamed as bullets and cannon shells churned up the water. There was no time for fear as we fought back, firing as the fighters came into range. There was the stench of cordite from my guns, then a Perspex panel in my turret blew out so I felt as if I was sitting in a hurricane. I could see that the WOP/AG in the aircraft next to us had been hit and there was blood all over the back of his turret. One of our formation, obviously hit, crashed into the sea and disintegrated, but this success did not satisfy the enemy who still came in to attack, though one of the fighters, obviously damaged, with its undercarriage hanging down, finally withdrew. After what had seemed like an eternity, the others flew off, either due to lack of ammunition or fuel. I found I had no ammunition left for one gun and only ten rounds for the other.

'At the conclusion of the engagement one Blenheim piloted by Flight Lieutenant F. M. "Tich" Thorne, who had joined the squadron with me, had been very badly damaged – to such an extent that I doubted if he would make it back to base. We were unable to stay with him, as we had to limp home with damage to both wings and the tail. We landed at our parent 'drome, Horsham St Faith, after an operation that had lasted 4 hours. We had not been on the ground for many minutes when we

Horsham St Faith, 1944

Aerial view of Horsham St Faith

saw another Blenheim, obviously in some difficulties, coming in to land. The pilot successfully landed and as the aircraft taxied towards us we could see that it was so badly damaged it looked like a sieve. Miraculously it was "Tich" Thorne and his crew, none of whom, despite the enormity of the damage, had received a scratch.[1] We now made enquiries to find out "who had got the chop" and were told the news.

It is difficult to describe feelings after the loss of so many friends, for while we mourned their loss, we could not suppress a sense of elation at having survived ourselves. The only way you could carry on and retain your sanity was believing, no matter what, you would be the one to get back.

'On Thursday 6 June the Prime Minister, Winston Churchill, and two crews of each of the squadrons in 2 Group visited West Raynham. In addition to the Bristol

---

[1] Flight Sergeant David Keane, pilot, Sergeant George 'Jock' Duffus, observer and Sergeant Ian Gow. Wop/AG 'Titch' Thorne were subsequently KIA 24 July 1942

Blenheims there were Short Stirling, Handley Page Halifax and Flying Fortress I aircraft, and the twin-engined Avro Manchester. These aircraft, with wing spans of nearly 100 feet, looked enormous beside the Blenheim with its wing span a mere 56 feet. "Winnie", as Churchill was popularly known, appeared, accompanied by members of the Government, and sundry senior officers. He mounted some steps used for the inspection of aircraft engines and invited us to gather round him. We did, with alacrity. During his speech he referred to 2 Group as his "light cavalry". In his address he began by reminding us that 43,000 civilians had been killed in air raids on Britain in the previous 12 months and that his promise that the RAF would retaliate by day and by night had not yet been fulfilled. He had come personally, he said, to explain the importance of the special tasks we would be undertaking in the next few weeks, when our operations were likely to have a major impact on the course of the war. He then gave us some more unpalatable facts. German intervention in the Middle East was turning the war against us in that theatre. "Germany must be forced to move her fighters westwards," he told us. So, escorted by large numbers of fighters, we would attack targets in the West that Germany would have to defend. Our purpose was to relieve pressure on other fronts and to ease the stranglehold on our lifelines. "I am relying on you," were his closing words. There is little doubt that the personal visit of this determined individual with his magnetic personality was greatly appreciated by all of us who were present. He made us feel that the operations in which we were involved were well worthwhile. The great man made a second visit to the Group shortly after Germany attacked Russia on 22 June 1941. On this occasion he reiterated his

New Douglas Bostons arriving at Great Massingham

Douglas Bostons in flight

determination to carry the war to our enemy in every possible way in order to assist our new Allies.

'On 17 June we flew over to Horsham St. Faith for a briefing for a raid that we would never forget. We found that we were to take part in a *Circus* attack on the Kuhlmann Chemical Works at Chocques near Bethune in northern France. We would be accompanied by a large fighter escort and were to fly in one large formation of 24 aircraft in 8 Vics of 3, stacked up one slightly below and behind the other. We also discovered that we had drawn the "short straw" in our position, as we would be the last aircraft in this large and unwieldy formation. Later in the war, no matter how many bombers took part in a raid, we never flew in boxes of more than six aircraft, which could manoeuvre sufficiently to carry out evasive action in response to attack by flak or fighters. At 1745 hours we taxied out, with my excitement having some difficulty overcoming my fear, and took off, the last in the queue. Flying down to meet our escort, looking forward I could see this enormous formation of Blenheims, while looking back over the tail there was an empty sky. Whenever I see a flock of birds I am always reminded of that moment. Hurricanes, our close escort, closed in around us while the Spitfires flew high above forming a protective umbrella. They were certainly a most comforting sight.

'We droned on towards the French coast, having climbed to our operational height of about 10,000 feet before being met by a heavy barrage of flak. We carried on towards the target, by which time our Vic was lagging behind the main formation and we attracted the unwelcome attention of a number of German fighters who had managed to avoid our escort, which itself was also under attack. The sky was full of fighters whirling around in combat while we were under constant attack. One determined character actually flew up between us and the No 2 in our formation, but although I was surprised, I immediately reacted and fired a burst as he went past. My instant reaction must have been due to the training I had received. The fighters were armed with cannon, so on occasions they could stay off out of range of our machine guns and take pot shots at us. They hit us in both wings and put our port engine out of commission. (The port engine supplied the power for the landing gear and the turret.) Losing power on the port engine initially made our kite swing to the left, although George somehow managed to manoeuvre underneath our colleagues for mutual protection. Sadly, they gradually pulled away from us, leaving us an unfriendly and persistent Messerschmitt for company and a heavy flak barrage to speed us, if that is appropriate in this instance, on our way back to base as we crossed the coast at Cap Gris Nez. Fortunately one of our escorting Hurricanes came to our aid and we heard later that he had shot down our "German friend" near the English coast.

'The Blenheim was not noted for its ability to fly on one engine, and George had to fight with the controls to keep us in the air and on course. Apart from sending a message back to base notifying them of our problems, there was little I could do but cross my fingers. We could have landed at any aerodrome once we crossed the coast, but George was determined to get us back to Horsham St. Faith, which he not only did but also brought us in for a perfect landing. It was, by any standard, an example of marvellous flying.

'I flew my last op with 18 Squadron on 5 July; another shipping patrol, and then I was posted as an instructor to 13 OTU, Bicester, having completed 49 operational sorties without a scratch.

'Between 12 March and 14 July 1941 2 Group had lost 68 Blenheims and their crews (15 from 18 Squadron). There were only 12 crews on a squadron and 8 squadrons in the Group so it represented a very heavy loss rate. I spent a frustrating time at Bicester where I made repeated requests for a posting. However, they continued to fall on deaf ears, so when in September 1942 Flight Lieutenant Johnny Reeve, who was in charge of the Gunnery Wing asked me to crew up with him and Pilot Officer Freddie Deeks for another tour of operations, I jumped at the chance.

'Johnny was a rather complex character who I never really got to know, whereas Freddy, who had worked in Fleet Street, was most interesting and easy to get along with. Like myself, they had both completed one tour of operations on Blenheims, Freddie being one of the few who had survived a tour in Malta during the winter of 1941/42 where the loss of aircraft and crews had been absolutely appalling. The air gunner who normally flew with us was an extremely likeable Newfoundlander called Johnny Legge. On 30 September 1942 we joined 88 Squadron at RAF Oulton. My posting had coincided with my promotion to the rank of Pilot Officer. After having flown many hours in Blenheims we now found ourselves members of a Squadron equipped with the Douglas Boston, a really first-class twin engined medium bomber. It was ideally suited for low level flying, highly manoeuvrable, faster and carrying a larger bomb load than the dear old Blenheim. It also meant living in Blickling Hall again, which for me was like going home, except that this time I lived in the Officers' Mess, with the services of a batman!'

Another officer at Oulton who was also billeted at Blickling Hall was pilot Jack Peppiatt.

'We were at Blickling from September 1942 to the summer of 1943; a most wonderful period on several levels; high drama in terms of the war and the seductive delights of a country mansion during the quiet moments. We had visits from ENSA troupes who performed in a barn near the house; elegant evenings with all present to see people like Reg Dixon and Tessie O'Shea. Afterwards they were invited into either the Sergeants or Officers mess. On one visit Tessie came with her pianist and manager to our anti-room after a tiring day of travel and performing. The beautiful room was crowded with RAF and invited visitors from local forces units. As usual she was being asked to do a song for us as a favour, but Tessie wasn't the favouring kind in private life I fear. She refused briskly but after a lot of – slightly drunken – prodding she agreed with poor grace to do just one. She set off; the room was packed as people pushed in to get a view. Then, in the distance, the skirl of the pipes, and into the room marched two burly pipers from the Black Watch having been told in their innocence to do so by a troublemaker. Tessie O'Shea's response was several four-letter words, which in those days were not often heard in mixed company.

'For a period of two or three weeks the Squadron moved down to a forward airfield leaving three or four crews to hold the fort at Blickling. We lucky ones lived the life of Riley. We fished in the lake, poached game and every evening we had a banquet. We roamed the house looking at the treasures that were still tucked away. At Christmas 1942 we had a wonderful party in the dining room – stuffed pike and even swan. There was great competition to secure the affections of the local vicar's niece (I believe).

'A popular bit of 'fun', so we thought, was to carry a Verey cartridge into the dining room, surreptitiously held behind the back, stand before the ornate fireplace until the chosen victim was eating and then toss it into the fire and walk smartly out. The room would fill up to neck level with black smoke. This became less popular after someone did it whilst the CO was having his breakfast.

'I suppose because of the splendour of the surroundings we all tried to live up to them and evening dinner was a well dressed performance; however the usual behaviour always followed. I can clearly see us all seated around the walls in the small first ante-room. The door to the dining-room was open and the floor cleared on our side. A beer mug was placed on the carpet behind a table. The idea was to gain speed in the dining room, dive through the door over the table and do a forward roll, placing the head in the mug on landing. Participants removed tunics and ties…this whole process was carried out in a decorous way with the CO commenting on style and content of performance.'[1]

---

[1] Oulton became a satellite in 2 Group for Swanton Morley (where timber for Blickling Hall was felled in the 17th Century) and Douglas Bostons, flown by 88 Squadron, would soon arrive. These were to be the first in a continuous line of American-built aircraft at Oulton, which would extend to the end of the war.

MEMORIES OF BLICKLING

*I*t was on the 3rd April 1941, as a 20-year-old I first saw Blickling Hall. My first view, looking down the drive towards the main entrance is one which is as fresh today as it was 63 years ago.

At that time I was a Sergeant Wireless Operator/Air Gunner in 18 Squadron, which was equipped with twin engined Blenheim Mk.IV medium bombers. This aircraft had a crew of three: pilot, observer and wireless operator/air gunner. We had moved from the airfield at Great Massingham to Oulton, a couple of miles from the Hall. The Squadron remained at Oulton until 13th July, during which time we lost fifteen aircraft and had forty-three aircrew killed.

The Sergeants' Mess was situated in what is now the Stewards' Room, the entrance being in the southwest corner of the Hall. The main entrance and the staircase were not accessi-

ble to us but the remainder of the Hall and all of the grounds were our 'home'. The beauty of the Hall was not lost on me but being a native of Wensleydale it was the lake and grounds which were for me, the greatest asset.

At that time we were under a great deal of stress and the peace and tranquillity in which we found ourselves was an ideal setting in which to unwind. In the basement by the kitchen on the west side of the Hall was the telephone exchange. I can still picture cheese sandwiches waiting in the Mess for our attention on returning from an evening out. It was quite a pleasant summer and we regularly swam in the lake under the disapproving eye of the resident swan. We had no licensed bar so the Buckinghamshire Arms became out 'local' if we didn't have the desire to sample the 'fleshpots' of Norwich or Aylsham.

In June my 19-year-old brother Peter, who had just qualified as an electrician, was posted

Jim Moore, after a swim in the lake

to the Squadron. His quarters were in a dormitory above what is now the restaurant. He also worked on the Flight which I flew with and it must have been very traumatic for him when we were on operations. This situation was made worse when our aircraft was *damaged as a result of enemy action. On those occasions we would land at our parent 'drome, Horsham St. Faith, and leave the aircraft there to be repaired. Despite this experience, in August 1942 he re-mustered as an air gunner, losing his life on his first operation on 28th May 1943.*

At the beginning of July my crew was posted to the Middle East but, as I had been hospitalised with pneumonia at the beginning of the year, I was posted to 114 Squadron at RAF Leuchars.

As a nation, with only the Commonwealth countries as our allies following the succession of defeats, we truly had our 'backs to the wall'. Despite this, as a small Squadron (compared with what was to follow in May 1944), our morale was excellent. There was a good relationship between all ranks and there was a sense of belonging. Considering our losses, this may seem illogical but it is true.

I was to return to the Hall on 30th September 1942 as a newly commissioned Pilot Officer to join 88 Squadron, which was equipped with the twin-engined Douglas Bostons MK III.

The Officer's Mess was located in the East Wing of the Hall with the entrance in the South-East corner. Our circumstances were somewhat more luxurious than on my previous

On the lawn to the west side of the Hall

stay and my room looked out towards the Temple. An elderly batman took care of our needs. On this occasion we had our bar in the Mess and the sergeants had theirs in a single storey building on the west side of the Hall. By this time the outlook for our nation was looking decidedly brighter with the Americans now our allies, the 8th Army's victory at Alamein and before the end of the year the landings in North Africa. Both the Squadron and I were to remain at the Hall until 31st March 1943 when we moved to RAF Swanton Morley. The major operation in which the Squadron took part was on Sunday 6th December when we led 86 medium bombers on a daylight raid on two Philips Valve Works in the centre of the Dutch town of Eindhoven. The raid was successful despite the loss of fourteen aircraft but none from our Squadron. In the New Year some of our aircraft were taken to re-equip squadrons in North Africa, so we were for a while, non-operational. Compared with my first visit we had no fatalities yet, being rather under employed, it made us feel rather restless.

On my return I had renewed my relationship with Norma, a native of Norwich, so at every opportunity that fair city was my 'target'. We married on the 18th February 1943 and in 1993 we celebrated our Golden Wedding.

Before the end of the war I was to complete three tours of operations and fly 92 operations, yet the summer of '41 is the period which will forever be imprinted in my mind. It was the most exciting yet frightening time, contrasting to the beauty and peace provided by Blickling Hall.

Jim Moore DFC

Wellington crew boarding their plane

4

'ONE OF OUR AIRCRAFT IS MISSING'

Oulton is about as rural as it gets in Norfolk. On the other hand, the historic city of Norwich was and is a thriving city and in WWII the Norfolk capital and its 126,000 inhabitants were a target for *Luftwaffe* bombers. Following an attack by 234 RAF bombers, mostly carrying incendiaries, on the old Hanseatic City of Lübeck on the night of 28/29 March when about half the city, some 200 acres, was obliterated, Hitler ordered a series of *Terrorangriff* (terror attacks) mainly against English cities of historic or aesthetic importance, but little strategic value. In Britain they became known as the *Baedeker* raids, after the German guidebooks of the same name. Night after night terrified civilians were forced to cower in their cold and stinking Anderson shelters at the bottom of gardens in the weakly defended towns and cities in the West, south and east of the country while over-head the few RAF night-fighters available struggled to blunt the terror attacks. Loss of life was heavy. Teenager Nora Norgate, was one of thousands of Norwich citizens who in spring, 1942, was forced to endure frightful German bombing and deprivation.

'When war was declared in 1939 I was 15 years old and lived in a terraced house, 31 Belvoir Street, Norwich. My aunt was responsible for my upbringing after I'd lost my mother when I was four years old. After passing the school examination in July 1940 I stayed on at Blyth Secondary School for Girls, Norwich, to take a business course in shorthand, typing and book keeping. As the course progressed we went out for job interviews because many of the men were being called up into the

Norwich Thorpe Railway Station

services and were being replaced by girls. I was ready to leave for school one Monday morning in 1941 when a letter arrived informing me that I was to report for clerical work at the Goods Office, Thorpe Railway Station, Norwich, at 8:30 that same morning. There was no time to prepare: one minute I was a schoolgirl, the next a wage earner! At that time, both my elder sister and younger brother worked in a shoe factory in Norwich. I had worked at the railway station for about a year when the city was bombed very heavily by the Germans in a series of quite devastating raids. Being near the East Coast we witnessed many low-level attacks by German fighters and bombers.

'On 14 April 1942 the *Luftwaffe* had begun a series of attacks on Norwich and the East Coast, flying in below 3,000ft to avoid radar contact and flying home again flat out at speeds approaching 300 mph to make the task of interception very difficult. (For four consecutive nights, beginning on 23/24 April, Rostock was devastated by incendiary bombs and by the end only 40 per cent of the city was left standing). At 2015 hours on the night of Monday 27/28 April 28 German raiders were identified on radar heading for Norwich and twenty Ju 88s of *Kampfgeschwader (KG) 30* laid mines off the coast. Only three AI (Airborne Intercept) equipped Mosquito night-fighters, nine Beaufighters and ten Spitfires were available to intercept and the city was not protected by enough anti-aircraft batteries. Though AI radar contacts were made none of the raiders was shot down. This was the first raid by *I/KG2 'Holzhammer'* since converting to the Do 217E. Together with *IV/KG30* and *II/KG40*, from 2340 to 0045 hours, they dropped 185 HE bombs and incendiaries weighing 50 tons on Norwich, killing 162 people and injuring 600 more. Fourteen of the victims died instantly when their shelter near the Dolphin public house took a direct hit. Thousands of buildings were damaged and 84 people were dug out of the rubble alive. Some reports said that the enemy bombers machine-gunned the streets.'

Nora Norgate would never forget that night.

'The air-raid sirens began their mournful wailing at about 11 pm. We stirred in our beds waiting for the distinctive sound of the hooter, which told us enemy bombers were getting closer. It went almost immediately and we scrambled from our beds, hurriedly dressed, grabbed our torches and had just began to race downstairs and out to the Anderson Shelter in our backyard when the first of many bombs came whistling down. We cowered helplessly on the stairwell in the middle of our house hearing the frightening whine of falling bombs, the awful droning of the enemy planes and the house-shaking explosions. Then the windows suddenly shattered and were blown inwards, closed doors were blasted open, ceilings cracked, then collapsed in clouds of choking dust around us. We were absolutely terrified and were convinced we wouldn't live to see the morning. My sister, aunt and I clung closely together while wondering if my younger brother, who was at that time a messenger for the Air Training Corps, was in the immediate area. [It later transpired that he was quite safe.] Flares lit up the whole city like daylight as they floated down from the stream of bombers, dozens of swaying searchlight beams raked the sky, streams of bright tracer bullets were flying, anti-aircraft guns boomed defiance. I can't remember how long it all lasted, but it seemed forever.

'When we could no longer hear the bombers overhead we ventured out into the street. Shocked, shaken and in tears, we saw an unbelievable scene of destruction. Most of the houses in Belvoir Street were damaged. A few had been reduced to scattered piles of fiercely burning matchwood and rubble. Many people had been killed, even more injured, some seriously. Other areas of the city had been hit much harder. By some miracle Number 31 appeared to have been one of the least damaged houses in the street, but it would be some time before we got our windows replaced and all the repairs completed.

'The sound of the anti-aircraft gunfire, the strict "black-out,' the Air Raid Precaution warden, the food and clothing ration books issued to each family, gas-mask drills, steel helmets at work, sleepless nights in the shelters, shortages, and long queues for everything, and evacuation drills, were a part of every-day life.

'Two nights later [on Wednesday 29/Thursday 30 April] Norwich was again the target for German bombers. More high explosive and incendiary bombs fell, causing more fires and more loss of life but we were in the comparative safety of our Anderson shelter that night. [In all 69 people died and 89 were injured as 112 HE and machine gun fire reigned down on the city]. Many people were so apprehensive that they left the city during the nights, sleeping in any kind of shelter available in the surrounding countryside and returning to their homes the following morning. During the next seven or eight days after those two air raids, our family would leave our home after tea, walk out of the city, carrying blankets, pillows, sandwiches, hot tea in flasks and our torches to the Mile Cross Bridge and sleep under the bridge each night. We were up early the following morning, walked home and then went to our various places of work. About thirty barrage balloons were installed around Norwich shortly after the two raids and in early May 1942 they proved their worth because there was another, larger air raid, but the bombs fell on the outskirts of the city.'[1]

While Norwich reeled from the constant bombing at least its good citizens could draw some small measure of satisfaction knowing that brothers (Nora's brother was one who joined the RAF), fathers and cousins away in the services were 'dishing it

---

[1] George Swain in *Norwich Under Fire* states: 'By the end of 1944 we had more than 1,450 alerts. 670 high-explosive bombs and 25,000 incendiary bombs: 330 of us had been killed and 1,100 wounded: 30,000 homes had been damaged, more than 2,000 of them beyond repair'.

out' in good measure. As Air Marshal Sir Arthur Harris, who on 22 February was appointed C-in-C RAF Bomber Command, said,

The Germans entered this war under the rather childish delusion that they were going to bomb everybody else and nobody was going to bomb them. At Rotterdam, London, Warsaw, and half a hundred other places, they put that rather naive theory into operation. They sowed the wind, and now they are going to reap the whirlwind...

A new British directive calling for 'area bombing' of German cities had been sent to Bomber Command seven days before Harris's appointment (though for the rest of the war he became synonymous with the attacks on German cities). The Air Ministry decided that bombing the most densely built up areas would produce such dislocation and breakdown in civilian morale that the German home front would collapse. With the new directive bomber operations at night entered a new phase that was not restricted to one side of the divide. During May-August 1942 Harris unleashed 'Thousand Bomber' raids on Cologne, Essen and Bremen, though he could only accomplish this by pitching in untried crews from the Operational Training Units (OTUs), many of them flying Wellingtons, but even Blenheims and Hudsons were used. When 1,046 aircraft were sent to bomb Cologne on 30/31 May, 599 were Wellingtons and no fewer than 367 of the aircraft came from OTUs. For 98 minutes a procession of bombers passed over Cologne. Some 898 crews claimed to have reached and attacked the target. They dropped 1,455 tons of bombs, two-thirds of them incendiaries. More than 600 acres of the city were destroyed. In all, 40 bombers and 2 Intruders were lost, a 3.8 per cent loss rate; 116 were damaged, 12 so badly that they were written off. The fires burned for days and 59,100 people were made homeless. The second 'Thousand Bomber Raid' took place on the night of 1/2 June when 956 bombers including 347 from the OTUs went to Essen. 31 aircraft (3.2 per cent) failed to return. A third 'Thousand Bomber Raid' took place on the night of 25/26 June when 1,006 aircraft, including 102 Wellingtons of Coastal Command, attacked Bremen.

As the RAF night bombing offensive gained momentum the stark obituaries began to fill the newspaper columns. More often they read: *"Dead, MIA – believed killed."* Replacements for the losses came from the same OTUs that had contributed many hundreds of young aircrew for the Thousand Bomber raids. Canadian Flight Sergeant Delmer Mooney skippered one crew, which arrived at Marham, Norfolk in June 1942 to join 'A' Flight in 115 Squadron, which was equipped with Wellington bombers. His front-gunner/bomb aimer was Sergeant Joe Richardson and his tail-gunner, Sergeant Bill Margerison. Sergeant Eddie Killilea, the wireless

NORWICH 1943/4

Sgt Don Bruce

operator/air-gunner (WOP/AG) was quite a womaniser and could sing and dance as well. His easy rhythm on the dance floor had helped him during Morse training and he had finished top of his course. Sergeant Don Bruce, a 21-year old Londoner, was the observer and fifth member of the Wellington crew. He had already escaped serious injury in an Anson crash at Air Navigation School.

It was the practice for 'green' crews to fly their first op with an experienced pilot. Thus, Sergeant W. C. 'Norrie' Norrington was to be the crew's pilot for their first op, on 6/7 June. Sergeant Don Bruce recalls.

'A bomber operation began in the morning early. After breakfast we reported to the Flights, A and B, for nominal roll call by our Flight Commanders, approximately eight crews in each Flight plus the reserves. We were allotted our aircraft for local flying or air testing. Our kite was KO-A, a newly delivered machine, which we would write off temporarily in a crash landing at Exeter aerodrome after having been badly shot up by flak over Brest but that was for the future. Now we were to take it up for air firing, 'George' test – Automatic Pilot, and Homing practice – GEE. After an hour we landed and taxied to dispersal. As we passed through the Flights we saw instructions to the ground crews chalked up on the boards. Six hundred gallons of petrol and a 'standard' high explosive bomb load, six five-hundred pounders and a thousand pounder to drop in the middle of the stick, for KO-A. We then knew that we would be on "stand to" that night. Speculation was rife as to the target. Had it been 450 gallons it could have meant "Happy Valley", which is the nickname for the heavily defended Ruhr Valley or even a cushy trip to Paris and the Renault factory.

'After lunch we spent the time relaxing as far as possible and then around teatime we were briefed and told the target was Emden. From then on I was busy preparing the Flight Plan. At this stage of the war we were still given a certain amount of freedom in choosing our route and the height at which we would bomb. Another tense period of waiting followed, in which time I collected my bag of navigational instruments, a met report, and operational rations for the crew – usually chocolate, oranges or raisins, chewing gum and six thermos flasks, two of black coffee, two of tea and two of Bovril. Finally we were seated outside the Flights complete with flying kit and parachutes ready for the transport to take us to the aircraft at the dispersal points.

'As each crew arrived at their dispersal we wished them luck. Then we were seated on the grass by KO-A. It was still light. We had a long wait as we were near the end of the take off sequence. Some 24 aircraft from 218 and 115 Squadrons would be airborne before it was our turn. I looked over the hedge and saw a farmer ploughing his field. It was all so peaceful. I wished desperately that I could change places with him. Tense and nervous we urinated against the wheels of the aircraft for good luck. This was a standard practice among aircrews, later to be prohibited by Air Ministry order as the subsequent corrosion was causing undercarriage failures. As our take off time approached [2335 hours] I climbed into the aircraft and set the detonator and diffuser on GEE and its map container. It was warm inside and strangely quiet compared to the noise of the aircraft outside. I was alone for a moment and I looked around the observer's compartment trying to visualise a burst of cannon fire from a night fighter ripping through the cabin. Now the rest of the crew were climbing aboard. The pilot was starting the engines and I was too busy with my duties to think of anything else.

'We taxied along the perimeter track maintaining strict W/T silence. The aircraft ahead of us got the 'green' from the Aldis lamp and then we were swinging round to face the take off strip. No one spoke to the pilot. He must not be distracted. His aircraft is heavy and would take all his concentration to get it off the ground. He would do an 'operational take off'. The heavy tail turret complete with gunner must be raised off the ground first so he jammed on the brakes, and pushed the throttles up to the gates. The Wellington shuddered and roared. He pushed the stick forward until it almost touched the instrument panel. Slowly the tail lifted and when the nose was pointing slightly down he released the brakes and we trundled off. Momentum gathered and at 100 mph he was holding her down. At 120 mph we lifted off the ground. As I lifted my hands off the log to note the time we were airborne I saw that the place where they were resting was moist with sweat. Take off with full petrol and bomb load was extremely dangerous.

'We climbed on course. The next hazard would be if we passed over a British convoy sailing down the coast. A convoy would open fire on any aircraft passing directly over it. We were low and vulnerable and although we knew its approximate position this could be quite inaccurate as the convoy maintained strict W/T silence whilst in these waters. Some aircraft had been badly damaged in the past by convoys. We passed out to sea without incident, still climbing. The gunners called up for permission to try out their guns. The whole structure of the aircraft shuddered as the guns opened up and the reek of cordite pervaded the atmosphere in the cabin. We hoped that no patrolling night fighter had spotted our one-in-five tracer.

'Approaching the Dutch coast we unfolded and locked in position the armour plate doors. These doors were protection for the cabin and cockpit from a rear attack. Still climbing on course, the wireless operator in the astrodome assisted the rear gunner in his endless search for night fighters. This is where the area began, the Dutch coast, the beginning of the night fighter belt. The aircraft started to weave gently from side to side as the pilot attempted to uncover the blind spot below us for the gunners. Ten thousand feet, cold but not unpleasant, we began to use oxygen. The pilot had difficulty in engaging the S blower (supercharger). If he failed we would have to stay at 10,000 ft. I asked the pilot the outside temperature but he couldn't tell me as the indicator had fallen off the dial. He was worried that the oil temperature on the port engine was too high. He throttled that engine back. The rear gunner was experiencing difficulty with his turret. Would I check the recuperator rams, which indicated the hydraulic pressure? I put my hand out and felt them. They were flat. The turret could only be operated manually. Should we turn back? The pilot decided to carry on. Twelve thousand feet. We could see the glow from the target. Apart from the odd flak gun popping off miles out of range we had experienced little hostility. I worked out the course to bring us out of the target towards the sea.

'The gunners were now calling over the intercom warning the pilot of pockets of flak. We started to weave violently. I moved forward to the bomb aimer's position setting the course on the pilot's compass as I went past. Lying prone along the bombing hatch I got a good view of the target which was well alight. It was like a running red sore in the blackness of the night. For a brief moment I felt sick with horror and thought of the human beings below. Then I was too busy to care. I set the rotor arm that would space the stick of bombs and removed the bomb release from its holder. This automatically fused the bombs. I lined the target up in the wires of the bombsight. The flak was heavy and the pilot weaved desperately. Red balls of light flak started lazily from the ground. Gaining in impetus they appeared to come straight for my stomach. I sucked my breath in. They passed like lightning to one side of us and were arcing above us. This confirmed what we have been told that the light flak at Emden reached 14,000 feet. We were menaced by both heavy and light flak. I got a glimpse of the target. No time for standard bombing pattern now. The gunners were yelling for the bombs to be dropped. They wanted to be away. All was noise, confusion, flak, searchlights and roaring, lurching, aircraft. I saw the target again. *Get over to port man. Hold it. BOMBS GONE!*

'The bomber rose, unburdened and free. We swung round on course and I scrambled back to the cabin. We left the target behind in a shallow dive to increase our speed. We were away to the comparative safety of the open sea.

'Everyone relaxed. We were flying parallel to the coast and danger was remote. Perhaps a patrolling Ju 88 night fighter but the chance was slight. I was busy with my navigation. The wireless operator poured coffee for us and took an empty milk bottle up to the pilot so that he could relieve himself. 'George' was u/s so he could not get back to the Elsan toilet. The pilot was still concerned about the oil temperature. It turned out later that the gauge was reading incorrectly. The final stretch of sea and then the English coastline. I switched on the IFF. We didn't want to be intercepted by our own fighters and for the same reason we stayed at a predetermined height. Crossing the coast and moving inland, eyes were peeled for Norwich and its balloon barrage should we be off course. We picked up the aerodrome and started to circle. The pilot tested the undercart and the red light stayed on meaning the wheels would not lock.

'We called up the ground. "Hallo Waggon Control, this is Reveille A Apple". No reply. We repeated several times, then it dawned on us that the transmitter had packed up. The receiver was working. We heard another aircraft calling. The aerodrome replied. It is not Waggon Control. We were over the wrong aerodrome. Panic for a moment until we found our bearings and arrived over Marham. We crossed the flare path at right angles and fired the distress signal, double green. Then we flew over again flashing "A" on our downward identity light. They were calling us from Waggon Control and telling other aircraft to get out of the circuit. To cheer us up they told us that the ambulance or "blood wagon" and the fire tender were standing by. They didn't know we were receiving them so they flashed a green from the Aldis lamp. We made a pass but the pilot overshot. We were braced ready for a crash landing. Second time round we made it. A perfect landing. The undercart locking light wasn't working. We climbed out. Suddenly my parachute harness weighed a ton. A quick debriefing with Intelligence and then cool, smooth sheets and wonderful, deep sleep.'

Some 233 aircraft, including 124 Wellingtons, had set out for Emden that night. Nine bombers failed to return. Crews reported good bombing results and this was confirmed by later photographic reconnaissance. Emden reported that approximately 300 houses were destroyed and that 200 were seriously damaged with 17 people killed and 49 injured.

In between 'ops' aircrews let their hair down when they could. On 12 June Bruce, Killilea and Margerison visited nearby King's Lynn. Killilea, attracted by a tall blonde in the doorway of the Eagle pub, suggested they paid it a visit. Bruce and

Margerison were hungry and went their own way to a cafe. A short time later, a Dornier, exploiting a hole in the clouds to excellent advantage, made a hit and run attack on the town. Bruce and Margerison finished up under the table. Further down the road the 'Eagle' was flattened. Killilea was among the 42 bodies pulled from the wreckage.

Jack Goad replaced Killilea and Flight Sergeant Del Mooney returned to captain the crew. On the night of 17/18 June the crew of KO-A Z1648 were part of a small force of 27 Stirlings and Wellingtons which flew an operation to St. Nazaire while another 46 aircraft carried out mine laying off the French port and in the Frisians. Aboard Mooney's Wellington were sixteen 250lb bombs but the target could not be identified in poor weather and only six aircraft bombed.[1]

Bruce had trouble with his compass and the ETA for landfall in England came and went. When Bruce finally got his pinpoint worked out he nearly had a baby on the spot! He shouted over the intercom:

'We're right over Brest'.

Just at that moment the searchlights came on and coned us. Del started to weave the Wellington but the flak was already bursting closer. He climbed 500 feet and then dived 500 feet. It was rather sickening for us and as we dived the gravity sucked the fuel from the engines and they cut out. We did not know if we had been hit. Only Del knew that. I was absolutely paralysed with fear and what with the table going up and down I could not plot a thing.'

Suddenly, Del Mooney snarled over the intercom,

'Give them a stick!'

Eight 250-pounders whistled down into the night and as they exploded the searchlights went out. However, the port engine, which ran the hydraulics and the radio, had been put out of action. Mooney turned and limped away from Brest in a northerly direction. Over the sea the remaining 250-pounders were jettisoned. White managed to get his transmitter working off batteries and sent out a Mayday distress call, which was acknowledged. Bruce was so dejected that he swore if they got back he would never fly again. However they did get back. Mooney suggested they crash-land but the Englishmen aboard warned how hilly the West Country is. Mooney thought they should crash land on the beach but the crew was worried about mines. Bruce, now standing in the second pilot's position, saw runways passing below the bomb panel. He exclaimed,

'Hey! We're over an aerodrome'.

---

[1] RAF crews were not allowed to release bombs over France if the target could not be determined.

It was Exeter. Mooney banked carefully and the aerodrome put its light on. As they made their approach a searchlight was swung onto the Wimpy, almost blinding the swearing Canadian. Exeter was a fighter airfield and had a different system of lights, which no one understood. Mooney ended up going downwind at 110mph. Bruce looked back at the undercarriage and could see the wheels hanging down. Grimly, he gripped Mooney's seat and as they touched the concrete runway, the wheels folded and the Wimpy collapsed onto its belly. Great streaks of sparks shot back from the fuselage. Fortunately, the starboard engine was still operating and it slewed the bomber around in a 180-degree arc as 'blood wagons' chased them along the runway. They finished up facing the opposite direction. Everyone got out safely but KO-A was a write-off. No one was sad to see the end of it for the gun turrets had never worked. In the afternoon Squadron Leader Cousens flew down from RAF Marham to take the crew home.

Next day Bruce had got over the Brest episode. On the night of 19/20 June the RAF raided Emden. Some 194 aircraft, including 112 Wellingtons took part. Of these 131 crews claimed to have bombed Emden but bombing photographs revealed that part of the flare force started a raid on Osnabrück, 80 miles from Emden, in which 29 aircraft eventually joined. Emden reported only five HE bombs and 200-300 incendiaries with no damage or casualties. The RAF lost nine bombers including six Wellingtons. On 20/21 June 185 RAF bombers made a return raid on Emden. Mooney's Wellington carried a 4,000-pounder in the bomb bay. The crew returned safely once again but eight aircraft including three Wellingtons, were lost. Two nights later, on 22/23 June the RAF returned again to Emden when a force of 227 aircraft, comprising 144 Wellingtons, 38 Stirlings, 26 Halifaxs, 11 Lancasters, 8 Hampdens was dispatched. Some 196 crews claimed good bombing results but decoy fires are believed to have drawn off many bombs. Emden reported that 50 houses had been destroyed, 100 damaged and some damage caused to the harbour. Six people were killed and 40 injured. Bomber Command lost six aircraft; four of them Wellingtons.

On 25/26 June the RAF mounted the third and final 1,000 Bomber Raid, to Bremen. Some 1,067 aircraft were dispatched, mainly Wellingtons and Halifaxs and including over 100 Hudsons and Wellingtons of Coastal Command. Although the raid was not as successful as the first 1,000 raid on Cologne on 30/31 May, large parts of Bremen, especially in the South and East districts, were destroyed. The price Bomber Command paid for this raid was very high. No less than 48 aircraft were lost; the highest casualty rate in the war so far.

On the night of 27/28 June Del Mooney's crew were one of 55 Wellington

P/O BILL HANCOCK

F/SGT DEL MOONEY

SGT BILL MARGERISON

BASE – 115 SQUADRON MARHAM

SGT DON BRUCE

SGT RON ESLING

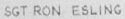

DUISBURG
NIGHT 13/14TH JULY 1942
BAILED OUT NIJNSEL/SON

OBSERVER

REAR GUNNER

bombers among the 144 aircraft that visited the city again. Of these, 119 aircraft bombed blindly through cloud after obtaining Gee fixes. Nine aircraft failed to return but Mooney's crew landed back at Marham safely. Their run of operational bombing sorties was interrupted towards the end of the month. On 30 June Mooney's crew made two search operations over the North Sea for a missing aircrew. Bill Margerison moved from the rear turret to the front and a new rear gunner, Sergeant Ron Esling, joined the crew as WOP/AG and flew with the crew on the night of 2/3 July when Bremen was bombed again, this time by 265 of the 325 bombers dispatched. Some 13 aircraft were lost.

Mooney's crew's next operation was to Duisburg, Germany on the night of 13/14 July when 194 aircraft including 139 Wellingtons, were despatched in what was the first of a series of raids on this industrial city on the edge of the Ruhr. Mooney and his crew were given a new Wellington Mk III, KO-K, to replace KO-A. By now they were old hands on the squadron, with six weeks' operational experience. This operation would be Don Bruce's eleventh trip; unlucky thirteen if he counted the two search sweeps over the North Sea. All through briefing Bruce's mind was on the bomb load they would be carrying deep into Germany. It was a lightly cased 4,000-lb dustbin-shaped bomb studded with detonators. For maximum blast effect it had a protruding rim to prevent it penetrating too far into the ground. The Wellington had to be stripped of its bomb-bay doors and flotation bags to accommodate the sinister weapon which meant that the bomber would not be able to fly on one engine or float for long if they had to ditch. Mooney's crew was to follow in the wake of a main bomber stream. There would be a lull after the main force had finished bombing and the Germans would assume that the raid was over. Their rescue services would be in full swing and the KO-K would arrive over Duisburg to drop its maximum blast bomb, effectively wiping out any rescue services.

The briefing room was crowded and hot. Thirty-one year old Wing-Commander Frank W. Dixon-Wright DFC, the 115 Squadron CO, addressed his crews.

'Go for the centre of the town, boys. Plenty of old dry timber there. It will burn well...after all they do it to our towns so we do it to theirs.'[1]

Mooney's crew left the briefing and prepared to take off for Duisburg. Bruce recalls,

'Prior to take-off I was busy preparing the Flight Plan. I collected my bag of navigational instruments, a met report and operational rations for the crew: the

[1] Dixon-Wright was to die a fortnight later, on 27 July, bombing Hamburg.

usual chocolate, oranges and raisins, chewing gum and six thermos flasks. As before we were seated outside the Flights, complete with flying kit and parachutes, ready for transportation to the dispersal point. We sat on the grass by KO-K. It was still sunlight and we had a long wait. Forty aircraft from two squadrons were getting airborne at approximately two-minute intervals.

'We climbed aboard. Del started the engines and we taxied along the perimeter track maintaining strict W/T silence. The aircraft ahead of us got the 'green' from the Aldis lamp and then we were swinging round to face the take-off strip.

'We climbed on course, passing out to sea without incident. Still climbing, the gunners test-fired their .303in. calibre guns. Nearing the Dutch coast we unfolded and locked into position the armour plate doors. Still climbing on course, the WOP/AG in the astrodome helped Ron Esling in his search for night fighters.

'Approaching Duisburg and running in at 13,000 feet, Mooney became cautious, steering the bomber around the town. Suddenly, he spotted what he had been seeking, another Wellington about 500 feet below and making its run across the target. It was attracting the flak and the searchlights. KO-K followed unmolested. When things became too hot for the crew, the other Wimpy banked away in a dive. KO-K maintained its position, right in the centre of the target.

'The Wellington bucked as the 4,000-lb bomb was released. The defences tried to bring them down. All hell was let loose and the blue "radar" searchlight on them was joined immediately by other searchlights, forming a cone around them. Mooney had forgotten to put his goggles on and was blinded by the glare. Esling, who had been wounded by flak once before, was shouting over the intercom for Mooney to get out of the beams.'

Bruce thought to himself,

'We have very little time before our height and course are predicted. Can't shake them off. They are hitting us.'

He heard a sound like a stick rattling on corrugated iron.

The port engine is hit.

The pilot in desperation pulled the nose up and up. There was an inert sensation throughout before the stall, and then Mooney swung the bomber over in a stall turn. The Wimpy was now diving in the opposite direction. The searchlights lost the bomber in its exacting gyrations but would the Wellington stand up to the great stresses Mooney was imposing upon it? The bomber plunged to 9,000 feet. Inside, the crew was floating in space. Only the navigation table held Bruce down where it pinned his knees. Maps, stray nuts, bolts and pencils floated past his face. All this time his eyes remained glued to the Observer's airspeed indicator. The needle had started on the inner circle: 320, 330, 340, 350 mph. He read the ever-increasing airspeed indicator with alarm, thinking of the red warning plate mounted on the pilot's control panel which said,

THIS AIRCRAFT MUST NOT BE DIVED AT SPEEDS OF 300 MPH.

Down and down the Wellington dived. Gravitational force pressed on the hands and arms of the crew, making them feel as heavy as lead and forcing Bruce down into his seat and onto the navigational table. His eyelids began to close involuntarily.

Before the 'final squashing process' Mooney somehow managed to pull the Wimpy out of its near fatal dive. The crew could hear him, panting with exertion through his microphone. They were as one with this terrible load that was wrenching at every rivet in the aircraft. As suddenly as it had begun it was over, and incredibly the bomber was back on the straight and level. All manner of debris littered the table and floor. The case containing the rations had burst open showering the Observer's table with raisins. In the dim light Don Bruce watched an earwig emerge from the sticky heap.

Bruce gathered his maps from the floor near the bed while Mooney was still fully employed with the control column and rudder, desperately trying to keep the port wing, with its dead engine, on an even keel. He climbed 500 feet but the starboard engine could not do the work of two and began overheating. As the aircraft levelled out it dropped back to 500 feet. It lost height so rapidly that the crew realised that they would not make the coast. A hurried consultation between Mooney and Bruce resulted in the immediate order of

'Jump, jump, rear-gunner!'

There was no reply from Esling. Bruce was about to investigate when Mooney cried out,

'Don't bother – he's gone.'

The Canadian could tell from the trim of the aircraft, which was flying light in the tail, that he had baled out. If Bruce had been required to turn the turret using the 'dead man's handle' it is doubtful whether he and Mooney would have got out in time.

The forward escape hatch in the Wellington was for use by the pilot, wireless operator, front gunner and the observer. Bill Margerison went through the forward escape hatch first after taking some time to find his parachute, which had been dislodged during the stall turn. Bill Hancock started but almost at once returned to his position to retrieve his gloves. Bruce removed his intercom to prevent strangulation during the parachute descent, loosened his tie (the RAF dressed for war!) and fastened his parachute to his harness. Mooney grinned and gave Bruce the thumbs up.

'Good old Delmer, he's a great guy', thought Bruce.

The Wellington had a diamond-shaped escape hatch on the starboard side, near the bed. It was cut away in the geodetics and either covered with fabric or a trapdoor. This was to be used only in extreme emergency but Bruce doubted whether anyone could exit through it with a parachute pack. He was not about to try. He moved to the forward escape hatch and gingerly lowered his legs through the hole. The slipstream caught them like chaff in the wind and he was swept along the underside of the fuselage, his parachute pack jamming against the hatch in the process. Finally, Bruce was away – down into the night.

'THE RIPCORD! Pull the ripcord you fool!' Bruce shouted to himself.

There was a sharp slither of fabric as the pilot 'chute tugged at the main fabric arid then a crack like a pistol as the cords holding the harness across his chest broke free. There was a terrific jolt and the umbrella of silk opened. He felt sick and hung limply in his harness. Dim shapes began to form. He got into a sitting position. The parachute trailing ahead in a light wind caught in a tree. Bruce swung into soft earth and grazed his elbow. He had, in fact, landed near a farm at Nijnsel in Saint-Oedenrode owned by Mr Van Dijk. Bruce shouted

'Hello!'

A woman gave a piercing scream and both Van Dijk and his 17-year old son, William, who were outside thinking a German aircraft had crashed, ran inside because there was a curfew and Dutch people were not allowed outside at this hour. They peered out through a window and saw Bruce take off his Mae West and make off down the road. He was alone in a strange country.

William van Dijk recalls:

'All of us hadn't realised Bruce came down so near behind us, till suddenly a wind blew against our backs, and, surprised, we looked back and saw his chute hanging in a tree. However, we were so surprised that we ran indoors but we had not yet seen him. When we were indoors we looked through the window and saw an airman taking off his Mae West. He made off down the road. However we did not let him indoors, as we were of the opinion a German plane had come down and we thought he was a German. Moreover, then there was still a curfew so we were not allowed to go outside at this hour. His parachute was taken by the German patrol and the German soldiers asked us, "Where is the Tommy?"

'We explained by signs (we could not speak German) that he had gone away, but they didn't believe it. Then one of them pointed a gun at my father; ready to fire, while four other soldiers searched the farmhouse. Big iron pins were stabbed into the hay in the loft. During this time we were very afraid as it had been possible the airman had crept indoors. When the Germans had searched everything and every place, they went away. Some hours later we heard that the airman and a friend had been taken into the house of Mr Bekkers. But still another friend had parachuted closer to the burning plane. However, he had broken his ankle and was taken by the Germans at the same time.'

The Wellington had been shot down at approximately 0330 hours. Ron Esling, the first man to bale out, had landed in a farmyard. His first reaction was to go to sleep; a sure sign of shock. He did not sleep long. He decided to open his survival kit. Not wishing to be caught with what was essentially a 'spy kit', Esling proceeded to eat all the edible maps, water purification tablets, uppers and downers' pills and chocolate! Feeling drunk and after trying, unsuccessfully, one of the many farm labourer's houses around the farm, Esling tottered into the village of Son. Esling hammered happily on the door of a most imposing house which, as it turned out, belonged to the *Burgomeister* and his charming and pregnant wife. The Burgomeister was a pleasing fellow and he took the fallen flier in.

Esling was hardly the picture of sartorial elegance and so the mayor called for a barber. A shave and haircut improved the airman's morale. However, the mayor informed him that, much to his regret, he would have no option but to turn him over to the authorities because he had already attracted too much attention in the district. He asked Esling what branch of the military would he like to take him into custody. Esling replied, '*the Luftwaffe*'. In his current state of mind he would not have been surprised to have said, '*the Gestapo.*' The pills were having an effect and Esling dozed off to sleep again. A *Luftwaffe* field policeman standing before him and shouting at the top of his voice awakened him. Esling thought he looked like someone in a play. The German had just shaved because he still had talcum powder on his face. Around his neck hung an illuminated plaque and he wore the familiar 'piss pot' helmet on his head. There the comedy stopped. Amid a tearful farewell, Esling was marched into custody.

Meanwhile, Bill Hancock had also been captured. He had almost landed on top of the burning Wellington but had managed to pull the shrouds of his parachute and just missed a fiery death. He landed in a field full of cows, twisting his ankle in the process. While he struggled to his feet two very young German soldiers rushed him and arrested the fallen airman.

Don Bruce had left the scene of the crash at the Van Dijk's farm. Bruce met a man out of the darkness pushing a bicycle. He eyed the British airman suspiciously. Bruce discovered only much later that in this particular part of Holland the Dutch had not seen RAF personnel before and to them the RAF uniform was very similar to the German one. After an amusing tug of war over the bicycle the Dutchman realised that Bruce was not a German and he led him to a cottage. Bruce tried unsuccessfully to converse in English and then French. Just at that moment footsteps could be heard along the road. They were Germans! The Dutchman panicked, shut the door and left Bruce standing alone on the porch. Luckily, the German patrol ignored him. Taking no further chances, Bruce ran down the road in the opposite direction. The following morning he had another close shave when a German staff car roared past but did not stop. It was just another example of what a RAF airman on the run could get away with at this stage of the war.

Bruce eventually arrived at Nijnsel. He remembered what he had been told at evasion briefings: 'Head for large houses where the inhabitants are thought to be better educated and therefore able to speak English.' Bruce chose a large building but it turned out to be the presbytery of the village church. He knocked at the door and a grille opened to reveal a face. Bruce pointed to RAF brevet and said, '*RAF*'.

The figure replied, '*Nein. Nein*'.

Later, Bruce was told that it was a woman cleaner and that she was stone deaf!

It was the final straw. Soaking wet from a rainstorm and suffering from shock he wandered around the village in despair. He thought of giving himself up. No one appeared to want to help. Although he did not know it, there was no resistance group in the area and there was little chance of getting back to England. In desperation he approached some of the congregation who were leaving the church. Van de Laar, a seventeen-year old Dutch boy, listened to the airman. He did not understand that Bruce wanted a telephone so that he could give himself up. The Dutch took Bruce to the house of Pieter Bekkers, the village baker who had a telephone. People from miles around came to see the British airman on whose country so many Dutch pinned their hopes. Many peered through the baker's windows and others came inside and shook Bruce's hand.

Anna Bekkers, the baker's wife, asked Bruce how old he was. By means of sign language he drew the figure '21'. Mrs Bekkers threw her arms in the air and began crying. Bruce thought,

'My God, does she think I'm too young to die?'

He was physically and mentally exhausted by now and really believed he might be shot by a firing squad.

Meanwhile, Bill Margerison had had better luck. He had fallen in a wheat field about three miles from where Don Bruce had landed. He lay low until the following morning when a passing friendly Dutch civilian escorted him to a farmhouse between Son and Nijnsel. Van de Laar was despatched to find him. Margerison accompanied the young Dutchman on a bicycle and was reunited with Don Bruce at the Bekkers' house.

Pieter Bekkers wanted to hide both the British airmen but Bruce knew the situation was hopeless and told him he must hand them in. Bekkers reluctantly telephoned the Burgomeister. He agreed with Bruce. So many people had seen the two men that one might inform the Germans. The Burgomeister summoned Police Chief Eikenaar, head of Dutch Police in the area, and aided by *Luftwaffe* officers he arrested the two British airmen.

Bruce and Margerison were taken to the *burgomeister's* house in Son where Ron Esling was under house arrest. All three men were taken to a *Luftwaffe* airfield at Eindhoven where they were joined by Del Mooney. The Canadian explained that he had baled out of the doomed Wellington with great difficulty. Hancock had clipped on Mooney's parachute but had only fastened it on one side. It was never easy to exit from a Wellington in distress because the pilot had to crawl underneath his seat and leave by the escape hatch in the floor.

As Mooney left his seat, the Wellington began rising on its one remaining engine and started circling. As if that was not enough, Mooney had to get his parachute clipped on properly and fight his way down to the escape hatch. When he had finally got to the floor the Wimpy had lurched into a dive, hurtling to earth at frightening speed. It had taken a frenzied surge of strength on the part of Mooney to extricate himself. He just managed to get clear at only five hundred feet. The time lapse between his baling out and the Wellington crashing was so slight that he had almost landed on top of the burning bomber.

The crew was re-united with Bill Hancock and after four days at Eindhoven they were put on a train for Amsterdam. There they were put in cells below ground for two days. Hancock was retained for more questioning and then sent to *Stalag Luft III* but Mooney, Margerison, Bruce and Esling were sent to the *Dulag Luft* Interrogation Centre outside Frankfurt. (*Stalag Luft III* was for RAF officers only.)

Their train steamed across the flat lands of Holland and through the German countryside to Cologne. The city had been devastated three weeks before by an RAF 1,000-bomber raid and feeling among the German civilians was running high. The station was extremely crowded with the evacuation still in progress. The sight of RAF uniforms aroused deep hatred and the prisoners had to be locked in a small room for their own protection.

Although the train was overcrowded the escort party and their prisoners had a reserved compartment. Bruce sat down and glanced casually through the window towards the platform. An elderly German rushed over, fixed his eyes on the British airman, swore profusely and then spat on the window. Apparently, he objected to the RAF having seats and, eventually, he succeeded in getting them moved out of the compartment. Bruce and his fellow crewmembers spent the journey to Frankfurt standing in the corridor.

At *Dulag Luft*, Mooney's crew signed the visitors' book, checking to see if there were any other crews that had been shot down on the Duisburg raid. It was not until after the war that Bruce discovered that they were one of five crews shot down on the raid and according to the visitors' book, the only survivors.

The four airmen were marched away to solitary confinement, interrogation and eventual processing for onward transmission to POW camps. On 19 July they were despatched to *Stalag Luft VIIIB* at Lamsdorf to begin almost three years of tedious and sometimes painful internment behind barbed wire. Ironically, their route took them past Duisburg. Much to the amusement of the escorting German Officer, Bruce and his fellow crewmembers were surprised at the lack of bomb damage around the city.

5

YANKEE DOODLE COMES TO TOWN

A respite from bombing – combat crews playing softball whilst formations of Liberators return from bombing missions

'*Achtung, feindliche Flugzeuge!' Jagdfuhrer* or Fighter Control, Holland had picked up four three-plane elements heading across the North Sea. Immediately *Luftwaffe* fighter units were alerted. German radar had picked up twelve US-built Boston medium bombers thundering low across the North Sea to four airfield targets in Holland. Six of the aircraft carried RAF crews while American crews of the 15th Bomb Squadron (Light) manned the other half dozen. Significantly, it was 4 July 1942 – American Independence Day – and the first time American airmen had flown in US-built bombers against a German target.

Being the first American airmen to fly a mission from England was probably furthest from their minds when the officers and men of the 15th Light Bombardment Squadron aboard the P&O merchant cruiser HMS *Cathay* had docked on 14 May, at Newport, Wales. They were the first Army Air Force unit to arrive in the theatre since America entered the war at the end of 1941. The USA had been dramatically shaken from its isolation and was pitched headlong into the tumult of global war on 7 December when Japanese bombers operating from carriers in the Pacific Ocean carried out an unprovoked assault on Pearl Harbor and other military installations in Hawaii. Germany declared war on America the following day.

The 15th Bomb Squadron (Light) was symptomatic of America's almost total unpreparedness for war. It had no aircraft but some of its personnel had worked on the Douglas A-20 Havoc (Boston) and a few had even flown them. Shipped to England as nightfighters, the 15th was never part of the high-altitude daylight precision bombing offensive using heavy bombers envisioned by American war planners. Its use was a hasty stop-gap measure resorted to by AAF General Henry 'Hap' Arnold after promising British Prime Minister Winston Churchill on 23 May, '*We will be fighting with you on July 4th.*' Arnold had in mind a scheduled B-17 Group for this job, but dire events interfered. On 4th June the Japanese initiated a major offensive in the Pacific, attacking Alaska and Midway Island. B-17s about to depart for England were immediately diverted to the American West Coast. With the turning-point Battle of Midway over, original orders sending the B-17s to England were reinstated but the delay caused by the shuttle exercise made it impossible for any of the Fortress squadrons involved to fly a mission to Germany before mid-August. That left the 15th, the only AAF squadron in the 8th Air Force, to fulfil Arnold's promise to Churchill.

The 15th entrained for Grafton Underwood in Northamptonshire, the first of four bases it would occupy during its stay in England. The American squadron was given a warm welcome by the RAF CO, as Captain Bill Odell, a mid-westerner originally commissioned as an Anti-Aircraft Artillery Officer in 1938, recalls.

'Beside him, US Brigadier General Ira C Eaker, representing the 8th Air Force, also greeted the newcomers, speaking with inspiration and pride when he said their arrival marked the first time in history that any American fighting unit set foot in England. 1st Lieutenant Philip Hennin, a pilot whose mother was active in the Burlington, Vermont 'Daughters of the American Revolution' chapter (an exclusive women's patriotic society restricted to female descendants of the men who fought in the War of Independence), glanced around at the blue-uniformed RAF officers present to catch any adverse reaction. Then he muttered, "I wonder if General Braddock said something like that to his redcoat regiments that marched across Pennsylvania in 1775?" Hennin was known for his off beat sense of humour and his rather dour outlook on life. General Eaker's closing comment, "All those who come after you, by comparison, will be recruits," was meant to be complimentary, but cool scepticism showed on Hennin's face.'

Bill Odell said in an undertone,

15th Bomb Squadron crews

'We aren't here for manoeuvres; this is for real. The general should have said "replacements", not "recruits."'

Hennin then added a final remark,

'Anyway, that's the last we'll see of him.'

He was to be proved wrong. In time, Eaker would visit the squadron again, along with the two highest-ranking American generals in the ETO to make note of a memorable event.

The 15th were at the mercy of the RAF and soon learned the meaning of wartime rationing. RAF cooks were running the mess and the only palatable food for Americans used to peacetime fare was black bread and cheese. Everything else was slop. After a week or so the American Mess Sergeant and cooks took over the kitchen and the food improved but some rations defied their best efforts.

The 15th Bomb Squadron had been despatched to England with the first influx of US troops in the UK to learn how to operate the airborne searchlight used by the RAF's Havoc (Douglas DB-7) night fighters. Airborne radar had replaced the airborne searchlight and the Americans were moved around East Anglia. Frustration was creeping in. The 15th still had no aircraft and the men were becoming tired of quaint English village stone walls, vine-covered churches and warm beer. They liked still less the constant rejoinder: 'It's rationed you know' and 'There's a war on Yank!'

On 4 June Lieutenant Cook went over to Swanton Morley for some first hand experience from the RAF on their way of doing things. Lieutenant Howard Cook was no more happy with the state of affairs in the 15th than anyone else and probably this led to his first big mistake when he tried to tell the RAF how to fly low!

While at Grafton Underwood, on Thursday 6 June, the 15th Squadron suffered two fatal accidents shortly after receiving its first DB-7 aircraft. The cause of the first accident was never discovered but the second was due to pilot error. Practising low level flying, Lieutenant Raditsky flew the aircraft into a high-tension cable. One cable caught the aircraft at the junction of the metal and Plexiglas, shearing the entire nose glass covering section from the bombardier's compartment where Lieutenant Notorwitz was sitting. The pilot managed to avoid a crash and brought the aircraft home safely. Jack Stone of the Engineering Office hurried to meet the aircraft, not knowing what to expect, but certainly not prepared for the macabre sight that met his eyes.

'The Plexiglas had been sheared off and the decapitated body of the bombardier remained strapped in the seat. The force of the wind through the open compartment had whipped the body against the jagged edges of Plexiglas. The compartment was a horrible bloody mess and blood covered the sides of the plane from nose to tail.'

On 7 June Captain Kegelman, acting squadron commander, was ordered to vacate the base to make room for the incoming 97th Bomb Group equipped with B-17s. Flights in training with the RAF were recalled and all flying activity was halted while the move to Molesworth, a new airfield constructed especially for US heavy bomber use, took place. No explanation was given for the sudden move, a mere seven miles distance. Much to their chagrin, the move put them within sight and sound of other bases where aircraft could be heard going on missions. While pilots in the 15th Squadron were awaiting radio equipment and aircraft to arrive from the States before anything else could be done most of the ground crews were passing the time away at Molesworth, waiting for something to happen. By 25 June, by which time equipment had arrived, there was no place to store it and no aircraft either, as the Bostons and Kegelman, Crabtree, Odell, Cook and six other pilots and gunners had started training under the direction of 226 Squadron.

Bill Odell recalls:

'Senior Flight Leaders, Captains Kegelman, Crabtree and myself had been commissioned officers at least four years before our arriving in England, had flown the A-20 aircraft almost two years and each had over 1,000 hours flight time. Our junior pilots, like Lieutenants Hawel, Loehrl and Lynn, had completed flying school in December 1941. The only advantage we Yanks had was largely technical. We learned by flying in the RAF manner on the wing of battle-experienced pilots. There was much to learn. At the same time, the 226 pilots discovered we flew the Boston differently than they did. In a subtle way we demonstrated a different technique when taking off in formation. While the RAF leader approached

Martin Crabtree, centre with life jacket

the end of the field still on the ground the US pilot wingmen would be airborne and flying alongside with their wheels drawing up into the wheel wells. The RAF mechanics were particularly grateful; damaged nose gear wheels and struts had become a major headache for them.

'From the beginning, Wing Commander Lynn, CO, 226 Squadron, recognized that the senior ranking US pilots – Captains and 1st Lieutenants with up to two years flying the A-20 – knew and flew the Boston aircraft better than his own. Even the 2nd Lieutenants who had completed AAF flying schools in late December 1941 had more technical knowledge and mechanical aptitude than any newly trained RAF pilot being posted to his squadron. The training they had received and absorbed was consistent with that given RAF crews being readied for daylight sweeps or night intruder missions. They had recently conducted simulated attacks and live bombing runs on sunken ships near the coast or land targets on isolated spits of land and there was little doubt that their RAF training was in its final phase. All they lacked was actual combat experience.

'In that regard, Wing Commander Lynn had advised his superiors that aside from providing an initial baptism of fire, his ability to further the Americans' pre-battle education was limited. They had already participated in combat-related activities by flying with the host squadron aircraft, ranging far beyond the English coastlines on post-mission sea searches for downed RAF aircrews. Lynn believed the American aircrews placed in his custody were fully familiar with the local topography and able to comply with all RAF flight procedures. They could be turned loose anytime and be perfectly confident of finding their way around in the dark.'

On 4 June at Great Massingham ten officers in two groups, one under Cook and the other under Odell left early in the morning to go to operational stations. Odell recalls,

'I was also given ten sergeants, who hoped to make a show as aerial gunners. We arrived at West Raynham just at lunchtime, so booked our meals and went to a briefing of the Boston Squadron. Time had to be wasted, so we watched the installation of a power mount for the twin guns of the Boston. It seemed quite practical, since it had almost all advantages of a turret, yet none of the tremendous weight. I was anxious to see what results were obtained after practice firing.

'The briefing took place in the ops Offices. The target was a 480-ft tower in the docks at Dunkirk. The route was almost direct using the tactics of sea level flight to foil the radio aircraft-detection system until about 13 minutes from the coast. At that point a 1,000-ft climb was to begin and we would drop four 500lb bombs at 10,000-ft. We watched the take-off and saw the English method was much different to ours. Namely, their engines were run from ten to twenty minutes on the ground before flight. The members of this squadron were all Blenheim trained which might have accounted for such procedure. The Bostons were kept on the ground with all three wheels until a bounce forced the pilot to fly it. One new pilot took off with upper cowl flaps open and reported back to the Squadron CO that he thought for a long while it was the bomb load causing the different flight characteristics. They attempted to take off in formation but didn't seem to hold it very well and didn't become organized until after four-five minutes of flying. They had a much more open formation than we did.

'We left the field for dinner after a talk with their Engineering Officer about engine trouble and booster coils as well as brake and landing gear problems. The average British pilot seemed to know very little about his ship. One Blenheim pilot didn't know how many cylinders there were in his motors! Their Engineering Officer seemed well trained but had trouble convincing the pilots of their errors. All through the meal Wing Commander Lynn (the CO) kept a close check on the flight by checking his watch. As soon as they left the target we left the mess. Back at "Ops" we learned very shortly that only five of the six that went on the run would be back. Pilot Officer Skinner and crew ditched their ship and were all in the dinghy. Shortly the five showed up over the field, one circled and shot a red flare to show he was in trouble.'

On 25 June after breakfast, the 15th Squadron contingent was driven to Swanton Morley. It was the night of the second 1,000-plane raid against Bremen and the Boston squadron was to make a low-level dusk attack on two German night fighter airdromes.

'After the briefing we watched the take-off. The raid was a success though one flight bombed a dummy airdrome. Next day there was an air raid on Norwich, eighteen miles distant, that took a helluva pasting from Jerry. A couple of the rascals were stooging around overhead but luckily didn't drop a thing. Next day Norwich was closed to everyone. The Huns must have done a lot of no good. King's Lynn too was out of bounds because of bombing. Someone saw a notice of a party at Watton, so I organized a group to go there. We were warmly welcomed and had a grand time discussing America with some Pilot Officers who were trained at Maxwell and Selma. Nothing much was doing for there were very few people circulating and the whole show folded up at 10:45. We drove home and piled into bed. Norwich was still smoking on Sunday, June 28th so we couldn't go there.'

On Monday 29 June Captain Kegelman and Lieutenant Bell represented the USA when 226 Squadron flew an operational flight in the afternoon to the marshalling yards at Hazebroek. Kegelman was a skilled pilot and fighter leader who inspired trust and confidence in his men and was well liked. He, Bell and Sergeant 'Bennie' Cunningham and Technical Sergeant Robert Golay, in DB-7 AL743 borrowed from 226 Squadron, flew as a member of the twelve-plane formation, led by Squadron Leader 'Shaw' Kennedy. Bombing from between 12,500 and 13,000 ft the formation recorded two hits on the railway lines at the eastern end of the yard and one or two were seen to burst on railway lines and sheds at the western end. The rest of the bombs fell on buildings to the south and north. No *flak* was encountered by the formation whilst over the target and all the aircraft returned. Not so fortunate were the escorting Spitfires who encountered German fighters en route to the target, claiming three destroyed for the loss of five of their own. Also providing cover for the first time on a *Circus* raid were Hawker Typhoons.

Odell recorded,

'The mission was just like manoeuvres because no *flak* at all was seen. All twelve planes returned and bacon and eggs was served to the crews. Immediately afterwards the beer began to be consumed. I took three officers and the two WAAF officers to their WAAF dance and remained to drive them home. I got into a grand discussion with a Scottish lieutenant and an English captain. We went through the military history of the US, me taking the part of the South on the question of slavery. Comparatively, the dance was dull. I was surprised at the charming young women the Group Captain (Colonel in our air force) and the Mess Officer married. Though both were over 40 and 30 respectively, their wives were not over twenty. I danced with them as a matter of courtesy and even as a matter of choice. A hell of a way to celebrate an anniversary – dancing with someone else's wife but I can't say I was joyously happy. After the dance dwindled down I brought the WAAF and RAF officers home. Later, about 1.30 a hell of a party was going on – as always after a successful op and Bell and Keg were signing their names on the vaulted ceiling 22 feet up. The rest were pouring beer down each other's necks and playing madly all over the place. I went to bed – just dozing off when a couple of sports came in and up-ended my bed, piling me into the wall with mattress and blankets on top of me. I finally shoved it out from the wall just as the air raid alarm went off. I couldn't turn on the lights; the main switch was off. So I tried to get organized in the dark just as the bombs started coming down. The windows rattled, the dull booming dazed me. Finally I got organized enough to get in bed but the bombs kept me awake for a while. The raid must have been on Norwich again although two of them hit Swanton Morley. It was a hectic night throughout.'

Harry Castledine in 226 Squadron recalls:

'The Americans were a really wild lot, but great fun. I was told they played cowboy and Indians in the woods around Bylaugh Hall with live ammo! At the All-Ranks dances you might think that they would win a jitterbug contest, but a lot depended

Lt Leo Hawel (2nd from left) and his crew

on the partner and the WAAFs were not so experienced.'

Lieutenant Leo Hawel, another American pilot, added:

'On July 1st Captain Kegelman put all nine American pilots' names in a hat. Six were marked with a 'yes' and three marked 'no'. I drew a 'yes' and later discovered I was one of six American pilots who would fly the famous 4th July raid over Holland. The six pilots drawn were Captains Kegelman, Crabtree and Odell and Lieutenants Lynn, Loerhl and myself.'

On Thursday 2 July Generals Spaatz and Eaker arrived and Kegelman talked with them. The generals wanted the Americans to put on a *Circus* without fighter escort. Odell wrote:

'Just shows you how much our brass hats know or how they value the cost of men's lives…Spaatz, Eaker and Eisenhower met the crews going on the sortie on 4 July and shook hands with all of us. Not only were we surprised, but a little embarrassed by them coming to make such a big deal out of what aircrews of 226 Squadron considered to be just another mission not unlike many others to their credit. It seemed a little ironic that they had been pressed into taking part in an American Independence Day celebration commemorating the severance of ties between our two countries. Then it was off to dinner and the food did some good. At six o'clock we got our kit and at 6.30 we were briefed. Four flights were attacking four fighter airdromes at low-level in daylight

Squadron Leader Shaw Kennedy was leading, with Kegelman and 2nd Lieutenant J. Loehrl. Their target was De Kooy. The three Bostons flown by Flight Lieutenant Ronald A. 'Yogi' Yates-Earl, Pilot Officer C. F. Henning and Lieutenant S. Lynn, were heading for Bergen Alkmaar. Three more, flown by Squadron Leader John Castle, Captain Martin Crabtree and Lieutenant Leo Hawel, headed for Valkenburg. The final three, flown by Flight Lieutenant A. B. Wheeler, Pilot Officer A. 'Elkie' Eltringham and Captain Bill Odell, headed for Haamstede.

Odell, like the others, had been awakened at 05.15 and served coffee in the mess hall before going to the operations room.

'We turned in our papers and got packed for combat flight (concentrated food, water purifier, compass and French, Dutch and German money). More dope on the trip and then out to the airplane. Had no trouble but was a bit anxious on take off.'

General Dwight D. Eisenhower, newly arrived in England to command the US Forces in the ETO, was to recall in his autobiography, *Crusade in Europe*:

To mark our entry into the European fighting I took time to visit the crews immediately before the take-off and talked with the survivors after their return.

The first of the Bostons had begun taking off at 0709 hours. The rest of the formation followed in the next five minutes. The first formation led by New Zealander Flight Lieutenant 'Digger' Wheeler reached Haamstede at just before eight o'clock. Behind Wheeler came Pilot Officer A. 'Elkie' Eltringham, followed by Captain Odell. Odell continues:

'After getting in the air we settled down and flew right on the trees to the coast. Then we went down to the water. Nice ride until the other Vic left us. Felt a little uneasy because there was a cloudless sky but no fighters appeared. Found land ahead and could spot the landmark of the lighthouse a long way off. Swung over the edge of the coast even lower than the leader and stayed right on the grass. I opened the bomb doors, yelled to Birleson and then it started. I fired all the guns for all I was worth and Birly dropped the bombs. I saw the hangar but that wasn't my dish. I saw Germans running all over the place but I put most of my shots over their heads. Our bombs were OK. I thought we would crash any moment for I never flew so reckless in my life. The next moment we were flashing past the coast and out to sea – the water behind us boiling from the bullets dropping into it all around. I kicked and pulled and jerked from side to side. I didn't look at the airspeed; I was trying to miss the waves. Over the target we were doing 265 but shortly after I opened up a bit. "Digger" claims he shot his guns into a formation of troops lined up for an inspection – his bombs hit well where they should have. 'Elkie' was a bit behind but he got rid of his load. He got a broken radio antenna and a mashed-in wing edge. I picked up a hole just above the pilot's step and a badly knocked-up bomb door. We zigged and zagged while eight miles out and then closed up waiting for fighters. None came. We reached the coast and were the first ones home.'

At Haamstede hits were achieved on administration buildings, a hangar and dispersal points. On their way across the airfield Wheeler's burst on his front guns had dispersed a parade of some 160 German aircrew in flying kit. The rear gunners on all three aircraft machine-gunned other targets as they swept across the field. As the formation left the target area much smoke was seen over the south eastern area of Haamstede.

At Bergen Alkmaar the three aircraft led by Yates-Earl in *Y-Yorker* arrived at two minutes past eight. Difficulties in identifying the target caused the formation to attack at 100 feet in line astern, starting fires on hangars on the north side of the airfield. The Boston flown by Lieutenant Stan G. Lynn and his American crew was hit by *flak* after bombing and crashed on the airfield killing all on board. Another Boston flown by Pilot Officer C. F. 'Hank' Henning left the target area after bombing but was intercepted by a Messerschmitt Bf 109 of *Jagdgeschwader 1* fifteen miles from the Dutch coast and was shot down. The Bf 109 had taken off from Bergen Alkmaar during the attack and had chased the formation to the coast.

The formation attacking Valkenburg found themselves too far south after crossing the coast to turn correctly onto track for the airfield. Lieutenant Leo Hawel recalls:

'Our flight hit the Dutch coast south of the point we had planned and our course took us through the main part of The Hague. We were so low, I saw two young ladies eating breakfast right out of my side window. I recall flying under some telephone wires and had to lift my right wing to avoid a church tower. (Frank H Donnelly, his bombardier-navigator, felt that he was "looking up at a few honest burghers"). The target came up very fast and we were briefed to open our bomb bay doors when the leader opened his. I instructed my gunners to fire with their machine guns, and I did the same as we settled down for the bombing run.'

As they ran in Squadron Leader John Castle, leading the formation, found he was unable to open his bomb doors through an error in selection. On the run in to a target Boston pilots normally had the bomb doors selected to 'neutral' and then placed them to 'open' before dropping their bombs. Castle discovered too late that he was still selected to 'closed' and moving the door control had only placed the doors in 'neutral' failing to open. Captain Martin Crabtree and Leo Hawel waited in vain for the leader's bomb doors to open as the signal to drop their own bombs.

Sqn Leader Castle explaining why he failed to open his bomb bay doors

Instead, the formation used their machine guns on airfield buildings and three dispersed Messerschmitt 109s, setting one on fire. All three aircraft were forced to bring their bombs back.

The formation attacking De Kooy also came in just off track and, finding itself unable to turn, were forced to fly through three miles of *flak*, which Squadron Leader Shaw Kennedy, the formation leader, was to describe later as the worst he had encountered in over sixty operational missions. The intense *flak* prevented all three Bostons from bombing. Kennedy machine-gunned ack-ack positions and personnel near the airfield. On the way home he attacked a 250-foot trawler with bombs and machine guns, the bombs unfortunately overshooting. He also attacked a second trawler with machine guns. Behind Kennedy Lieutenant Jack Loehrl was hit by *flak* north of the airfield. Apparently, Loehrl made the fatal mistake of making a normal turn, allowing the *flak* gunners to anticipate his course. Loehrl crashed on the beach. He and his two gunners, Sergeants Wright and Whitham, were killed. Lieutenant Marshall Draper, the bombardier, survived and was taken prisoner.

The other wing ship, with Kegelman at the controls, and crewed by Lieutenant R. M. Dorton, the navigator, and Sergeant Bennie Cunningham, rear gunner, and Technical Sergeant R. L. Goley, dorsal gunner, was also badly hit. The starboard engine took a direct hit and burst into flames and the propeller flew off. Kegleman's right wing tip struck the ground and the fuselage actually bounced on the surface of the airdrome, tearing a hole in the belly of the bomber. Golay recalls:

'We were flying so low over the target when I felt us take a hit, and then saw a propeller go sailing by. My first thought was, I hope that isn't ours! Then I felt us hit the ground and the bottom oilcanning under my feet.'

Lifting the Boston back into the air on one engine, Kegelman headed for the Channel. He was debating whether or not to set his crippled ship down on the sand dunes when over the interphone he heard his rear gunner exhorting him enthusiastically to 'Give 'em hell, Captain.' Kegelman duly obliged. A *Flak* tower on Den Helder airfield opened up and the young captain returned fire with his nose guns. He lifted the Boston over the tower and headed for England with the right engine on fire. The fire went out over the Channel and Kegelman continued home to Swanton Morley hugging the waves across the North Sea.

At Swanton Morley the first returning Boston piloted by Kennedy landed at 0814 hours. During the next forty minutes the others landed. The last to touch down was Kegelman, who despite the loss of one engine made a good landing and taxied to the control tower before shutting down. Inspection of his aircraft revealed scratch marks on the belly of his Boston where he had touched the ground. The experienced 226 Squadron crews were all of the same opinion that the *Flak* encountered on the raid was the worst the squadron had ever experienced. Odell concludes:

'All came back except Loehrl, Lynn and Henning. Loehrl was hit by a heavy shell and hit the ground right in the middle of the airdrome. "He flew into a million pieces", one gunner said. And I owed him £1 10s. I felt like a thief! Lynn was following before the flight hit the target, but never came away from it. His wife was to have a baby in November. He really wasn't cut out for this game. At breakfast he was salting his food, trying to hold the salt spoon steady, and yet throwing salt over his shoulders! I hoped he didn't crash. An Me 109 that took off just ahead of him shot down Henning. He tried to get it, but it turned, got behind him and set one motor on fire. He crashed into the sea. General Eaker, General Duncan and Beaman were there at the start and finish and didn't look so happy at the finish. They must have thought it was a "piece of cake" until three turned up shot down – two being American. Thus, we celebrated Independence Day! Beirne Lay and some Major from HQ took down our names and addresses, as it would probably be recorded for the folks back home. A party started shortly after breakfast (10.15) and kept up till lockout. I have to admit that this was the first day in history when I had a scotch and soda before breakfast! Everyone went to bed after dinner. I went to Norwich with Hawel and Bell and bought a shirt. Norwich took a real pasting because it was in worse shape than it was last time I saw it. One factory was completely demolished. Good shooting on Jerry's part. There was a big party that evening but I wasn't in the mood to enjoy it. Shortly after the buffet supper, which was excellent, I went to bed.'

Leo Hawel joined in the roaring party at Swanton Morley.

'When you lose a bunch of good boys, you *have* to get good and drunk, otherwise you'll get pretty browned-off with the whole set-up.'

In the middle of Ambassador John C. Winant's Fourth of July party at the Court of St. James in London, Captain Harry C. Butcher, General Eisenhower's Naval aide, was called to a side room in the J Pierpoint Morgan mansion to take a 'phone call from General Charles L. Bolte. He passed the results of the first American raid to General Eisenhower. Of the four airfield targets, only one had been attacked successfully. Of the six American crews taking part, only one had engaged the *Luftwaffe* with good results.

General Ira C. Eaker, the theatre commander, later penned Kegelman in for a Distinguished Service Cross. He was promoted Major and ordered Stateside with his crew (after an 'agonizing' tour of duty in the USA helping to sell war bonds, he returned to the 15th Bomb Squadron). Three others received the Distinguished Flying Cross. Of the RAF crews taking part, Flight Lieutenant 'Yogi' Yates-Earl and his observer Pilot Officer Ken Houghton, were awarded the DFC and his gunner, Sergeant Ted Leaver, the DFM, for their part in the attack on Bergen Alkmaar. Next day, after reading the British newspapers and talking it over among themselves, the mood of the American ground crews changed. The maintenance men came to the inevitable conclusion that they could claim no credit; RAF ground crews had performed their work. The enlisted men did take over though, after this.

On 5 July Captain Odell slept late and after lunch went to the ops room to see the photos of the target they took from behind. Leo Hawel recalled that everybody was 'feeling mighty rough – me included'.

There was quite a discussion as to the advisability of low-level raids. Our losses were the biggest the station had had in one operation. It all boiled down to this; in a high altitude bombing circus the chances of hitting your target are slim (in these Bostons) and you don't always have clear weather for them. In fact, it was very seldom you had a cloudless day. In low-level raids, you have the element of surprise, and that's about all. Jerry wasn't surprised because off the coast he had many small boats called 'squealers', who radio warnings to the land. The squealers were tapping like hell just as soon as we crossed the coast of Holland and continued until we had made good.'

The Americans continued with their training and were allocated 23 Boston IIIs

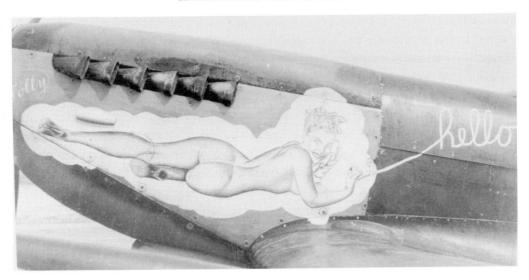

from RAF stocks. The 15th recommenced operations on 5 September 1942, when Major Griffiths led them against the heavily defended docks at Le Havre. Missions were flown using the normal box formation at 8,000 to 12,000 feet, bombing individually, the formation being covered by substantial Spitfire escort. On 11 September the 15th moved to Podington. Had joint USAAF-RAF plans to equip the 1st Pursuit Squadron (NF) with radar-equipped Beaufighters reached fruition, the fate of the 15th Squadron might have been different. However, the idea was postponed through lack of electronic equipment. At the end of September only twelve DB-7s were on hand, and the prospect of getting more Bostons was slim. Six pilots were transferred to wing HQ and on 1st October Captain Bill Odell was posted to 8th Air Force HQ at High Wycombe. Only Howard Cook of the original cadre of pilots remained. On 8 November the 15th Light Bombardment Squadron was transferred to the 12th Air Force, moving to North Africa to take part in Operation *Torch* on the 15th. Based at Youks le Bain, Tabessa, Algeria, the squadron arrived five days after the invasion and was operational within a week. The 15th was later absorbed into the 47th Bomb Group in Africa and inactivated.

Charles Kegelman rose rapidly in promotion. In April 1943 he was a lieutenant colonel in command of the 48th Fighter Group at William Northern Field, Tennessee until 8 November. On 12 November he assumed command of the 337th Fighter Group at Sarasota, Florida as a full colonel. On 16th November 1944 he assumed command of the 42nd Bomb Group at Sansapor, New Guinea, which by March 1945 were operating North American B-25 Mitchells from Moratai. On 10 March Kegelman's aircraft was involved in a mid-air collision with his wingman and he was killed. Kegelman Field, near Cherokee, Oklahoma, is named in his memory and is used for touch-and-go landings by T-37s and T-38s from Vance AFB.

6

'DINTY'

Jim Moore DFC

(l to r) FO Freddie Deeks, navigator; Flt/Lt Johnny Reeve, pilot; Flt/Sgt Johnny Legge, air gunner; FO J. W. 'Dinty' Moore, WoP/AG in front of *Excreta Thermo*

Life at Oulton and the other stations in 2 Group in Norfolk during the winter of 1942-1943 went on much the same as before. On 15 October 1942, nine Bostons of 226 Squadron from Swanton Morley and three of 88 Squadron at Oulton set out to attack the German raider *Neumark* in Le Havre harbour. However, when the formation arrived over the port, they discovered that the ship had gone so bombs were dropped on other shipping in a dry dock instead. At Oulton on the night of 31 October, at 2200 hours, six armourers were killed in an explosion while they were loading up a Boston.

'We flew our first op in a Boston on 16 October 1942, part of a formation of six Bostons in a *Circus* attack on the *Neumark*. We flew down to Ford in the southeast where we rendezvoused with our escort. The usual flak barrage was awaiting our arrival over the French coast, although it cannot have been too accurate as we flew on to bomb the target before returning home. The *Luftwaffe* stayed away from the party and we landed back, unscathed, at Oulton, feeling on top of the world after completing our first mission. Our first flight in the Boston was a revelation, for here we had a fast, manoeuvrable aircraft, with a terrific rate of climb, capable of carrying a bomb load of 2,000 lb, twice the weight carried by a Blenheim. Unlike the Blenheim, the Boston could, with one propeller feathered, still climb without causing the pilot too many problems. With this beautiful, highly manoeuvrable and powerful aircraft we were better equipped to carry the war to the enemy than we had been during the summer of 1941.

'On 9 November 1942 preparations for Operation *Oyster*, a daylight precision strike on the Philips radio and valve works in Eindhoven, Holland went ahead. Production was centred in two factories, both in built-up areas within the town, which demanded precision bombing from a very low level to minimise the danger to the local people. On 17 November a full-scale practice was held on a route similar to the one to be used, with the St. Neots power station as the "target". By 2 December preparations were complete. At 2030 hours at Oulton we gathered in the briefing room with eleven other crews from the squadron. There was a great deal of animated discussion. Various characters claiming to be "in the know" told us what the target was going to be, followed by an expectant silence when our CO, Wing Commander Pelly-Fry, stepped on the dais and the cover was removed from the large target map. The operation would involve 84 aircraft from the Group: 36

Bostons, 36 Venturas, and 12 Mosquitoes. In addition, our withdrawal was to be covered by four fighter squadrons of Spitfires, Mustangs and Typhoons, who would meet us at the coast, while the Americans were to launch a high-level attack with flying Fortresses on Lille as a diversion.

'After the briefing we were confined to camp, the telephone was put out of bounds, so we settled down for a disturbed night. The following morning we climbed into the flight trucks and made our way up to the 'drome all keyed up for this special operation. We collected our parachutes with the usual comments from the packers such as "Bring it back if it doesn't work" and made our way out to the aircraft. It was then that the unforgivable happened and we were informed that the operation had been postponed. It is difficult to describe your emotions at a time like that, for although you might feel a sense of relief you know that you will eventually fly on this operation so the overriding reaction is one of frustration. Having been briefed for the operation there was no way that the authorities were going to let us loose on the community in case word got out about our plans. They dreamed up a variety of service-type devices to keep us occupied, for which we displayed little enthusiasm.

'Thankfully, the morning of 6 December dawned and we were told that "it was on", so we were driven up to the 'drome again, with the predominant feeling being to get it over with. At 1115 hours we took off, forming up as No.3 to our "Wingco" and setting off on a course that took us directly over Norwich on our way to the coast. The noise of this large force of low flying aircraft brought many of the citizens to their doors to see what was going on, including my girlfriend, Norma. The instructions to fly at no more than 50 feet over the sea to avoid detection by German radar were strictly adhered to as we careered across the North Sea. The "Wingco" had the good fortune to have an excellent navigator, "Jock" Cairns, who guided us to our correct landfall. It was a pleasant sunny day and as we skimmed over the flat countryside we saw some of the Dutch men and women bedecked in their Sunday best. Many of them gave us a friendly wave. Despite the occasion and the obvious risks, the sense of speed, flying at about 20 feet, was truly exhilarating. On our way to the target I saw a lone Fw 190 fighter, whose pilot must have had quite a shock on seeing the approaching aerial armada and sheered off.

'Finally, I heard Freddie saying the target was straight ahead of us and, turning around, I could see the factory towering above the surrounding houses. 88 Squadron approached the main site at the lamp and valve factory from the south side at rooftop height and immediately began climbing to 2,000 feet in order to make shallow dives on to the factory. The leading pair, whose bombs had 11-second-delay fuses, ploughed straight in at low level, while Johnny led the remainder of the formation up to our bombing height of 1,500 feet. By now the Germans had opened up with light flak from batteries around the town, and one that was on the top of the factory itself. We dropped our bombs on the target, returning to nought feet without delay, and looking back I could see heavy explosions in the building, so it was evident that the bombs had landed in the right place.'

Jack Peppiatt was in B Flight, behind John Reeve.

'I think my main feeling was just plain excitement. Flying on the deck was always thrilling and we watched each other from aircraft to aircraft. Crossing the coast was a bit tense for two reasons. One, you were anxiously looking to identify a landfall and, two, the ack-ack gunners had a head-on view of you; for this reason we came in firing our guns to make them keep their heads down.

'The journey across country was a circus really; we slid about keeping sight of our leader and watching to avoid airfields. The other hazard was overhead cables etc. and the trick was to look out to the sides ahead so that you could spot the lines of pylons, which could reveal where the invisible cables might be. Although there was a lot of apprehension there was also a great thrill in it as I look back.

'Talk over the intercom went on the whole time between the navigator and yourself, discussing where you were, where the leader was going and did you see that railway or canal etc. I can still see the landscape flying by with brief flashes of recognition; a house, some people, vehicles. As we neared the turning point south of Eindhoven it did get taut, we all knew that if the target was missed there would be no way of recovering. In front I had glimpses of the leading Bostons and we began to pack in as we saw the buildings of the factory way ahead. The first two went in low and we then sailed up to 1500ft and I can tell you that we did feel very vulnerable; we seemed to suddenly stand still and hang about waiting to be shot at.

'By the time we were over the factory it was all smoke and explosions, with Bostons all around at different angles and at that point there was a bang. *R for Robert* turned several degrees to port like a weather vane and I heard Len telling me there was a big hole in the fin just above his head. But the aircraft seemed to handle all right and at that stage I was more concerned with where we were to go next. We headed northwest after the gaggle of aircraft until both my navigator, Sergeant Kirk, and I began to wonder why they didn't turn west toward the coast; by now we were all down hugging the ground for comfort.

'We made a joint decision to do what would now be called "our own thing" and, as some of the aircraft made the turn, we went with them. They later proved to be

107 Squadron but we were also joined and passed by Mosquitoes as we went on. After a few minutes settling down it all went up with a bang as FW 190s appeared. The next twenty minutes or so were full of action and not a little confusion. Some ten or twenty aircraft were screaming along, full throttle, in a loose mass, no one wanted to be at the back where the FWs were coming in to attack and wheeling away for another go. They had one problem which I think was that, as they dived, they had to pull out early to avoid hitting the ground because we were all at zero feet. I can distinctly remember seeing cannon shells hitting ploughed fields in front of me and moving on ahead as the FW began to pull out. At one point a fighter slid past us and sat just to my right as he slowed; so close I could stare at the pilot and admire the yellow spinner. Meanwhile Len was calling for me to jink and then shouted that he had got one. If he did I really don't know how he did it as I was sliding and diving constantly. The astonishing thing was that we didn't collide, as aircraft constantly criss-crossed in front of each other.

'Over the Dutch Islands the attacks petered out and we flew steadily just off the water until Len quietly told me there was an aircraft sliding over us from the side obviously unaware that we were under him. It all went dark as a big black shadow arrived and I sat rigid, hoping he wouldn't come lower and then throttled back gently to get behind him. If you know the height of a Boston fin you will know how we felt!

'Soon after this incident an aircraft just exploded in front of us and we flew through the debris. It was so completely destroyed that there was nothing big enough to hurt us. We looked down and back to see just the yellow stain of the marker from the dinghy...all that was left in just those few seconds.

'As we left the coast of Holland yet another Boston went in on our starboard side; possibly the pilot had been wounded earlier. These were both 107 Squadron aircraft as far as I know. These two events perhaps weighed more on us than anything else.

'As we approached Oulton I thought about the damage to our fin and Len tried to assess what might happen as we landed, as he could see to some extent. I realised the hole was through the pilot-head and as a result I had no altimeter or ASI. That meant coming in faster than usual. When we reached the airfield and flew over I could see Pelly-Fry's aircraft belly-flopped on the grass in the middle of the longest run and I felt I needed all the 1,100 yards for my performance; so it was off to Attlebridge where there was a long concrete runway. We plopped in with a sigh of relief and waited patiently for transport to Blickling where we found they had all gone to Swanton for a party...which we missed. The episode over Holland had

Over Norwich

resulted in me sweating profusely, so much so that my battledress tunic was saturated and my bar of chocolate had melted into the fabric. I can still see the yellow spinners of those FWs as they tried to get amongst us.

'*Circuses* were a different kind of fun. Usually two boxes of six would fly in formation at sea level until ten minutes from the target and then climb at 1,000 ft/min. up to 10,000 ft for the attack. Flying in a box was something that took practise. As a new member you would be tail-end Charlie, flying below and behind the chap "in the box". He was directly behind and below the leader and could look up into the open lower hatch of the lead aircraft. In the formation there was no chance to look at anything except the man you were formatting on and the throttle was in constant action, particularly at the back.

'Over the target it was necessary to fly straight and level for the bomb-aimer in the lead aircraft to line up, and that was a painful few minutes as, we were told, the anti-aircraft guns only needed 15 seconds to get onto a target. I recall Le Havre had a box barrage, which just filled the cube of air above the harbour with lethal puffs of black smoke. You sailed through this space, holding formation and being aware of these woolly puffs that appeared and then immediately slid backwards as we passed them at about 300mph.

'As we heard "bombs away" the formation would turn and dive for the sea while air gunners would give a commentary on any fighter action they might see.'

Jim Moore continues:

'We headed for home although the "Wingco's" aircraft had been damaged by flak, so he was having difficulty in keeping it under control, which put us off course. We were encouraged on our way to the coast by the efforts of German anti-aircraft gunners. The remainder of our formation reached the coast without the attention of any German fighters, which may have been due to the fact that we were not returning by our intended route. We must have been well off course for we saw no sign of the fighter escort with whom we should have rendezvoused at the coast. Other squadrons who did return by the planned route were less fortunate, not only being harried by *flak*, as we were, but also by the unwelcome attention of German fighters. We landed back at Oulton after an exciting and memorable operation, which had taken us 2 hours and 20 minutes without a scratch, my only excuse to use my guns being to fire at some of the *flak* positions. The "Wingco", in the meantime, found his way home with difficulty, having attracted the attentions of a German fighter; without hydraulic power he had to come in with his wheels up, making a safe if bumpy landing. The aircraft looked in a sad way but the crew walked out, though "Jock" Cairns later found out that he had suffered a cracked vertebra.

'The following day the national newspapers carried the story of the raid with several photographs. The heading in the *Daily Mail* read "Heaviest Day Bombing Raid of the War" – "Big Dutch Radio Works Smashed". It did much to raise the morale of the British people, who up to the end of 1942 had had little to cheer about. As for me, as soon as I had been de-briefed I found a telephone to let Norma my girlfriend, who lived and worked in Norwich, know all was well. She had been looking in vain for us to return over Norwich, so she was beginning to worry. Next day I met her during her lunch-break and proposed. She agreed to marry me, so she was easily persuaded to take the afternoon off work so we could go and buy our engagement rings. The film of the Eindhoven raid was taken by Flying Officer "Skeets" Kelly, who had flown with us, and Flight Lieutenant Charlie Peace. I will always remember sitting in a cinema when one of their productions was included in the newsreel and the audience applauded enthusiastically.'[1]

'Early in January 1943 I returned from leave to Norfolk with Norma "to get on with the war". During January we were briefed to take part in four *Circus* operations with varying degrees of success due to the weather. It should not be forgotten that a method of identifying a target through cloud had not, so far, been fitted to our aircraft, although there would be a system known as *Gee H* brought into service within the next 12 months. On 9 January our target was Abbeville, so we took off "into the wild blue yonder", everything going according to plan, meeting our escorting fighters on schedule and crossing the French coast, where we enjoyed the usual hostile reception. We flew on until we were 40 miles from the target, only to find a thick layer of cloud that made it impossible for us to complete our mission. The risks were exactly the same as if we had actually bombed, so I'll make no comment as to our feelings as we landed.

'On the 18th the story was exactly the same, the only difference being that our target was to be Cherbourg, which, of course was screened by cloud. On the 21st we had better luck, the Met man having got his forecast right. The target was the Dutch port of Flushing, which I had last visited on 25 April 1941 with George and Ron. On this occasion, however, we did not take off alone, nor were we to fly at low level. This was to be a *Circus* involving 12 Bostons, flying in two boxes of six aircraft accompanied by our usual fighter escort. It was a pleasant day with excellent visibility, so much so that I could see the Dutch coast long before we reached it. We were obviously not welcome as large and menacing black balls of *flak* appeared in the sky ahead of us. The formation manoeuvred gently to avoid the threat, until we actually got on to the bomb run to the target, that anxious period when we flew straight and level. Finally, I felt the aircraft lift as our bombs left us. We now turned out to sea without any sign of the *Luftwaffe*, leaving the flak behind and returned to Oulton. Flushing was of special significance to us members of 2 Group as one of our

[1] Over 60 tons of bombs hit the factory buildings, which were devastated, essential supplies destroyed and the rail network disrupted, but 14 aircraft (nine Venturas, one Mosquito, and four Bostons) had been shot down. Photographs taken after the raid showed that both factories had been very badly damaged, fully justifying the decision to make the attack in daylight from low level. The Germans reported that 'Damage was caused to nearly all the work buildings'. The factory was in the middle of Eindhoven, so a considerable number of homes were also destroyed or damaged, yet the loyal Dutch patriots' spirits were bolstered and they praised the RAF crews for their precision bombing, which resulted in little loss of life on the ground. In fact, 107 houses and 96 shops were completely destroyed, and 138 Dutch workers and civilians living around the factory were killed and 161 wounded. Seven German soldiers were killed and 18 wounded.

squadrons in a *Circus* operation there was attacked by an overwhelming number of German fighters, with every one of our twelve being lost.

'On 26 January we went on a *Circus* to Abbeville. Everything went according to plan, meeting the escort, climbing rapidly over the sea to our operational height before crossing the French coast where we made our correct landfall. We then turned on to the course to the target, when we found it screened by a layer of cloud. Someone up there must have been looking after the interests of the good people of this town.

'On 18 February 1943 I married Norma in the beautiful St. Peter Mancroft church in Norwich. My brother, Peter, who was 21 years of age, and who had joined the RAF in December 1940 to train as an electrician, was my best man. On the completion of his training Peter had joined 18 Squadron at RAF Oulton on 1 June 1941, when I was flying operationally with that Squadron. After twelve months, by which time he had been promoted to the rank of corporal, he volunteered for training as an air gunner and he later became a mid-upper gunner on Stirlings in 218 Squadron at RAF Downham Market.

18 February 1943, St Peter Mancroft Church. The wedding of Jim and Norma Moore. Best man is Jim's brother, Peter, far left

'In the months to come, having experienced the pressure of life in 2 Group in 1940/41 I felt that as a Squadron we were under-employed. In the spring of 1943 our aircraft were needed in North Africa, so we spent some time converting from the Boston Mk III to the Mk IIIa. It was a period of preparation for the invasion of Europe and the development of close links with the Army, to which the Group would provide close support. On 1 April 1943 our days of living in the splendour of Blickling Hall came to an end and we moved the few miles to RAF Swanton Morley. At that time our morale was pretty low, as we had been non-operational since the middle of February. The reason for this was that the medium bomber Squadrons operating in North Africa had been equipped with Blenheim Mk Vs (Bisleys) which had been proved to be totally inadequate. Our lords and masters decided to remedy this by taking Bostons from the Boston Squadrons in 2 Group. We still had a few left but, until we received some more from the U.S. of A, which took until 28 June, we were to remain in the non-operational category. Our new home was a standard RAF aerodrome with comfortable accommodation but lacking the lovely surroundings and freedom of Blickling Hall. However, on the plus side, the food in the Officers Mess was excellent, as the chef had formerly been employed in a leading London hotel.

'On 28 May several of us had spent a very pleasant day with the Guards Armoured Division who were stationed nearby where they were foolish enough to allow us to try our hands at driving their Sherman tanks. On arriving back at Swanton Morley I went into the Officers Mess when I decided to check to see if there was any mail for me. I found a hand written note on a tiny piece of paper addressed to me. On opening it I found it to be a copy of a telegram which read "RECEIVED TELEGRAM. PETER REPORTED MISSING. DAD". On the evening of the 27 May Peter took off as mid upper gunner in a Stirling of 218 Squadron on his and his crews first operation. They had been briefed to lay mines in the sea-lanes off the coast of the island of Terschelling and had failed to return.'[1]

The following day I was flown over to Downham Market where I was given details of the operation by the Squadron Adjutant and handed some of Peter's personal possessions. I was then sent on leave where Norma and I tried to console my parents who were absolutely devastated

'On 1 June 1943 2 Group was transferred from Bomber Command to Fighter Command. 'Bomber' Harris and his heavy bombers had been directed to pulverise

[1] It was not until February 1991 that Jim Moore, through the good offices of a modern history student at Groningen University, Theo Boiten, found out that his brother's aircraft had been shot down at 0058 hours on 28 May, by Oberfeldwebel Karl-Georg Pfeiffer flying an Me110 night fighter.

German cities and towns and had no place for our medium bombers. In any case, our Group was to become part of the 2nd Tactical Air Force in preparation for the invasion of Europe. These momentous events occurred without in any way affecting the lives of we lesser mortals. At last came 28 June and we were deemed to be an operational Squadron again. On 12 July, my pilot not being on the Battle Order, I volunteered to fly with Flying Officer Peppiatt. We were briefed to carry out a low-level mission to Alost providing there was sufficient cloud cover. It was one of those frustrating occasions when, on our arrival at the enemy coast, not a cloud was to be seen so it was back to base carrying our bombs. On 25 July my pilot was again not on the Battle Order so I agreed to fly with a good friend of mine, New Zealander Johnny Wilson. During the briefing I had a very real premonition this was an operation from which I was not going to return. It was a weird sensation. I felt like a spectator to the events going on around me. Anyway we collected our parachutes and walked out to our aircraft. Johnny Wilson started the engines and prepared to taxi out for take-off when we were informed the operation had been cancelled. The following day, my own pilot was back on the Battle Order, so Flight Lieutenant Partridge took my place in Wilson's crew. At the briefing we found that our nine Bostons were to carry out a *Circus* attack on the *Luftwaffe* airfield at Courtrai. On our arrival over the enemy coast the *flak* barrage was much heavier than usual. As if this wasn't enough we were attacked by a number of Focke Wulf 190s who broke through our fighter escort so battle was joined in earnest. One of our aircraft was soon in difficulty, falling away from the formation. It was the Boston piloted by Johnny Wilson who managed to release his canopy so he and his crew could bale out. These were Johnny, the navigator, Pilot Officer "Jock" McDonald, my replacement and Sergeant Hunt of the RAF Film Production Unit. We were later very relieved to hear they had survived although they had become prisoners of war. It would seem my premonition had had some substance.

'On 19 August the Squadron moved to a new airfield at Hartford Bridge (now known as Blackbushe). We were joined the following day by 107 Squadron, and shortly after by 342 (Lorraine) Squadron to form 137 Wing. Our arrival at Hartford Bridge sparked off many rumours and a great deal of speculation, our aircraft being painted with new markings to indicate that we were part of the Allied Air Force, so we became convinced that the invasion of Europe was about to take place. The beginning of September was an opportunity for us to put into practice the time we had spent in laying down smoke screens for the Army. In this case though it was the Navy, which was carrying out minesweeping operations to within 7 miles of Boulogne, where they were threatened by batteries of heavy coastal artillery. Canisters were loaded into our bomb bay and we took off, flying low over the sea in pairs until we sighted the minesweeping flotilla, which was chugging its way towards the French coast. We flew in pairs between the ships and the coast, laying down a smoke screen. The next pair replaced the screen. It was a very satisfactory feeling to lay a smoke screen "for real" after the number of times we had done it in practice.

'On 4 September we led one of the formations of six Bostons in a *Circus* attack on the marshalling yards at Amiens, and the next day we were part of a force of 23 Bostons detailed to carry out a *Ramrod* attack on the *Luftwaffe* base at Woensdrecht. The *flak* barrage was particularly heavy over both the coast and the target, though the *Luftwaffe* once again declined to get airborne. Despite the attentions of the anti-aircraft gunners we were able to drop our bombs and return to Hartford Bridge.

'The climax to these combined operations, known as *Starkey*, which was obviously a rehearsal for the invasion, came on the 9th when we laid down another smoke screen for a naval flotilla eight miles off Boulogne. Johnny was then promoted to the rank of Squadron Leader and we were posted to 107 Squadron on the other side of the aerodrome.

'On Sunday 3 October Wing Commander Dickie England led the Bostons of

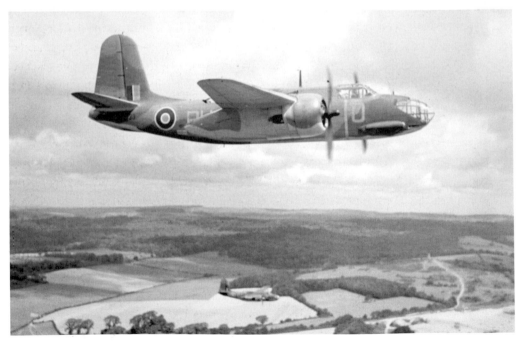

A Boston IIIa of 88 Squadron

107 Squadron off to attack the Chaingy transformer station. It was my 69th operation. It was a beautiful sunny day as the engines of the 36 Bostons of three squadrons were being warmed up prior to take-off. At 1240 hours we were airborne, forming up on Wing Commander Dickie England and setting course over the south of England, coming down, as usual, to nought feet as soon as we were over the sea. I felt a sense of occasion, as if we were taking part in something special, my excitement easily overcoming my fear. We made a perfect landfall, crossing the coast without opposition and speeding low across the French countryside towards Paris. Finally the outskirts of the capital city came into view with the Eiffel Tower dominant on the skyline. We had still not been challenged as we changed course for Orleans, although we saw first a Do 217 flying overhead, and later a tiny Fiesler *Storch* spotter aircraft, which were both too far away for us to engage. Indeed, our camouflage was so good that I doubt if the crews of either aircraft were aware of our presence.

'On our arrival at the target the two leading aircraft with delayed-action fuses on the bombs remained at low level while we led the rest of the formation up to 1,500 feet as we had done on the raid on Eindhoven. Every one of the 12 aircraft dropped its bomb load and as we turned away I could see the bombs exploding, completely destroying the transformer station. During the attack there was no enemy interference from any source, which was a pleasant change. On the return journey the only target that presented itself to me was a railway goods train, peacefully plodding its way across the countryside, at which I fired a few rounds as we flashed past. As we crossed the coast on our way home the Germans opened up with some light *flak* and one of our aircraft was slightly damaged. This was one of those occasions which must have been the answer to a planner's dream – effective navigation, avoidance of *flak* concentrations and the finding and bombing of an undefended target that was destroyed, the whole operation passing without a single hiccup. It was later established that this series of attacks had caused maximum disruption to the French electrical system and the railways, which were electrified, from Paris to Brittany.

'Early in November 1943 we were "screened" and we were to be sent on rest. My feelings were completely different from those I had experienced at the end of my extended first tour. I had taken part in only 18 operational sorties and we had been involved in so much training in preparation for the invasion that the news came as a sort of anti-climax. On 16 February 1944 I returned to Swanton Morley. It was now the 2 Group Support Unit, supplying men and equipment to the operational Squadrons in the Group, which now included Bostons, Mitchells

Halifax of 57 Squadron which put down at Old Buckenham after being hit during the
Venlo raid

and Mosquitoes. Thankfully the anticipated losses of aircrew had never been achieved and the re-employment of those of us who had survived our operational tours had become a problem. I was to remain there, virtually unemployed, until 22 April, when I was posted to RAF Manby to undertake an Air Gunnery Instructors course. On 6 June we were informed that the allied forces had at long last landed in France. I remember sitting back and thinking that here I was in the safety of a classroom while my old friends were involved in a truly historic event for which we had worked so hard and risked so much. I also wished that Peter and so many others I had known could have lived to see this day. I later learned how 2 Group's two remaining Boston squadrons, 88 and 242, had, in addition to bombing the enemy, laid smoke to screen the invasion force at one beachhead from the German coastal guns. Further, all of the squadrons, Bostons, Mitchells and Mosquitoes, had been heavily engaged in bombing troop concentrations, railways, Panzer divisions, indeed any target requested by the Army, with considerable success.

'On 27 March I learned that I, with my crew, had been awarded the DFC. Reading the kindly worded citation it was evident it was for surviving two tours with emphasis on the first in the Blenheims of 18 Squadron. I returned to Swanton Morley on 22 October 1944 ostensibly as Gunnery Leader of "B" Flight, 2 GSU, having persuaded the Group Gunnery Leader, Squadron Leader Jerry Levack that I wished to fly a third tour. It may seem crazy, but I was terribly unsettled and I became determined to return to 2 Group to complete another tour. I believe the reasons for this were threefold: first of all my second tour had been less than satisfying, secondly, the effect of loss of Peter and finally, hearing the heavy bombers flying over us every night on their way to bomb targets in Germany. I was delighted to learn that I was to fly as fighter controller on a 226 Squadron Mitchell with Squadron Leader Jock Campbell, whom I had known and greatly respected when he was on 88 Squadron. I was due to leave for France in an Anson on 15 November but we were delayed when the weather closed in and it was not until 19 November that I was flown over to RAF Vitry-en-Artois, to join the crew. On the date of my arrival I met "Jock" and his crew but they had been briefed to take part in an attack on Venlo in support of the Army so there was little time for conversation.

'I waited until I saw them take off, thinking that I would have plenty to talk about with them when they got back. I then got on with the usual routine of settling into the Mess and finding out the location of the squadron office and so on. While I was doing this Jock was leading his formation in their approach to the target when his aircraft received a direct hit from an anti-aircraft shell and broke up. He and his crew were killed. On the return of the remainder of the squadron I found it difficult to believe the tragic news they brought with them. I suppose, human nature being what it is, that my main reaction would be to thank my lucky stars that bad weather had postponed my arrival.'

7

'THEY TRAVELLED TOGETHER'

A Halifax of 35 Squadron

Bridge Farm, Bradfield, in the heart of rural north Norfolk, was the home of William and Matilda Gibbons, and their son Jack. Farming was pretty tough in the thirties and forties, with no cars, tractors or combine harvesters, nor a telephone or electricity in the house. October 8th 1943 had been just another day, and as is the habit of the farming community, they retired early. On the many RAF airfields across East Anglia it was a different story. Hundreds of airmen were preparing for take-off. Their bombers were fully laden with a deadly load to be delivered to the heart of the Third Reich. That night the main force of 504 aircraft was to visit Hanover, while a large-scale diversionary raid by 119 aircraft took place on Bremen. The crew of Halifax HR777 TL-Y of 35 Squadron, Pathfinder Force, 8 Group, at Graveley, Huntingdonshire, was one of seventeen Halifaxes used to mark the target at Bremen. HR777 took off at 2246 hours and headed off to join the formation. What happened after this is best described by Derrick Coleman, the 19-year old air bomber and radar operator.

'Ross Whitfield had gone to an Australian Squadron and his place as rear-gunner had been taken by a Canadian, Sergeant "Benny" Bent. About 50 miles from the target I had left the H2S and moved into the nose of the Halifax in preparation for a visual bombing run using the Mk XIV bombsight. There was no moon, no cloud and visibility was good in a bright starlit sky. To quote the official report, "Bent saw a Ju 88 at 200 yards on the fine port quarter slightly up and closing in fast. He told his Captain (Flying Officer Muller) to 'corkscrew port port'. The E/A (enemy aircraft) opened fire at 200 yards with cannon firing a very dull trace, hitting the Halifax and setting the port outer engine on fire. The rear gunner returned the fire with two short bursts, aiming point blank and hitting the fighter, causing it to pull up sharply. The Halifax was now in a spin and the Ju 88 appeared to Sergeant Bent to be hanging on its props on the starboard beam. He gave it another very short burst; observing strikes and saw it fall away, apparently out of control. By now the bomber was falling fast in a spin with flames pouring from the port outer engine. The pilot regained control after losing 8,000 feet in height, but as the port outer engine was u/s and the port inner engine appeared to have been damaged, the aileron and elevator controls also damaged, besides the turret being u/s and other damage to the aircraft, the bombs were jettisoned and course set for base."

'I was terrified during the spin as I was pinned to the floor of the bomb-aimer's position. I could not move and thought this was the end. Although the report states that the bombs were jettisoned, I recall attempting a bombing run on a solitary searchlight which was seeking us. The searchlight went out! Max Muller did a magnificent job in getting the aircraft back to England, gradually losing height all the way and using full right rudder to keep the aircraft straight. My brief attempt to help by tying my intercom lead round the rudder bar and pulling was very ineffective.

'We crossed the English coast in daylight, attempting to reach RAF Coltishall, but crashed a few miles short; just not enough power to hedge hop in. In the Halifax the bomb-aimer occupied the co-pilot's position for take-off and landing. I recall quite vividly the pilot struggling to keep the aircraft above ground. We passed between two trees, which we hit with the wings. It was a complete write-off although the nose and part of the fuselage remained reasonably intact. At least one of the engines had been torn away and was on fire. All the crew escaped injury except for Tommy Ellwood, the flight engineer, who had taken up his crash position behind the main spar and sustained a bad cut over one eye which subsequently required stitching There was a touch of humour at the end. Blazing petrol had landed on the back of Benny Bent's flying clothing but Hoop Arnott, the mid-upper gunner had seen this happen so he jumped on Benny (who must have wondered what was happening) to roll him over, so putting the flames out. A rather nervous couple living in a nearby cottage initially thought we were Germans, but when they realized we were RAF we were invited inside and given cups of tea until transport arrived. Flight Sergeant Emery was the navigator, and Pilot Officer Mac Maskell the WOP. There was no doubt in the minds of all crew that we owed our lives to the amazing ability and strength of the pilot, Max Muller.'

In a written account of the same incident by the Flight Engineer, Tom Ellwood, given to Max Muller's son, Derrick's recollections are confirmed. It includes the following extracts:

'By this time the Halifax was also in a dive and I was knocked off my feet. As I fell I struck my head on the main spar, cutting my face badly, but found I was unable to get up because the "G" forces were so great. The Halifax was obviously spinning out of control. To my great relief the plane eventually came out of its spin. I found Max grimly but firmly in control of a very damaged Halifax. He alone had used his great physical strength to pull the plane out!…The turret and hydraulic system was damaged, and petrol had been lost from two or three tanks…the bomb door…refused to close, adding drag. Max asked us all for our views and opinions on the unpleasant alternatives facing us – bale out now and risk being a POW, fly on and risk a possible ditching/drowning in the North Sea or try and limp home. After a brief discussion it was decided to fly on.

'Our Mayday was picked up as we approached our coast and we were directed to Coltishall. The dim lights from the airfield were a welcome sight. The port wheel failed to lock. By this time we were flying on one engine…The Halifax came down with a heavy jolt. It wavered and crashed finally grinding to a halt. It seems we had hit a tree which, fortuitously, had slewed us around and diverted our progress away from a farmhouse. Eagerly, we scrambled out as the Halifax now was on fire, to be confronted by two figures behind a wall who were relieved when they realized that we were not Germans. They helped us back to their farm and provided us with strong hot tea and sandwiches. Never had a cup of tea tasted so wonderful, nor has the feeling of being amongst friends felt so good, as we all sat in the warmth of that farmhouse.'

The farmhouse was Bridge Farm, and the nervous folks were the Gibbons family.

Jack Gibbons cycled to the next village of Antingham, and with difficulty managed to arouse the postmistress in order to phone the police. The Norfolk Civil Defence diaries record this call at 0438 hrs and show the crash happening at 0330 hrs. There is a question mark against this timing, since Derrick Coleman distinctly remembers the crash occurring in daylight. The crew were transported to the hospital at RAF Coltishall, and after the necessary care, were taken by road back to Graveley. The crew then split up.

The two Canadian gunners are believed to have completed their tours before returning to Canada. Tommy Ellwood's cut affected his eyesight and he was permanently grounded. He resumed his previous career as an engine fitter. Pilot Officer N. G. Emery, the navigator, was the only survivor of Halifax II JP123 TL-F, which crashed on the Stettin raid on 5/6 January 1944 killing Flight Lieutenant R. R. G. Appleby DFC and crew. He spent the rest of the war in the infamous POW camp at Sagan.

On the night of 22/23 May 1944 when Dortmund was the target for the bombers, Flying Officer Mac Maskell and Pilot Officer Derrick Coleman flew in Lancaster ND762 TL-E. The 35-year old Maskell was flying as a second wireless operator. Homeward bound, their Lanc was shot up by a nightfighter over Holland, and the Lancaster exploded, throwing out three survivors – the pilot, Flying Officer E. Holmes, Warrant Officer F. J. Tudor DFM and Coleman.

Maskell was one of the five airmen who died in the explosion, as was 37-year old Sergeant A. S. McLaren.

Derrick Coleman, who was not yet 21, avoided capture, was moved under the cover of Dutch and Belgian undergrounds, but was betrayed and ended up joining Emery at *Stalag Luft III*. Meanwhile, in February 1944, Squadron Leader Max Muller transferred to 25 OTU as an instructor, but returned for a further operational tour with 35 Squadron, this time piloting Lancasters. On 8/9 April, just thirty days before the end of the war, he volunteered for yet another raid over Germany, to Hamburg. His Lancaster was believed to have been hit in the nose by *flak* and Muller and five of the crew were killed. Flight Sergeant Charles Wilce DFM survived while Flight Lieutenant P. B. O. Ranalow died from his injuries on 10 April.

As for the Gibbons family, 81-year old William never really recovered from the trauma of that night. He died 55 days after the crash, and 75-year old Matilda passed away just seven days later. They were buried together in nearby Trunch cemetery. Their headstone is etched with the words

THEY TRAVELLED TOGETHER

A B-24 Liberator keels over after a direct hit in the fuel tanks

8

THE CURSE OF TUTANKHAMUN?

Liberators of the 44th Bomb Group – the Flying 'Eightballs' – regularly assembled over Norfolk and joined the bomber fleets of the Second Air Division striking out across the North Sea for enemy occupied Europe. Below, in tiny hamlets such as West Bradenham, close to Shipdham airbase, men on reserved occupation, like Fred Fawkes, worked the fields around the Bradenham Hall estate, helping to provide desperately needed food for an embattled nation.

Bradenham Hall is a two-storey Georgian house, set in several thousand acres of arable and fruit farmland, owned for a hundred years, from 1819-1919, by the Haggard family. Henry Haggard's great-grandson, Sir Henry Rider Haggard (of *King Solomon's Mines* fame) was born at Wood Farm on the estate in 1856. Haggard visited Egypt in 1887 and again in 1904, when he met Howard Carter, then custodian of antiquities at Luxor. The two Norfolkmen undoubtedly had much to talk about, for Carter hailed from Swaffham, six miles east of Bradenham.

Bombing up at Wendling

In November 1922, the famous Egyptologist came upon the hidden treasure of King Tutankhamun while concluding his exploration of the Valley of the Kings. That same year Haggard finished writing *Queen of the Dawn*, a story of ancient Egypt.

When the tempo of war increased with the arrival of the 8th Air Force in October 1942, American servicemen with a keen eye for history and especially English literature sought out Haggard's and Carter's ancestors and old haunts. Soon, B-24 Liberators of the 14th Wing, 2nd Bomb Division, were encamped around Swaffham, at North Pickenham, Shipdham and Wendling. Liberators of the 392nd Bomb Group – the 'Crusaders' – often flew over Bradenham towards Station 118, Wendling, a minute's flying time away in the parish of Beeston.

Meanwhile, men like Fred Fawkes, tending the land near Bradenham Hall, grew complacent with the sounds of the Pratt & Whitneys, because, by late 1943, they were almost commonplace. On 20 December 1943, this illusion was rudely shattered when *Exterminator, Old Bolts* of the 579th Squadron, 392nd Bomb Group, returning from a raid on Bremen, crashed in a field on the estate with the loss of all the crew. Some of the locals began to scratch their heads. Hadn't another Liberator crashed on the runways at Shipdham just a month before – on 18 November?

On that day the Liberators received a 'frag' order for a mission to bomb the Junkers Ju-88 assembly plant at Oslo-Kjeller and industrial targets in Oslo. Colonel Myron Keilman, 392nd Bomb Group, flying deputy lead, saw the target 'standing out in the late morning sun' and thought, 'It would be a shame to miss it.' Lieutenant McGregor, in the lead aircraft, held his ship precisely on altitude and airspeed and he and the 20 bombers following released the 210 500-pounders on the target simultaneously.

The 44th followed suit. On the return leg scattered clouds across the Skagerrak shielded the *Luftwaffe* from the B-24 formations. Suddenly, gunners spotted a dozen plus Ju 88s skimming across the cloud tops opposite to their line of flight and making fast diving passes as they circled in behind the bombers. The Libs moved into a tight formation as the fighters, diving in pairs, lobbed rockets and 20mm explosive shells into the 392nd. Tail and top turrets responded with bursts of machine gun fire and the ball turret gunners opened up below as the fighters broke off the attack.

Three Liberators, one each from the 93rd, 392nd and 44th, were forced to land in Sweden. Others dived for cover and sheltered in the clouds. For a time they played 'hide and seek' as the fighters circled. Eventually, the bombers were lost from view. Wave after wave pressed home their attacks but Staff Sergeant Forrest S. Clark, the tail gunner aboard Lieutenant Rockford 'Rocky' C. Griffith's ship in the 44th, succeeded in shooting one of them down.

'Sitting in the tail position I could look back and see a line of seven to ten fighters lining up to attack our rear. Suddenly, they attacked from all sides. Two shells went through the turret directly over my head, missing me by inches. One after the other the *Luftwaffe* pilots zoomed in at our tail and then dived beneath us to come up in front and swing and line up for another pass. Closer and closer they came as I tracked them with my twin .50 calibre guns, but could not get a good lead on any until they passed under us and then shot up again for the waist gunners to try.

'Finally, I fixed one in my sights as he levelled out and came in faster and faster. "So close", I said to myself, "He's going to hit us; he's going to ram us." I gripped the triggers of both guns and pressed. I kept holding the triggers down, hoping they would not jam the belts. I could see my tracers going out in long lines right into his wing roots. Bright flashes of fire and tracers kept boring into his wings until he came so close I could see the outline of the German pilot's head in the cockpit. Just as he slipped under us I saw a thin trail of smoke coming from the engine.'

Clark was almost completely out of ammunition and a 20mm shell hit the waist gunner, who was bringing him more rounds, in the head, knocking him unconscious and leaving him bleeding on the floor. Clark heard the bailout bell but at first he had difficulty in getting out of his shattered turret. Two men were getting ready to jump through the open camera hatch.

Clark prayed because he knew he would not survive long in the ice-cold sea if he jumped.

'I actually went down on my knees and prayed. Much to my surprise, just about that time, the fighter attacks suddenly stopped, and the Germans left us to what they must have thought was our deaths.'

During the same operation, Lieutenant Joseph L. Houle's B-24 was severely damaged. It tottered gallantly to within 50 miles of the English coast but, with safety in sight, his fuel indicators were reading zero and he was forced to ditch in the sea. The aircraft seemed to break in two and four figures were seen to slip into the icy waters of the North Sea. Griffith, himself flying on three faltering engines, circled over the scene while his radio-operator called ASR. With his own fuel supply running low Griffith dipped his wing in salute to his fallen comrades and turned towards his base. Tragically ASR was unable to trace any of the crew or the aircraft. Griffith's Liberator spluttered on barely above the surface of the sea.

Clark adds:

'More than once the call went out from the pilot to prepare to ditch but Sergeant William T. Kuban, the ball turret gunner, would surely have died if we ditched in the icy water. We limped on and more than once it seemed all engines quit and the plane stuttered as if in its death throes. But the plane would not die.'

Griffith and his co-pilot, Lieutenant L. G. Grone, got the Liberator back to Shipdham where the one landing gear failed to drop. Sergeant Earl J. Parrish, the flight engineer, tried in vain to crank it down by hand. Griffith called off the crash landing in favour of a belly landing but the stubborn undercarriage leg failed to respond when Parrish tried to retract the 'down' leg. Griffith refused to panic and ordered everyone except Grone and Kuban to bail out. Forrest Clark bailed out, fell to the ground and gripped it with both hands in a gesture of relief and thanksgiving. Griffith and Grone landed the badly damaged B-24 on one wheel. Kuban survived. Altogether, six B-24s were lost on the Oslo raid.

Two hours later repair crews checking the wreckage, found two unexploded 20mm shells in the one good engine that had brought the crew home. The discovery of the two shells is ironic in the light of subsequent events.

Forrest Clark gradually recovered and was trying desperately to get back on flying status when on 21 December he flew as a waist gunner aboard *Emmy Lou II*, a Liberator with a distinguished combat record, in a 44th four plane practice formation from Shipdham to the Wash. The flight was a combination of test hop (because the B-24 had been in for repairs after severe battle damage on a mission to Bremen) and group practice formation. *Emmy Lou II's* largely regular crew was captained by one of the most experienced pilots in the group, Captain Richard Butler, a Ploesti mission pilot with an outstanding record of combat. He had crash-landed *Miss Emmy Lou* at Catania, Sicily, on the return from Wiener Neustadt. Technical Sergeant Donald Eslocker, who was banned from flying above 10,000 ft. after suffering frostbite to his face and hands on a bombing mission, was aboard, as engineer, to qualify for his monthly flight pay. He stood on the flight deck behind

B-24s of the 44th Bomb Group, taxiing in early morning at Shipdham

Lt Griffith's crash, 18 November 1943

Butler and co-pilot, Jerry Grell on takeoff. Nick Garcia, from armament, was along for the ride while Kooken, Chamberlain and Boulanger, were gunners to be.

Butler recalls:

'The flight was routine enough until the formation break up. We were at 800 feet, in the pattern for landing, when there was an explosion in the No. 2 engine. With the explosion, the other three engines also quit!'

In the waist Forrest Clark heard over the intercom:

'We're going down!'

Butler wrote later:

'Nothing to do but land straight ahead. We were headed right at a large tree but I managed to avoid hitting it with the nose, and took it at about the No.2 engine area. We hit; skidded, hit a ditch and the plane broke open.'

Clark adds:

'Before we could take any crash positions we hit with a great jar, and wreckage went flying. Roy Neeper, who was also a Ploesti veteran, was standing near me in the waist position. The wings clipped off trees and ploughed into the soft farm field, sending showers of earth over us. This was the closest I ever came to dying, even more so than Norway. It is my firm belief that in the split seconds before the crash Butler managed, in some miraculous way, to soften the impact to such an extent as to save our lives. He narrowly missed a farmhouse. We could have lost the entire crew and the pilot, a great loss of manpower, to the 44th. I do not to this day understand how anyone got out.'

Emmy Lou II crashed at 1830 hours in farmer Percy Kiddie's field at Wood Farm (where Rider Haggard was born), now part of the Bradenham Hall estate. Clark sustained back injuries jumping out of the B-24 from the waist gun position. Butler was seriously injured. He says:

'I tried to open my seat belt with my left hand, but there was a 90 degree bend at my left wrist – broken. I managed to open the safety belt with my right hand and then went out through the left cockpit window, which was completely broken open. Upon getting out I found that I couldn't stand up – my left ankle was also broken. This was probably caused by the jolt received from the left rudder pedal when we hit the tree.

'People were coming out of the wreck from all kinds of holes. Fires had started and some shells were exploding. After taking roll, Nicholson, the bombardier, was missing. He and Coiner, the navigator, had been on the flight deck in preparation for landing. When I asked, "Where's Nick?" Loy Neeper went back into the wreck through the top hatch. I can still see him coming back out while reaching back in and with one hand, lifting the unconscious Nicholson out and dropping off of what was left of the fuselage. For this action, Loy Neeper received a Soldier's Medal – well deserved!

'We moved away from the wreck as, by this time, there was quite a fire with lots of exploding shells. I was crawling along as best I could and Neeper was dragging Nick. About this time, a farm worker came over and began helping some of us.'[1]

General Leon Johnson, CO, 14th Combat Wing, who had led the 'Eightballs' low over Ploesti oil fields on 1 August, had witnessed Butler's rapid descent from aboard his B-24, landed and led crash crews to the scene in his staff car. Dick Butler takes up the story again:

'I remember General Johnson helping to carry the gate and I was very embarrassed. Nick had regained consciousness by then and was doing a lot of moaning. We were very lucky! Besides my injuries, Grell had a broken right arm. Nicholson's injuries turned out to be some broken ribs and a bump on his head. Mason, my radio operator, was missing his left ear! When the explosion occurred in number two engine, metal came through the fuselage and took his ear off completely. Someone found it and at the hospital it was sewn back on and saved. Amazingly, that was the extent of the more severe injuries.

'There was a lot of speculation as to what really had happened. One theory was that there was an unexploded shell in the No.2 engine from the battle damage that finally let go. A hole in the underside of the number two nacelle had been patched, but the projectile not discovered. Another view was that we had encountered ice and that caused all four engines to quit but I doubt that it would affect all engines at the exact same time. And, it doesn't explain the explosion. Personally, I think the explosion severed fuel lines or the electrical system and that is why they all quit. There was a lot of damage to the left side of the fuselage along the flight deck before we hit the ground. Grell, Nicholson and Mason wound up in a Yorkshire hospital. Mason and Nicholson got out in a few days. Some time in January 1944, Grell and Butler got back to the 44th where it was decided that they would be sent

---

[1] In October 1992, Forrest Clark (who flew missions after the Bradenham crash before going down in Switzerland in April 1944), was reunited with the farm worker, Fred Fawkes, a sprightly 84 still living at West Bradenham, who was working 100 yards from the scene of the crash. Fred recalled the accident as if it were yesterday.

'I could see him comin' over the top of me. I thought, he won't get over that hedge. Well he didn't. He hit a tree, took the top off it, and landed in a pit. A chap on a tractor ploughing in the next field came up with me. Bullets were flying everywhere. We got this chap out of the plane. He couldn't walk so we took a five-bar wooden gate off the field, laid my big khaki coat on it, put him on and carried him up to the cottage in the meadow nearby.'

BASE
LIFE

The Curse of Tutankhamun?

home as hospital patients as it would take so long for their broken bones to heal in the English climate. Colonel Fred Dent, CO. 44th Bomb Group, was opposed to this action but the flight surgeon, backed up by Colonel Bill Cameron, Butler's squadron CO, prevailed.'

The peace and tranquillity at Bradenham Hall was not disturbed again until 9 October 1944. *P-Bar Peter, The Flying Crusader*, crewed by Lieutenant Alan 'Ben' Alexander, co-pilot Presley Broussard, navigator Tom Kirkwood, radio operator Frank Gallo, and engineer Rupert Sutphin, of the 392nd Bomb Group, took off on a 'typical dreary, low ceiling day shortly after lunch' from Wendling to test *Mickey* radar apparatus. *P-Bar* was the last original B-24 arriving with the group from the States to England. The crew were told that 'they wanted to have *P-Bar* chalk up 100 missions before it fell apart and it would be more likely to reach that goal as a lead ship rather than a wing ship.'

Ben Alexander describes what happened next.

'Above the thick overcast there was no problem checking out the radar navigation equipment, so, after getting a heading from Tom, I started my descent through the cloud cover. We broke out of the clouds at a low ceiling of about 300 ft,

B-24 Liberators of 392nd Bomb Group refuelling at Wendling, 9 September 1943

achieved visual contact with the base and, as we were readying our turn onto the base leg, the problems began. First, the number three prop ran away. With Presley's help on the rudder pedals, resetting the trim tabs, and with great effort, we slowly managed some directional control. I had Press pull the power off number three, lower the gear and help me get lined up with the runway. When we were about a mile from the field, I suspected we had lost another engine as we couldn't maintain desired altitude on our approach. We were over a small village above a street with businesses under and ahead of us when the left gear brushed the top of a tall tree.

'It was time to forget about reaching the runway. I hit the intercom button warning the crew to prepare for a crash landing, headed for a small field a short distance to our left and plopped the ship down about 50 ft beyond a 6 ft high hedgerow. We were in line with two large trees some 200 yards away. With very little directional control, I was depending mostly on hope and luck to pass between them. The left wing made it, but the right wing hit and completely sheared the trunk of the tree on the right about ten feet above the ground. Spinning rapidly clockwise, *P-Bar* bounced into the far bank of a four feet deep bog, breaking the fuselage open just back of the trailing edge of the wings. It came to rest with the left rear stabilizer and rudder resting atop the left wing, with fire engulfing a large part of the fuselage aft of the flight deck. At this time the flight deck was still fairly upright, and the crew, except Gallo, were able to climb up and out the escape hatch without injury. After counting noses and realizing Frank was still in the wreck, Press and I tried to work our way up into Frank's station. However, the fire and .50 calibre slugs screaming around us chased us out. I just hope Frankie never knew what hit him. We did realize that there was never a sound coming out of the plane.

'Next day, after everything had cooled off, Major "Pappy" Cornelius, the Group Engineering Officer, helped me reconstruct the plane's action. The centrifugal force set up by the spinning action caused by the wing hitting the tree I'm sure, saved us on the flight deck from serious, if not fatal, injury. Heck, my co-pilot hadn't even buckled his restraining belt! If we had hit that bog straight ahead, worse things could have happened.'

Incredibly, *P-Bar* crashed in the same field *Exterminator*, *Old Bolts* had piled into eleven months earlier!

Bradenham Hall's wartime chapter passed into history along with boyhood memories of Rider Haggard. The best selling storyteller had moved to Ditchingham House, near Bungay where he died on the morning of 14 May 1925. Major Cheyne, Haggard's son-in-law, was with him the night before.

'The window blind was up and the blaze from a large building on fire was visible in the distance. Rider rose up in bed, pointed to the conflagration with arm outstretched, the red glow upon his dying face.'

'My God!' said Cheyne to himself, 'an old Pharaoh.'

Another blaze occurred just before midnight on 30 April 1940, when a Hawker Hurricane of 504 Squadron at Martlesham Heath, piloted by Squadron Leader Rupert Hartley-Watson, the 28-year-old Squadron CO, developed engine trouble and he crashed on the driveway while attempting to land. The Hurricane was wrecked and Hartley-Watson was killed. During WWII the Hall on the estate was taken over for the care of wounded American airmen. Left behind at Ditchingham Hall's stables, used as a bar by the GIs and waiting to be discovered by a modern day Howard Carter, were cartoons, wall paintings of aircraft (at Shipdham and Wendling too) and scribbled names – some as indecipherable as Egyptian hieroglyphics.

Many American airmen who embarked on missions from England, died, like Tutankhamun, under the age of 20, never to see the fruits of their victory. And what of Bradenham Hall? In 1951, it was bought by Lieutenant Colonel Richard Allhusen and his wife Evelyn, who have lived in it ever since. In November 1992, two tragedies befell the stately home. On 9 November, burglars broke in and stole $100,000 worth of antiques and, later that same month, 6,000 gallons of ammonia-based crop spray were washed into the River Wissey after the storage tank capsized. It was exactly 70 years after Carter had discovered King Tutankhamun's tomb.

A LETTER FROM NORWICH

Another young woman who endured the terrible aerial bombardment in April 1942 was Kathleen Pye. A 20-year-old Red Cross volunteer and bank worker at the National Provincial in St Benedict's Kathleen lived in Brian Avenue and she wrote a letter just days after the second of the Baedeker raids to her brother Charlie, who was serving in the Royal Navy. In it she graphically describes the awful experience of so many ordinary people caught up in the war.

The siren went Monday night about quarter to twelve and about ten minutes later while we were still in bed there was a terrific 'crump'. We got up and came downstairs, grabbing our clothes as we came, and John and I and the dog got under the table and Mum and Dad got under the stairs. There we stayed for a whole hour while the planes roared around and dropped bombs unceasingly. Our doors and windows rattled and we thought we must have had a bomb in our garden.

However, at the end of the raid when we went outside, the house was OK but there was a terrific fire in the city. This was, as we found next day, Wincarnis, Victoria Station and City Station and one or two other fires which started in small houses. Dereham Road was badly bombed and all the Heigham Street area. Beers was burned down and they have since got temporary premises at Harry Pointer's. We only had three panes of glass broken in the bank, but Beryl Gedge is awfully worried as there is nothing left of Wincarnis. The Odol works weren't much damaged on Monday, but in Wednesday night's Blitz they too were gutted and all of the staff except about a dozen of the office staff have been dismissed. They are staying on in an office in the Close but when everything is settled they don't know what will happen to them.

You know Pauline Newby who was in the Pantomime. They lived in Patteson Road and Monday night their house received a direct hit. Mr Newby had put an incendiary out on his chicken shed and came indoors to take his wife and two children down to the shelter. While they were still indoors the house was hit. Pauline was rescued fairly quickly from under the rubble and she could speak to her father who was also buried but neither of them could do anything for themselves.

A fire started and Mr Newby could see the flames creeping up on all sides, but fortunately they were extinguished before he was burned. He was got out at five in the afternoon, having been buried since 1am and he was conscious all the time. Pauline is now out of hospital but she hurt her back and legs and was suffering from shock. Her Dad had two cuts on his head and bruises and his stomach hurt through the weight of the bricks.

About two days later Mrs Newby and Barbara, who was five[1] were dug out and they

---

[1] Her memorial plaque gives her age as eight.

Kathleen Pye, between brothers John and Charlie, a year after the air raids

were very badly charred. I don't know when they are going to be buried but some people were buried today in a communal grave. Maggie Pratt was bombed out of Elizabeth Fry Road and her furniture is nearly all ruined and the house is uninhabitable. Five Irishmen were killed in her road. This first night we only had about one gun firing and no fighters up and the wretched planes were diving wholesale. That was the worst part of it, they usually began diving over Lakenham and then dropped their loads – we escaped the bombs but it was dreadfully nerve-racking and also the wretched bombs were whistling past and every time this happened we kept ducking down lower. The remainder of Rupert Street was knocked about and (the bombs) absolutely knocked Jimmy Middleton's shop and others in that row off the face of the earth. I can't tell you everywhere that was hit, as it was so widespread. Practically every area had some bombs.

Tuesday night we had another raid, but it was only about a couple of planes and we had some AA fire and no bombs were dropped.

Wednesday night we had yet another and although it only lasted three-quarters of an hour it was worse than anything. Old soldiers of the last war and even people who were in the London Blitz said they never experienced anything like it. It was hell let loose.

To accompany the dive-bombing we had the noise of a lot of AA guns. We were quite pleased to hear that though.

It was awful under the table as we had seen the shambles of houses after the last raid and wondered how we would get on if we were hit. However, when there was a lull we thought we'd be better off in the open, so we got the car rug and coats and tore off down Hall Road, past the Tuckswood and got in a field under a hedge. There were lots of other people there and in other places along the road, as they seemed to appear from nowhere when the 'All Clear' went. It would have been a marvellous sight had it not been for the destruction. It appeared as though the whole of the city was ablaze and one or two smaller fires on the outskirts. Caleys was burned out in the old building and the wall of one part is all leaning in. The new part near Chapel Field was partly burned and all the windows were broken. Buntings was partially burnt and is not useable. Woolworth's, Curls and Brigg Street and Greens, Red Lion Street and Boots and Saxone are completely gone. It's like a wilderness – just masses of rubble and twisted girders. The Norwich Training College was burned-out but all the girls were safe, although some of them had a narrow escape. The Unthank College was bombed out and Duff Morgan's opposite the church is flattened and burnt. It had a direct hit.

The Carlton had a bomb hole in the side and people were standing about for a whole day looking at it when someone spotted the darned thing. It hadn't gone off. They got it out – it was a dud.

Freeman's house and others in Rowington Road had a direct hit, also Warrington's and

Lord Haw Haw claimed that *Luftwaffe* pilots discovered that the Norwich clock tower was six minutes slow.

another in that row and the blast made the houses opposite uninhabitable. Marshall's was bombed out; the bar part of the Smoke Room and the sitting room lay in Grove Road – a mass of bricks and mortar. Three soldiers in the house next door were trapped in the cellar but were got out and only one was hurt. An old lady died in Warrington's Morrison Shelter, but his wife and daughter were safe, but of course they had to be dug out. Warrington was on duty as a warden and of course he knew exactly where to find them and they were soon rescued.

A land mine dropped at the bottom of Grapes Hill and there's a terrific crater, which extends right across the crossroads. The bank and Hick's fish shop, the ironmongers and Boots etc, are now just a pile of rubble. I think this is one of the worst areas, as another dropped behind the bank and all round there's nothing but piles of bricks and mortar.

The only thing standing is the bank's strongroom, which was built of reinforced concrete. It has a crack in it through which the fireman managed to squirt some water; but everything inside was safe, although some things are a bit damp. My typewriter, which was on the shelf, fell off and is slightly broken but I think is repairable. Our caretakers were sheltering in the Crown Inn and although the upstairs floors were badly damaged they were safe in the cellar; but they've lost everything and poor Mrs Hare was worried to distraction as her mother had to have both legs off above the knee as a result of Monday's raid. We are operating at London Street at the moment but we don't know what's going to happen to us. We may be merged with Norwich or we may have our own department in one of the side rooms up there. We haven't got everything out yet but what we have is full of small stones and mortar, and of course we've lost quite a lot of stuff in the main office including one or two personal belongings. Although there's such destruction no one was hurt down there, as they were all in shelters further up the road.

Dereham Road got another packet and Beers had more incendiaries up at Harry Pointer's, but it wasn't much. Nearly all the laundries with the exception of the Pearl were bombed and burned and we've lost our laundry, as has half the population of Norwich. The Bowthorpe Institution had a direct hit on the old men's ward and killed one or two, but they were evacuated before Wednesday's raid to make room for the wounded. There were also some fires on the cemetery and the Angel Road area was bombed. Sheila was bombed out of Hillcrest Road. Arthur Pye was also bombed out of Livingstone Street.

I can't remember any more places in detail now, but you'll see it all when you come home although you won't see it at its worst as they are clearing up already. A shelter in Chapel Field Gardens had a direct hit and many were killed – when they decided the remaining people were dead they sealed it up.

I don't think we'll have any more dive-bombing as Norwich is waking up at last. Eileen Marshall is sleeping here in your bed and Mrs M and Cyril are out at Surlingham and old

B-24J Liberator *A Dog's Life* crashed at the junction of Spixworth Road and Church Street, Catton, 13 February 1945. All nine crew died and a woman civilian was injured.

B-24J *Lassie Come Home* crashed in the garden of 14 Spynke Road, Norwich, 14 January 1945. All but one of Lt John Clayborn's crew were killed, along with two children who were playing in the garden. A third child miraculously escaped injury.

St Benedict's, Norwich, after devastating German bombings

When *Curls* was bombed out, *Jarrolds* let them move in to their store

Carrow Road, home of Norwich City Football Club experiences an American rodeo

A Theatre Royal programme

Billy went to Thetford, but is back again today and is living with Aggie. I went to the Woodlands (Bowthorpe Inst) to help and, my crumbs, did we get some nice jobs. I won't put them on paper. I've also done a duty at Rosebery Road rest centre but it was not quite so bad as the Institution.

Poor old Billy Marshall has no clothes. All his things sailed down into the bar and then on into the cellar with the drawing room furniture on top of it. Cyril's bedroom was cut in two and it was all open to the sky but they couldn't get up there for a couple of days as the rest of the house looks as though it would fall in a high wind. However they've been salvaging today and when he looked in his chest of drawers he found that his new stopwatch and cigarette case were missing. Evidently someone had got up there and pinched them. Some money was also pinched from Freeman's house – or what remains of it. I think there must be some awful people about. Of course all this has its lighter moments and we've had some laughs and we all came through safe – thank God, and I hope we don't have any more.

Well, I must finish now I think this is the longest letter I've ever written and its taken three sittings to finish it as I've been so busy with Red X – we wanted plenty of blood last weekend. Directly my three months is up they're going to extract another pint from me. That will be sometime after May 15. They want a lot of Group 4 blood, as this is most useful... Well, cheerio and all the best,

Write soon,

Lots of love

From Kathleen. XXXXXX

VE day celebrations, Aylsham

9

A FINE ROMANCE

*N*ORA *N*ORGATE *C*AN*fi*ELD

'We'd become used to seeing strange-looking service men in Norwich from the early days of the war. When the "Yanks" first appeared in the city in 1942 they were also very noticeable in their different style uniforms, and different language, which was English and yet it wasn't! For example, we'd never heard of a drawing-pin described as a thumb-tack, a torch as a flashlight or petrol as gasoline. Completely foreign!

'I first met my husband-to-be Corporal Herman Canfield (later promoted to sergeant) of the 577th Squadron, 392nd Bomb Group, in May 1944 at a friend's home at Crane's Corner near Wendling. He'd arrived at Wendling in November 1943 and was a clerk in the Group Operations office where his work included the scheduling of practice missions over The Wash, North Sea, and eastern England for the flight crews. When we got engaged in August 1944, we immediately began the necessary procedures to obtain permission to marry.[1]

'He had to write a letter to the Chaplain at the base, giving my reasons for wanting to get married and that I was single, of good character etc. My aunt, who was responsible for my upbringing after I'd lost my mother when I was 4 years old, was also required to write, confirming her approval and giving her permission. Herman had to go for a personal interview with the 392nd Group Base Chaplain: "Why did he want to marry? Was he being coerced in any way? How long had he known me", etc, etc. Then began the waiting while Herman's record was investigated to see if he really was single or married or divorced, etc. We went ahead and planned our wedding for early December, as we knew it would take some time for official permission to filter through. Our banns were published in the local paper and we made all the necessary arrangements with the vicar and the sexton of my local Church. In mid-November, permission was granted and we were married on 2 December 1944. The reception was held at The Volunteer, which was owned by my uncle, Harry Brock. Herman and I went to Blackpool for our honeymoon and as I had a free rail pass and he was a serviceman it didn't cost much.'

Herman left Norwich on 3 July 1945 and Nora followed the next February having spent three weeks being 'processed' at Tidworth. Nora was given permission by her office manager to go out to the train platform and say goodbye to Herman.

[1] Servicemen had to seek the approval of their commanding officers two months in advance of a proposed wedding.

'It was a very emotional parting, as we really had no idea when we would see each other again. We began our lives together eight months later when after 13½ days of seasickness I arrived in New York to a reception of snow and the bands playing.'

Nora and Herman Canfield

By October 1945 some 60,000 G.I. brides were still waiting to be transported to the States. Nora's friend Ivy Seabourne, who was also brought up in Belvoir Street, had loaned her wedding dress to Nora to wear, and she too sailed for America, on the *Queen Mary*, in February 1946.

'There were four of us in the cabin with babies. One of the girls was seasick all the time. She couldn't get to the dining room for meals so we would bring her crackers.'

Ivy was on war work in Luton and during a weekend leave to Norwich in October 1943 she went to the Odeon cinema and was offered a cigarette by an American, Charles Holston, a cook in the 44th Bomb Group at Shipdham, who was sitting next to her. Ivy didn't smoke but she pretended she did. She and Charles arranged to meet later outside the Post Office. They corresponded and met in London or Norwich when they could get leave. Charles, who worked 24 hours on, 48 hours off, would cycle the 18 miles from Shipdham to Norwich.

'The first day I thought I'd never get there' he recalls, 'but each day it got shorter'.

They married on 20 May 1944 and a year later their eldest daughter Diane, was born in Thorpe Nursing Home three days before VE Day. After arriving in America Ivy and Charles travelled by train for two days to Elkhart, Indiana. Their second daughter, Sharon, was born in Elkhart and they have stayed there. Charles worked in the dry cleaning business and Ivy worked in a bank. Today their elder daughter lives with her three children in Washington State and the younger one is in California. Ivy and Charles are avid square dancers and enjoy gardening and travelling.

Nora found it took some adjustment to become a farmer's wife in Indiana. They have a dairy herd and grow corn, wheat, soya beans and hay. They have 5 sons and 7 grandchildren.

Nora and Ivy, who once both lived in Belvoir Street, now live 180 miles apart, still keep in touch, and visit each other two or three times a year.

MIRIAM THORPE AND EDWARD J. ISRAEL.
ST. JOHN'S R.C. CATHEDRAL

Miriam Thorpe, daughter of Mr. and Mrs. Walter Thorpe of Norwich, Norfolk, was married on June 14th to 1/Lieutenant Edward J. Israel, son of Mr. and Mrs. John Israel of 923 Garden Street, Hoboken. The Reverend Father J. P. Fagin performed the ceremony held in St. John's Catholic Church, Norwich, England. Following the afternoon ceremony, a reception was held at the home of the bride's parents. The bride was given away by her father. She was attended by her sister, Miss Enid Thorpe, a WAAF, and Captain Nicholas C. Cianakos of Blackstone, Virginia, was best man. A royal blue bolero ensemble with wine accessories worn by the bride blended with the multi corsage with iris and red roses. Lieutenant Israel was the Base Technical Inspector of the 448th Bomb Group at Seething. A graduate of Stevens Institute of Technology, with a degree of mechanical engineering, the groom continued engineering training as an aviation cadet in the AAF at Chanuso Field, Illinois and was commissioned in September 1942. Prior to his arrival in England in September 1943, Lieutenant Israel served as an engineering officer at Army Air Ease, Columbia, South Carolina; MacDill Field, Tampa, Florida; Barkesdale Field, Shreveport, Louisiana; and Atterbury Air Base, Columbus, Indiana.

Captain Ed Israel

LILIAN BURNETT

'I was born in London but at the height of the war my family moved to the coastal town of Ipswich in Suffolk. It was there that I gained my first impression of real live Americans. During the war years I left school at fourteen and went to work. We had long since learned to respect the air raid sirens that told us when enemy planes were approaching. We had learned to live in a world of darkness, as no light could be visible from a home, church, factory, car, or even our bicycles, because a light might lead the German bombers to us. I remember the first time I was fitted for my gas mask, how I galloped home to show my mother, dad and sister. I was twelve at the time, but it soon became second nature to pick up our gas masks and tin hats when we left home. War or no war, life went on. Everyone was doing their part. Our fathers who were too old for the army were recruited into the Home Guard. Women were recruited for Air Raid Wardens. Both men and women were fire fighters.

'I was too young for any of these jobs, so I volunteered to work weekends at the YMCA Canteen where we served what food we were allowed. All types of food were strictly rationed and there wasn't much variety. We managed to have tea, coffee, toast, and sometimes some little plain cakes, which often became the brunt of the soldiers' jokes, as they would say, "If we ever run out of bullets, we can always use these cakes." There were three of these canteens in our town, and we worked in whichever one needed us. At first it was only our English boys that used them.

'I grew to love my work at the canteen. In a small way we helped to pass time for some of the soldiers who were lonely. There wasn't any dancing or recreation, only a few tables and chairs, an old piano, and a radio. It was just a place for the soldier to go to get in off the dark streets, especially if one didn't have much money. I have seen many a homesick soldier come in just to find someone to talk with. There was a friendly atmosphere in our canteens, so if someone could play the piano, it wasn't long before he would be surrounded by a crowd of fellows singing the songs that had literally become a part of England.

'English people have always been said to be reserved and stuffy. I believe that it was the singing and laughter that brought us through the six years of war. Never let it be said that Englishmen haven't a sense of humour because I know differently. We learned to laugh at Lord Haw Haw, who night after night broke in on the BBC broadcasts to inform the English people exactly where the German planes would be dropping their bombs that night. Invariably some soldier would mimic Lord Haw Haw, and everyone would end up in fits of laughter. I always thought that little bit of German psychology backfired, for while these nightly messages were meant to frighten the people, it always ended up as the joke of the evening.

'When the first Americans reached our town, it did not take most of them long to find our number one landmark, the English pub. I will never forget the first American soldiers I saw. There were about five of them who were very much under the influence of alcohol. Their hats were on the backs of their heads, and their ties were every way but the right way. Two of them were sitting on the kerb, and the others were holding up a lamppost. They were singing. My immediate thought was, "If this is a sample of the Americans who have come over to help us, heaven help us".

'In the next few weeks the town literally became full of American soldiers. My first encounter with these GIs left the impression with me that they were loud showoffs. They would call, "Hey there Limey," after the girls as they walked down the streets. This used to embarrass us English girls to death.

'As time passed, we had servicemen from several different countries coming to the canteen regularly. One Saturday in January 1945 I was working at the little canteen at the Railway Station. I was alone at the time, as my two girl friends hadn't shown up yet. I was trying to keep a supply of good hot coffee and tea, while washing and drying cups and saucers, and waiting on the servicemen who came in. I was beginning to get a little panicky when through the door came an American soldier that I had never seen before. It was all I could do not to giggle. This soldier [Clarence Burnett] seemed so different from the other Americans I had seen. He was big built and of course his Army overcoat made him look all the bigger. His face was round and covered with freckles. Under his cap was the brightest head of red hair that I had ever seen. His manner was very kind and friendly. By this time he had sized up the situation. Only he wasn't looking at me, it was I looking at him. He was looking at the stack of dirty cups and saucers that I was struggling with. I was quite unprepared for his next statement when he asked, "Can I help you wash dishes?"

'Well, by the time I could bring my thoughts together he had his coat off, sleeves rolled up, and his hands in the dishwater. At the same time he was saying, "I don't mind washing dishes, but I won't dry them." At those words I sprang toward a tea towel, after all what else could I do? We washed dishes side by side for quite a while, hardly saying a word to each other, until a British MP walked in the door and demanded of my dish washer, "What do you think you are doing behind the counter?" It was quite obvious; he was washing dishes. But the MP said, "Don't you know that servicemen are not allowed back of the counter?" I tried to come to the defence of my dishwasher, and the MP softened a little, saying to me, "It's nice that the boy should want to help you out, but orders are orders."

'Both my American soldier and I were a little embarrassed by the incident, and it wasn't long before the soldier put on his coat and left the canteen. I hadn't even found out anything about him, so I decided to call him "Red."

'The next weekend I was on duty at the canteen, about a block from the Railway Station. My two girl friends and I were kept pretty busy. I turned around from my job of filling up the cake tray to find myself looking into the face of my freckle-faced redhead. He said, "Hi! How are you?" I replied with, "Hello, can I get you something?" He said that he would like a cup of coffee and cake. The English coffee is a bottled liquid and you put one teaspoon-full in a cup and fill it with boiling water and milk. Milk was hard to get, and it was really a luxury if one could have a cup of coffee made with milk. I remembered how nice "Red" had been to help me the week before, so I decided to give him a real treat, a cup of coffee made with milk. I thought Americans like sweet things so I put in two teaspoons of sugar.

'I carried the coffee out to him with the same elegance that a waiter in tie and tails would carry in a roasted duck. I thought to myself, "He will be so pleased when he sees the trouble that I have gone to." I put the cup down in front of him, and then he spoke the words that shattered me to pieces. "What on earth is this?"

"Why it's the coffee you ordered," I said.

"You call that coffee? What did you make it with?" he demanded.

I told him, "I made it with boiling milk and used two spoons of sugar, which is a luxury these days. Believe me, any English boy would be glad to drink it."

I was unprepared for his next statement. He simply said

"Well, let some English boy drink it then, because I don't want it."

'Boy, was I hurt! I took my special cup of coffee back and gave him a cup of the regular coffee and cake. I took his money and walked away, thinking to myself that I might have known that he would turn out to be rude like most of his fellow Americans. I thought, "If he comes in again, I just won't speak to him."

'The next time he came in, I had my girl friend, Vera, wait on him. He said, "Hi" to me. I felt like sticking my tongue out at him, but I remembered my manners. "Red" came in almost every week for several weeks. I finally decided that I could at least be civil to him. After a time, I was quite surprised when he asked me to go to the pictures with him. You will notice that he didn't say that he would take me.

'After I got off at the canteen we walked to the show, where I ended up paying my own way. As if this wasn't bad enough, it seems that he didn't have quite enough money to pay for his own ticket. It was lucky for me that I had enough. Needless to say, I was beginning to have some pretty mixed feelings about this Yank. He did pay me back and explained that he was just broke that night.

'Weeks went by, and he would walk me home from the canteen, though sometimes he would complain that it was too far to walk. We would talk about his plans for the future. I realized that he was just walking home with me because he was lonely. This was all right with me because I was writing to a boy that I had known for years who was now in the Royal Marines.

'In the weeks that followed, Red and I learned quite a lot about each other, as well as about the countries that we both came from. My mother invited Red, along with my two girl friends, to tea for my birthday. He said that he would try to make it. But when I came home on the day, he wasn't to be seen. It was then that I realized that I was disappointed because he wasn't there, and that it mattered that he hadn't come. Then, as I entered the house, someone grabbed me and said, "Happy Birthday." He had come.

'April was upon us. The war in Europe was rapidly coming to an end. Red's Group had been away while their runways were resurfaced. When he returned on April 1st he did not talk much, but did say he had missed me very much. Later that day he asked me to marry him. I thought it was an April Fools joke. But he asked me again a few days later. I told him that he would have to ask my dad. To this he said, "Why, I don't want to marry your dad?" But ask dad he did. Dad wasn't surprised, but my mother wanted to know if I had thought about leaving home, family, friends and customs to move to a new country. It was a hard decision for a girl of 18 to make. I wondered, "Would love and understanding be able to outweigh the loneliness for the folks you know and country you love when it came time to leave them?" We were married on 20 May 1945 in St. Clements Episcopal Church in Ipswich.'

The wedding of Clarence 'Red' Burnett from Chillicot, Illinois and Lilian Lambert was witnessed by bridesmaids Betty Lambert, Lily Harbour, Vera Harbour and Gwen Pallant. Norman Protsman from Cincinnati, Ohio, Red's friend from the 860th Bomb Squadron, 493rd Bomb Group, was best man.

10

'THE BEST YEARS OF OUR LIVES?'

Larry 'Goldie' Goldstein

Larry Goldstein and Rose, Brooklyn, New York,
17 July 1943, just before going overseas

In July 1942 B-17 and B-24 heavy bomb groups of VIIIth Bomber Command began arriving in England in ever increasing numbers. Nearly 100,000 acres of Norfolk farmland were eventually taken over for USAAF use. The first US B-17 Flying Fortress raid from these shores took place on 17 August 1942 and by 1943 the Eighth Air Force numbered over a score of heavy bomber groups. By 1945 it had become one of the mightiest air forces in history. GIs from every state of the union and from every walk of life in America were inducted, trained, and sent to England, or the European Theatre of Operations (ETO) as it was known. Most of the airmen were like their counterparts in the RAF, in their late teens and early twenties. And just like their RAF cousins the 'Yanks' were expected to fly a tour of

Landing at Knettishall, 1944

missions in the B-17s and B-24s, or die in the attempt. In the USAAF a tour varied according to what period of the war they happened to arrive in England. In 1942-43 a tour in the 8th Air Force stood at 25; later the magic number would rise to 30 and finally, 35, because higher command insisted that missions had 'become easier'. The months of 1943 when a long-range fighter such as the P-51 Mustang was not yet available to escort the bombers all the way to their targets and back again, is generally considered to be the worst period for American bomber crew survival in WWII.

One of the men who beat the odds was New Yorker Larry Goldstein, who flew a tour of 25 missions as a radio operator on B-17s in the 563rd Bomb Squadron, 388th Bomb Group at Knettishall.

'I was born in Brooklyn, 10 February 1922, the fourth child of Lena and Maurice. My sister Marion was the eldest, with my brothers Irving and Bernard following. My father was a hard working successful businessman. His occupation was a plumber and later a builder, and for a man with limited education, he was extremely successful. We had a beautiful home managed by a warm loving Jewish mother who we respected and revered. My father was not a strict disciplinarian but we respected his opinions and his personal observance of our Jewish traditions. When it was time to go to temple in the holidays we were there to accompany him.

'Dad's business was operated from the backyard of our house. The property was rather large with room for a house, an office and a four-car garage, workshop and storage area. Marion worked for my Father and so did my brother Irving. Marion ran the office and Irving worked as a mechanic. I can recall many men working for my Dad and a great deal of activity every day. Mar-Bern Plumbing and Heating Corporation was the name of the company and I was proud as a child of the small empire that my Father had created.

'I graduated from Erasmus Hall High School in 1940. I was not a great student, studies got in my way, sports were important to me. I was devastated when I did not make the High School football team. I was a fierce competitor and hated to lose. I thought I was a great player and was known on the sandlots of Brooklyn as "Snake Hips" because of the way I was able to run on the football field.

'Sometime in the early 1930s, just after the financial disaster of Wall Street, our family life style began to change. As the youngest member of the family I did not notice these changes which were subtle at first. The little things that I took for granted were not there any longer. The situation got worse and I really could not understand why things could not continue as before. I was destroyed, but being the tough guy that I was, I managed to survive.

'When I was in my early teens I had a talent for drawing and was rather good at copying any picture that I saw but I could not draw anything on my own. I thought of attending art school but other things got in the way and nothing ever developed of this interest of mine. My first job after high school was as an apprentice in a commercial stationery store in New York. Naturally this was to be my future, a tycoon in the stationary business. This dream ended when I became an apprentice draftsman for a city agency. This was it, my true love, a career that I would enjoy, and as a matter of fact from this experience I applied for and was accepted by the US Coast and Geodetic Service, a government agency. I was to be trained as a typographical draftsman and worked on mapping areas of Africa that would become famous in WWII. It was an interesting job and I enjoyed every minute of it.

'Things were soon to change for every American. Pearl Harbor was an event that angered everyone. From a peace-loving nation we became a nation of enraged patriotic citizens. Everyone was for America and the young men all asked the same question, "Where do I enlist"? While waiting for my draft number to be drawn I too was caught up in this patriotic fervour that swept our country. I went to the Marine recruiting office and was told by the Sergeant in charge to go home and

Larry Goldstein

wait for my number to be called, and this after I had passed the physical. He was right and within two weeks my draft number was called and I waited for my actual reporting day.

'Just before entering the Army I met Rose Mandel, my first real serious romance and the girl that I wanted to be waiting for me when my service was over. We had about six months of dating before I entered the Air Corps.

'My military service began 16 October 1942 and little did I know that I would volunteer in the near future for flying duty. I was classified by the Air Corps as a potential radio operator and was sent to Chicago to attend a school. The army had taken over several of the large hotels as barracks and schools. Chicago in the winter was a cold place to be, especially when we arrived from Miami in November in our summer uniforms. From November, when I arrived, to March when I left

Chicago, after graduating as a radio operator, I suffered through a very cold winter with a great deal of snow, ice and very cold winds. We all found out why this city was called the 'windy city'.

'The course finished in March and within a week I was reassigned. I was sent to Boca Raton Florida to a special radar school, promoted to Corporal and after arriving there several of my buddies and I decided that this was not the army job we wanted, thinking that we might be sent to some island in the Pacific. Each Friday we had to take a written test and if you failed you were immediately shipped out to another base. I found myself in Salt Lake City at a replacement depot. It was here that I volunteered for flying status. Along with my GI friends I was impressed with the glamour of flying and all that went with it: the silver wings of a gunner, the promotions and the flight pay. I was hustled off to aerial gunnery school before I had a chance to rethink my decision. I was not aware that at that time the Army Air Corps was in the process of building the largest combat air force in the world and had plans to take the aerial war to the enemy over his territory. I attended gunnery school at Wendover, Utah, not at the regular air base but way up in the hills. If ever a place could be classified as a sample of hell this was the place. The months of June and July, the height of the summer with temperatures ranging near one hundred degrees, was unbearable.

Wendover is so remote that some months later, crews that were to train for the atomic bomb group were sent here. This was a top-secret mission and it was felt that there would be no contact with the outside world. How right they were. The GI comment about this base was that a man going AWOL for five days would only be charged for three because he could be seen walking on the salt flats of Utah for the first two days. It was so hot that every day I had to cool off with a shower whenever possible, usually several times a day and this was not easy because we had to rely on water trucked in from the air base on a twenty four hour basis. Despite these hardships I survived and graduated and was awarded my crewmember wings along with a promotion to Sergeant. This was a proud moment in my life because I knew that I was about to participate in the making of history. Perhaps my GI pals and I were unrealistic to what was ahead of us. Flying as a crewmember seemed to be a glamorous thing to be a part of.

'I was sent to Moses Lake, Washington where I was assigned to a crew as a radio operator. These were the men I would be going to war with and we would train as a unit. Our pilot, Belford J. Kiersted, was a strong quiet man from Uniontown, Pennsylvania, a tough coal town. "BJ" had a dark, brooding look about him. He and his sister Dorothy had toured the country before the war as

L to r: Sgt Jack Kings, Sgt Robert Miller, S/Sgt Larry Goldstein

the ballroom dance team of "Jan and Janis" (Belford and Dorothy apparently lacked pizzazz). At our first meeting BJ asked us to work hard, become proficient at our jobs and possibly some day one of us might be responsible for the rest of the crew's survival. He along with our co-pilot "Ace" Conklin prodded us to achieve perfection and at the same time were also working hard to sharpen their own skills. Cliff Conklin was a Jock from New Paltz, New York. When Conklin was assigned to Keirsted's crew he was crestfallen. He thought, "I don't want to be with this crew – we've got a ballroom dancer for a pilot!" but Keirsted proved he was on the ball and more than just a set of twinkletoes. Quiet, reserved, he exuded a calm authority that was universally respected and admired. More than that the men liked Keirsted. "He was just a nice guy, period," Conklin would say. "He never had a bad thing to say."

'All of this training was to pay off later on when we flew in combat. Our crew gelled immediately, and we worked well together. With any group of men there were individual personalities to deal with, but when we were flying our sole aim was to help the crew survive, nothing else mattered. Personally I had a great deal of faith in the abilities of BJ and Ace as pilots and I felt safe with them at the controls and they seemed to be aware of potential trouble that was always around us, and prepared to handle an emergency if it happened. This was a comforting thought when flying because there always was the element of danger present. Kent Keith was the bombardier, a sheep rancher from near Ekalaka, Montana.; Phil Brejensky, navigator, also Jewish and from Brooklyn too. In training Kent Keith had given him the nickname "Bloodhound", joking that there was a dog on his Montana ranch that could find his way home better than Brejensky. Jack Kings, waist gunner, from Huntington, West Virginia had never met anyone Jewish before. As a kid he fished for food. It was something to eat besides rice and beans. In the depths of the Great Depression his family was too poor to afford new shoes so they stuffed cardboard soles in the old ones. "We kind of came up the hard way" he recalled. Later, in combat his attitude was, "If you got hit, you were hit. If you didn't, you made it. I could never see any point worrying about it." E. V. "Pete" Lewelling the other waist gunner was a good ol' boy from Zolfo Springs, Florida. The tail gunner was Bob Miller, a lunk from Chicago, Illinois, and a loner. Howie Palmer, engineer, was from New Hampshire and Eddie Kozacek, an immigrant's son and farm boy from Coxsackie, New York, a gunner, was added as a replacement.

'As a crew we trained hard, flying the famous B-17 bomber and when we weren't flying we attended ground school classes. Our training was intensive, seven days a week, night and day. Within the three months we trained each of us realized how important our individual effort was for the survival of the crew. After a period of training reality struck – we were ordered to a staging area for overseas assignment. We were still very impressed with our importance as combat crewmembers, a very enviable position to most other GIs.

'In September 1943 we were on our way overseas and sailed on the *Queen Mary* from New York along with 15,000 other Army Air Corps personnel. Needless to say, this was a very crowded ship but after five days we arrived safely and disembarked in Scotland. With twenty-nine other crews we were assigned to a replacement pool and after five days we were rushed to the 388th Bomb Group at Knettishall as replacement crews for those lost. When we entered our barracks on a cold dreary night all we saw were empty beds. We were told that these were the beds of men who had been shot down a few days before. A very sobering thought for us as a group. Suddenly flying status was not that appealing. Someone said out loud, "And we volunteered for this?"'

'After a period of orientation, we flew our first combat mission. The training was behind us; this was the real thing. We were not certain what was ahead of us,

B. J. Kiersted's crew. Larry Goldstein 2nd from right, kneeling

because in training we were never awakened at 3:30 am, never had to shave in cold water, or had to eat breakfast on a nervous stomach. This was fun, I think. We flew under extreme conditions, the excessive cold, the use of oxygen for six hour periods, the scene of fellow airmen being shot down and lastly the ever present enemy anti-aircraft fire and fighters waiting to knock us out of the sky. It was not until we returned to our home base and we began discussing the days events that I realized how scared I was, but then again so was everyone else and not embarrassed to say so. This was only our first mission of a scheduled twenty-five combat tour before we could even consider a return to the States. Each flight became more dangerous as the air war was stepped up. Air Force history has recorded this period as the heaviest of WWII and the most important air raids on Germany were flown. If a crew survived eight to ten missions at this time they were considered lucky. We were able to complete the twenty-five: I guess someone up there was looking out for the "Worry Wart" crew. Every time that I entered the plane for a mission I never thought that our crew would not return that afternoon. Every flight was an adventure; so many things could go wrong. We had our share, but fortunately none were bad enough to cause any harm to any of the crew. Except on one occasion. We made a forced landing with one engine on fire, with a full gas and bomb load but we were able to evacuate the aircraft safely – with one exception, Howie Palmer was injured rather severely when he stumbled into a part of the propeller just after it came to a halt. He never did fly with us again as he was hospitalised for many months.

Perhaps our darkest day was Thursday 30 December 1943 (we were assigned Ludwigshafen and the I G Farben Industrie plant) because on that day we lost a crew from our barracks, a crew that we had trained with and had become very close friends with. Men living together as closely as we did made us feel almost like family. To lose a friend and to actually see it happen was devastating to us all. I had been with Technical Sergeant D. Letter since Gunnery School at Wendover, Utah, and all through phase training and into combat. [Letter was the radio operator in 2/Lieutenant A. W. Carlson's crew on *Satan's Sister*, which was involved in a collision with *Joho's Jokers* on the bomb run when the 388th formation ran into severe prop wash from the group ahead]. As I looked up and out of my radio hatch I saw Letter's plane in the high group swing back and forth several times. Suddenly, it flipped over and broke in half right in the middle of the radio room. Our morale was at its lowest point, especially when we returned to our barracks and saw their empty beds. We did not know whether they had survived the parachute jump, or had been killed.[1]

'We did not have time to mourn their loss because we were called out for another mission the very next day and as was the case, our own survival was on our minds. It was about this time that I realized that this was a dangerous game I was a part of. Was the glory of being a combat crewman worth it? I never knew if I was a brave man, I had never been tested. Our crew never once discussed the possibility of our chances for survival, but I am sure that we all thought the same thing. When we first began flying together our goal was to not take chances and to put our faith in our pilots. 'BJ' kept repeating that we will make it, and on one occasion when we met our first ground crew chief when our own plane was assigned to us, 'BJ' asked him how many crews he had. He said, "You are my third, the other two went down". 'BJ's' answer to him was, "We will make it, you can mark it down". We were not as sure as he was, but his self-confidence rubbed off on us. When I saw another plane get hit and go down, I watched for the parachutes to open. I immediately felt

[1] Letter, Carlson, and four others on *Satan's Sister* were killed.

sorry for them but just as quickly I found myself saying, better them than us. Self-survival can play mean tricks with the mind.

'Our 25 missions were not simple, each one seemed worse that the last, but when we were briefed on 4 March 1944 for our twenty-fifth and last we had hoped for an easy run and then home to the good old USA but that was not to be the case. The target this day was to the first daylight raid on Berlin. It was the worst possible news that the "Worry Wart" crew could hear. We went though our pre-flight ritual as we always did, but this one had a special meaning. All went routinely until we were well into the flight, when suddenly the entire force was recalled, the best possible news that I could hear over my radio. The fact that we were going home was sweet music to our crew when I told them of the recall, but someone said, "Can we take our bombs home on our last mission?" We all said no so we dropped back out of formation away from the protection of our fellow bomb group, probably the dumbest thing that we could do because any enemy fighter pilot that saw a lone bomber immediately saw this as a kill and that is exactly what happened. We unloaded our bombs on a railroad yard and began our climb back to the formation, which now was miles ahead of us when suddenly there was a loud explosion and we immediately dived for the cloud cover below us. This quick action by our pilots probably saved our plane and us from destruction. When we checked in by position, no one was hurt and we saw no battle damage. Every time we left the cloud cover there was more enemy fire at us, but we managed to escape. When BJ asked me for a radio position report from the RAF rescue station I was not sure I could handle it, but even through German jamming of the message I was able to receive the position report, passed it on to our navigator and he plotted a course for England. When we came out of the clouds over the English Channel and saw the White Cliffs of Dover it was the most beautiful sight that I could ever hope to see. At this moment I did not realize the importance of my radio work, I had been too scared, but my training had paid off.

'Our landing at the base was not routine. We had no brakes and as we hit the runway we kept rolling until we left the end of the apron and came to an abrupt stop in a farmer's ploughed field. When the emergency vehicles reached us they wanted to know how bad the radio operator was hurt, but as I was standing there in one piece someone wondered why that question was asked. When the damage to the plane was pointed out to us we realized how lucky we were to be home safely. A large hole in the radio room was pointed out to me and it was then that I knew I was fortunate not to be injured. The hole was where my head might have been but somehow I had ducked and lucky for me that I did. The next morning we all went out to the plane to look it over more closely, and when we saw the many holes and damage to the outer skin it was then that we all said our thanks in our own way. A few days later BJ came into our quarters and ordered us all to accompany him to the base chapel and there we really became one crew that was thankful for completing our missions without a major injury.

'When a crew finished their combat tour they were rewarded with a trip back to the States. We were told about all the nice things that would happen to us when we reached the USA. Most of my crewmates left almost immediately, but I was chosen along with seven other men to train new crews that would be arriving in England. I was told that the assignment would be for three months, but I had a choice, accept a direct commission to 2nd Lieutenant and have to stay overseas for the duration of the war, or sweat out the three months. I chose the three months because I initially planned to ask Rose to marry me when I returned home. As things turned out, my decision was a wise one, as I remained just two months. When our students flew their first combat mission, I was released and left the base within hours of my notification. En route to my base to be shipped home I had to pass through London and who could miss a week of leisure in the international capital of the world. I was there for a few days when I met several US Army infantrymen. It was unusual to see anything but Air Force people in town, and when I inquired why they were there I heard something that immediately made me think that the invasion of Europe was about to occur. I decided to exit London before things changed and I was on the first train outbound to a small base near Liverpool. Most men in the Eighth Air Force were certain that if they were still in England at the time it was on, their trip home would not come until the end of the war. We all believed that if the invasion happened, we would be forced to fly additional missions. This was definitely a good time to leave London and to proceed to the next base where I would be processed for the trip to the USA. When I arrived, I was told that I would be there for about two weeks but after I was there for just a few days an announcement was made that Allied troops had landed on the beaches of Normandy, France. This was 6 June 1944 and within minutes a rumour began to spread throughout the camp that all airmen would be returned to fly more combat missions. There was a collective sigh of relief when we were notified before the day ended that we would all return to the States as scheduled. We were not aware of the heavy losses that our fellow combat crews were undergoing. We were needed in the US as instructors for new crews in training. Finally on 9 June I was on a large ship that left Liverpool for home. Not until the ship was two days out did I have the true feeling that I was really on the way home. It was a great day for me, I had finished my combat flying, and I was on the way home to be married.

'Sailing into New York Harbor past the Statue of Liberty was a thrilling event. I had seen this scene many times before but on that day in June it was the most beautiful sight that one can imagine. I was part of a group of GIs that were given the royal treatment. At this point, very few soldiers were returning from overseas, most were on their way over. We were treated as returning heroes. There was steak and fresh vegetables and fruit. We were extended all the help we needed including the promise of a long leave and the opportunity to bring a new wife to the next army facility, which in my case would be Atlantic City in mid-summer. After we were fed and babied, we were granted twenty one day furloughs and told that if we could bring our new wives with us for a honeymoon at Uncle Sam's expense.

'I was ordered to Atlantic City for rest and recuperation, but first I wanted to stop in New York to talk about marriage, but when I returned to my home, my parents were away for the weekend so I had to wait several days to see them. Rose and I were young and in love and wanted to be married as soon as possible. I had to return to the army base for a few days to be processed as the army called it. Then finally I was on my furlough and there was so much to do. For my first few days home I was welcomed and kissed by so many relatives that I was almost worn out. It was a terrific feeling to be with my family and Rose and right then everything seemed to be going well. I picked the most opportune moment to talk to my father about getting married.

'At first he took the fatherly stance, the war was going on forever, I had no prospect for a career and all the other arguments against marriage. In the end he relented and after a discussion with my mother they both gave their consent for our marriage. They both embraced Rose and her parents did the same for me. We began to make wedding plans, but when we visited the first Rabbi we were told on a Monday that if we were not married by the following Sunday we could not have a Jewish wedding for forty days because of a religious holiday. However we made all the arrangements for the wedding, though at first the Rabbi said the hall was not available for the day we selected, but my Father brought a little pressure to bear. Coincidentally the synagogue needed some plumbing work; of course, Morris Goldstein the plumber came through.

'The summer heat and humidity in New York for July 4th 1944, our wedding day, was abominable. With no air conditioning it was almost unbearable. At the photo session under the hot lights, with the heat and the excitement, I passed out. My father revived me and the wedding went on. Rose's family wondered whether she was marrying a sick man. We were off to Atlantic City for our honeymoon at the expense of the Army Air Corps. This was supposed to be rest and recuperation for the returning war vets and they treated us royally for twenty-one days. Most of my fellow airmen at their physical examinations were classified as having battle fatigue and were sent to another rest area for additional recuperation, but when I was examined I was classified and marked for active duty. I was shipped out to Galveston, Texas to attend instructors' school and also to do a great deal of flying. Rose and I lived in town, but the accommodations and the heat and humidity were too much for her and I had to send her home to New York temporarily. When I completed the course I was assigned to a base in New Mexico only a few miles from Galveston but I was allowed to go home to New York for a short leave and then Rose and I left for my assignment in Clovis, New Mexico. The town of Clovis was the typical army base town, small with very little to do. Rose and I lived off base and were able to spend much time together even though I flew a great deal. I was a radio instructor on B-29 bombers and when I first saw this airplane I was overwhelmed by its size and wondered if it could even get off the ground. After I had several flights I realized the capabilities of this plane. It was comfortable and

Larry and Rose, California 2003

was the first military airplane to be pressurized. Rose and I lived a pleasant life with other married GI couples and we made the best of the situation.

'For the next year I flew regularly and logged about five hundred hours. When "VJ Day" was declared I grounded myself and worked a desk job primarily because Rose became pregnant and it was just a matter of time until I was discharged. Exactly three years after my entering the service my discharge came through and it was then that I realized how lucky I was to have survived the war without injury.'

Larry Goldstein later found the California Chapter of the Eighth Air Force Historical Society in a decaying state. He began, with the help of a newfound friend, to revive the history of the Eighth Air Force in California. He says his last claim to fame is that his fellow veterans elected him President of the Society. He says he is honoured by this recognition and will work hard to make certain that the efforts of his fellow airmen in World War II are recognized and remembered forever.

11

THE MAN FROM LARAMIE

James Maitland Stewart

In July 1944 James Maitland Stewart, better known as Jimmy, was coming to the end of a very distinguished Liberator flying career. Everywhere the Hollywood actor went he was recognized. On duty, in the air and on the ground, he was treated like any other officer – almost. Born of Scottish-Irish parents on 20 May 1908 in Indiana, Pennsylvania, where his father was a hardware merchant, Stewart studied architecture at Princeton University, New Jersey, where he acted while a student. After summer stock in Falmouth, Massachusetts he made his professional debut in *Goodbye Again* and went with it to Broadway. By 1940, when he appeared on Broadway again, in *Harvey*, he had appeared in over twenty movies and had won an Oscar for best actor for his role in *The Philadelphia Story*.

Then in 1941, to everyone's amazement, he gave up his $16,000 (£3,250) a month salary in the movie industry and at 32 years of age, tried to enlist in the Army Air Corps. Stewart owned his own aircraft, had logged over 200 hours of civilian flying and possessed a commercial pilot's licence. However the gangling 6ft 4in actor weighed only 147lb, 10 lb too light, and he was rejected. In less than a month he had reached the prescribed weight but before he could enlist, his draft number came up.

'First lottery I ever won,' he drawled.

Stewart reported to Moffett Field, California on 21 March 1941 where he completed his basic training. Publicity-conscious officers tried to make sure Stewart remained a public relations figure for the Army Air Corps while he did little or no flying. Stewart shunned the publicity and logged another 100 hours' flying at his own expense during weekend passes. All he wanted was to fly, preferably in combat. However it was not until January 1942 that he received his commission as a Second Lieutenant and 'wings'. On 7 July 1942 he was promoted to 1st Lieutenant. He flew Curtiss AT-9 Jeep advanced trainers at Mather Field. It was thought that his constant desire for combat was too much in the Hollywood tradition and for six months he was restricted to checking out bombardiers at the Bombardier Training School, Kirkland Field, Albuquerque, New Mexico. Stewart took a heavy bomber course at Hobbs Field, New Mexico, where he came out as first pilot, or aircraft commander, before being sent to Gowen Field, Idaho for nine months as a B-17 instructor. He became Operations Officer and checked out four-engine bomber pilots in emergency procedures at 2nd Air Force Headquarters at Salt Lake City.

Finally, in the summer of 1943, after countless requests for a transfer, Stewart was posted to the 445th Bomb Group, equipped with B-24 Liberators, at Sioux City, Iowa, as Operations Officer of the 703rd Bomb Squadron. After only nineteen days, on 9 July 1943, he was promoted to captain and given command of the squadron on merit. In November 1943 the 445th left for Tibenham, Norfolk, on the Southern Ferry Route to become part of the 8th Air Force and Stewart went with them. The 8th Air Force already boasted one Hollywood movie star, Clark Gable, who had served on B-17s but had flown only five missions – to get the Air medal (B-24 men said) before rotating home to the USA. James Stewart not only stayed longer – to the end of the war – but also flew 20 combat missions in B-24s, including fourteen wing leads and one division lead.

Stewart's first mission was on 13 December 1943,

Clark Gable during a visit to Bodney, Norfolk 1943

L to r: 2nd Lt James N. Kidder, navigator; 1st Lt Charles S. Wolf, co-pilot; 2nd Lt Rowland Swearngin, armaments officer; 2nd Lt Donald Daniel, bombardier; front row, James Stewart, co-pilot; 1st Lt Lloyd, pilot

when he led the high squadron to bomb the naval docks at Kiel. At Bremen three days later and on a mission to Calais on the coast of France on Christmas Eve, Stewart showed his mettle, demonstrating a high degree of training and leadership ability.

On 7 January 1944 420 B-17s and B-24s caused considerable damage to the *I G Farben Industrie* chemical and substitute war material plants at Ludwigshafen and the engineering and transport industries in the twin city of Mannheim. Stewart led 48 B-24s of the 445th to Ludwigshafen. As the bomb doors opened, a shell burst directly under his wing, but Stewart managed to regain control and complete the bomb-run. After the target he joined the wayward 389th Bomb Group, which had strayed off course and although eight 389th B-24s were lost, his action probably prevented that group from total annihilation. George Makin, bombardier in the deputy lead ship in the 389th Bomb Group flown by Norbert Gebhard, recalls:

'Stewart, a great individual who we all admired for his theatre performances, saved my life and the lives of many other men in the 389th Bombardment Group. I am referring to his skill, airmanship and discipline.'

The details of what happened on that January day can best be described by quoting a December 1945 *Saturday Evening Post* article and noting passages from the official Air Force Records, which state that '...slight enemy fighter action was met from the IP to the target. Those attacks were successfully repulsed. Not so, however on their return, as there were determined attacks of the FW 190s and the Me 109s south of Paris. The 389th led the 2nd Combat wing – Major Caldwell was the air commander. The wing formation, after the rally point, found the leader increasing air speed and taking up a course south of that as briefed. At first the other aircraft thought the leader was making a dogleg to fall in behind the B-17s. But when it became evident that this departure from course was being adhered to, attempts were made to call the leader. The excessive air speed caused groups to string out. At 1308 hours the 389th found itself alone and unescorted south of Paris. About 35 FW 190s and Me l09s made vicious attacks. In the running battle, the leader, Captain Wilhite with Major Caldwell, was shot down.

'When the leader was shot from the sky, it was Jimmy Stewart who moved his entire group over the top of the new leader, Norbert Gebhard. It was this move that saved the 389th from annihilation because planes were spread out all over the sky and the aggressive yellow nosed fighters would surely have made their kill. I became a believer in the leadership abilities of Jimmy. He placed his aircraft over the new leader and the remaining planes of the 389th got back into tight formation for the trip back to England.

'When it was noted that the lead aircraft was off course, two alternatives were open to Stewart, both of them bad. He saw another formation leaving Ludwigshafen on course and knew he could easily switch over and tack on behind it, thus ensuring the safety of his own group. But this would have meant abandoning to its lonely fate the group that was blundering away from the main procession – an easy prey for fighters which were sure to single it out on the way home. And yet, if he continued, for the sake of wing integrity, to follow a leader who was heading for disaster, he must accept the certainty of sharing concentrated fighter attacks and extensive flak damage. With a hollow feeling in his stomach, Jimmy told the new leader of the 389th that he was sticking with them, He closed the 445th Group in for support and the new leader changed course, came home safely with no more loss of aircraft or lives.

'Colonel Milton Arnold wrote a letter of commendation to the 445th Bomb Group and James Stewart in particular. One statement from the letter commends the group on the splendid display of superb air discipline. It further states that "the good judgement of Major Stewart, your Group leader, in maintaining an excellent group formation, yet making every attempt to hold his position in the Combat Wing formation, is to be commended."

'...to me, this was Jimmy Stewart's Finest Performance.'

On 20 January 1944 Stewart was promoted to major, a rank he had previously refused to accept until, as he said, 'My junior officers get promoted from lieutenants' and he took command of the 703rd Bomb Squadron. Next day he led the 445th Bomb Group to Bonnier, France and the 2nd Combat Wing to Frankfurt on the 29th. While at Tibenham a troubled Stewart wrote:

'Our group had suffered heavy casualties during the day. As the big ships settled in for landings, wings and fuselages bore ragged holes from fighter attack and anti-aircraft fire. Bright red flares soared from planes carrying wounded, and ambulances raced to meet them.

'Men on the ground anxiously counted our squadron's incoming planes...nine... ...ten...eleven...then only an empty, grey sky. Where was the twelfth? Worried eyes swept the misty horizon, straining for some tiny dot, as hearts hoped against hope. But crewmembers in the returning planes knew that the missing ship would never land here again; German fighters had shot it down in flames.

'Tomorrow at dawn I would lead the squadron out again. Our target lay deep in enemy territory. Friendly fighters could accompany us only part of the way because of the distance involved. For much of the long flight we would be on our own – slow moving targets for the German fighters, the barrel-chested FW 190s, the sleek Me 109s.

'Imagination can be a soldier's worst enemy. My forehead was perspired as I visualized what would happen: my Liberator shuddering and lurching as we ploughed through curtains of *flak* – the sky filled with the ugly brown-black shell bursts – German fighters boring in from every direction.

'I slumped down at my desk but caught myself quickly. Fear is an insidious and deadly thing. It can warp judgement, freeze reflexes, breed mistakes. Worse, it's contagious. I knew that my own fear, if not checked, could infect my crewmembers. And I could feel it growing within me.

'I turned off the desk lamp and walked to the window. I pulled back the blackout curtains and stared into the misty English night, my thoughts racing ahead to morning – all the things I had to do, all the plans I must remember for any emergency.

'I thought of my grandfather, who had fought in the Civil war, and my father, who had served in both the Spanish-American War and the First World War. "Were you afraid?" I'd asked as a youngster back in Indiana, Pennsylvania, when we talked about Dad's experiences in France.

'I could remember the faraway look in his eyes as he nodded. "Every man is, son," he said softly. "Every man is." But then he would always add something else. "Just remember that you can't handle fear all by yourself son. Give it to God; he'll carry it for you."

'I had no illusions about the mission that was coming up. I knew very well what might happen. And I knew that fear would ride with it – and almost welcome it. Because, in its proper place, it would be an asset – sharpening perceptions, amplifying skills, and heightening the capacity for quick decisions.'

Stewart was to say many times after the war that he put his good fortune down to the fact that he always recited the 91st Psalm when over the target. It seems that his father had slipped a copy of the Psalm into his son's tunic pocket along with a note telling him how proud he was of him. The 91st Psalm reads:

> *He who dwells in the secret*
> *Place of the Most high*
> *Shall abide under the shadow of the*
> *Almighty*
> *'I will say of the Lord, 'He*
> *is my refuge and my*
> *fortress;*
> *My God, in Him I will trust.'*

Stewart was famous everywhere he went. Mary Thompson, manageress at the Reindeer Club for officers in Cork Street, London, recalls,

'One day, while in the dining room with the American Red Cross director, I saw an officer sitting at a table whose face was very familiar. I asked my director and she said, "Oh, that's Jimmy Stewart, the film star."'

During the 'Big Week' series of missions in February 1944 Major Jimmy Stewart led 28 Liberators of the 445th in the leading 2nd Combat Wing to Brunswick on Sunday 20 February. On this raid visual bombing was impossible so Stewart assumed the lead position and in spite of aggressive fighter attacks and later heavy anti-aircraft fire, held the formation together and directed an accurate bombing run over the target. The 445th lost three Liberators to *flak*. Stewart's actions earned him the award of the Distinguished Flying Cross. On 22 March he led the wing again, this time to Berlin. This was his first trip to Big-B and, when asked by newsmen if it was any more unusual than his others, Stewart said,

'Unusual? We hit Berlin, didn't we?'

By now the Top Brass considered that Stewart had been flying too many missions and he was moved on 30 March to the 453rd Bomb Group at Old Buckenham, Norfolk as Operations Officer to replace Major Curtis H. Cofield who had been killed in action only three days before. However, over the next few weeks Stewart still took his turn as Air Commander of bombing missions. On 13 April he flew 2nd Combat Wing lead against German aircraft manufacturing installations near Munich. All but one of the 453rd Bomb Group Liberators returned to Old Buckenham. Sergeant Melvin Borne, a ground crewman in the 733rd Squadron, recalls an occasion when Jimmy Stewart led the wing in *Whiskey Jingles*.

'After the mission, when he taxied into the hardstand, I went up on the wing to check how much fuel showed on the sight gauges on the flight deck. I could only get the bottom of the dipstick wet and told Colonel Stewart, "Sir, you taxied in on fumes." Well, two days later Stewart led another mission. Refuelling that morning he put a man on each wing tip and we would jump up and down rocking the aircraft and squeezing in about 40 more gallons by rocking all the air pockets out of the fuel cells. Then, before each aircraft taxied on to the runway, we would hand the flight engineer a gas hose up over the back of the wing and he would top off all the mains again until the fuel ran out and over the wing. That night they made it home with about 50 gallons left.'

In two months the group led the 2nd Bomb Division in bombing accuracy. By now the wiry, highly-strung Stewart was 36 years of age, and his combat career was coming to an end. People in high places rightly considered Stewart too valuable to lose and the decision was taken that he would fly no more missions. This really infuriated him. However, he was still on flying status and therefore had to fly so many hours each month to qualify for flight pay. He elected to fly the 453rd assembly ship,

Combat crew, 453rd Bomb Group, Old Buckenham

16 March 1944, ambulance men 'sweat out' the return of 453rd B-24s from a mission

The bar in the Officer's Club, Old Buckenham

Stewart with (l to r) 2nd Lt Robert F. Sullivan, Capt. Ray L. Sears and 1st Lt Arthur Cromarty following a raid on Berlin

Red Cross Donut Wagon at Old Buckenham

Wham Bam during formation for the mission to Bordeaux. Assembly ships were multi-coloured B-24Ds stripped of all armament and used to format the bomb group setting off on a mission. Their task completed, they would return to base, usually after about an hour.

On the mission to Bordeaux, Stewart took off in *Wham Bam* and flew the normal 'racetrack' course around the group's homing beacon, Buncher Six, until the 453rd had formed up. The assembly ship stayed with the group because it identified the group. *Wham Bam* flew on ahead and higher to allow the lead ship to take over. Normally, the assembly ship would then break away and return to base, its task completed. However, on this particular mission, Stewart pulled out to the left about a quarter of a mile and stayed there!

Wham Bam flew all the way to the departure point, at Selsey Bill, and by now his crew was getting a little anxious. They thought,

'He'll call in a minute and ask for the course home.'

'Up came the French coast and the crew thought, "Surely he'll turn back now," but he did not. He flew in position all the way to Bordeaux and back again with a very excited crew, conscious of the fact that they were flying an unarmed and highly colourful aircraft in a very hostile part of France. The crew were sworn to secrecy, but Colonel Ramsey D. Potts, the Group Commander, probably wanted to know where the crew had been for the past six hours! Altogether, Jimmy Stewart had flown 20 combat missions as Command Pilot, including 14 wing leads and one division lead.

Sergeant Melvin Borne:

'I flew with James Stewart on many occasions when he flew *Whiskey Jingles*. The biggest thrill of my life was the day he let me fly *Whiskey Jingles* back from Scotland to Old Buck. We went there to get some whiskey.'

On 3 June Stewart was promoted to lieutenant colonel and on 1 July he moved to 20th Combat Wing Headquarters at Hethel as chief of staff to Brigadier General

Ted Timberlake. By July 1944, apart from being awarded the DFC for 'exceptional achievement in combat while leading an attack on aircraft factories at Brunswick' he had also earned an Oak-Leaf Cluster to the DFC and the Air Medal (February 1944) with one Oak-Leaf Cluster (March 1944. A second OLC would follow in March 1945).

Harry H. Darrah of the 389th Bomb Group:

'Everyone had nothing but praise for Stewart for here was a man with nothing to gain and everything to lose taking such risks over the best defended targets in Germany.'

Darrah was co-artist for *Delectable Doris*, a 389th Bomb Group Liberator. He used a picture of a girl from a Vargas calendar. 'I painted the name

Damaged B24 Liberator of 453 Bomb Group after bombing raid on French coast, 20 April 1944

on using the style from a Carnation Cream can. Doris was the girl friend of the pilot, Bill Graff. The very next morning after the girl was painted on along came Jimmy Stewart who flew the bird on a tough mission.'

Stewart also performed other duties in his new capacity, as Jackson W. Granholm, a 458th Bomb Group navigator at Horsham St. Faith recalls:

'On 4 March 1945, 2nd Air Division Liberators bombed Basle and Zürich, Switzerland, by mistake. I had the unpleasant honour to be the defence counsel for the pilot and navigator of a lead squadron crew who put a beautiful bomb pattern on the railroad yards in Basle. They thought they had bombed Freiburg, Germany, and were tried in a general court for culpable negligence in the performance of duty. Because the questions were those of navigation, I was named to the defence board. The court was held at our group base at Horsham St. Faith. President of the court was Colonel James Stewart. We achieved an acquittal after a week-long court, longest in the history of the 8th Air Force.'

Hank Wentland of the 564th Bomb Squadron remembers the mission to Zossen on 13 March 1945.

'During briefing, a large groan erupted when the map of our mission was uncovered and we saw a long red ribbon heading straight to Berlin! Our concerns were not assuaged when informed that we were not really going to Berlin but to a small town 5 miles south of 'Big B'. Wow, hope the Germans understand this! In closing we were told our Command Pilot for this mission would be Lieutenant Colonel Stewart, who was in the back of the room. We turned and saw him, a tall, lean figure, nonchalantly leaning against the doorjamb. Oh, we caught the wrath of every 88mm battery on the way in. And before we reached the Initial Point Stewart came on the radio and said,

OK f-f-fellas…let's pull it in real t-t-tight!

'Having heard the actor Jimmy Stewart stutter occasionally in pictures, I thought it was a cute affectation and now realized he had a real little verbal glitch. Anyhow, the German Officer Training groups in Zossen that were housed in tents didn't

enjoy their reveille call that morning which consisted of 250 lb bombs raining down and through their housing facilities.'

On 29 March 1945 Stewart was promoted to full colonel. He served at 2nd Wing Headquarters as Executive Officer, Chief of Staff and finally Wing Commander, until 14 June 1945.

After the 7 April 1945 mission John B. 'Buff' Maguire, a pilot in 566th Squadron, 389th Bomb Group, who was flying his eleventh mission, his third as a deputy lead pilot, recalls that:

'The target was an ammunition and dynamite dump and we carried twelve 500 lb GP bombs. This particular mission is still very vivid in my mind. I guess it is because of the importance of our leading the entire 2nd Air Division on the mission that day, and we still were able to completely destroy the target and I had a ringside seat for the action…Another thing which is very vivid in my memory is the talk or speech that Jimmy Stewart gave at our interrogation, telling us what a fine job we did of destroying the target when the lead plane and the deputy lead plane were both lost at the IP commencing the bomb run. At the time Jimmy Stewart was Deputy Wing Commander. His remarks were just as impressive as any movie I have seen him in.'

By the end of the war Stewart had completed 57 months active service duty, 22 of them having been spent in the ETO. On 29 January 1945 the French awarded him the *Croix de Guerre* with Palm. On 28 September 1945 he became a colonel in the Reserve. Returning to acting full time in Hollywood in 1947 he starred in *It's A Wonderful Life*. In 1949, he married Gloria Hatrick McClean. More than most he was extra-specially qualified for some movie roles and he appeared in *No Highway in the Sky* in 1951, *Strategic Air Command* in 1955, *The Spirit of St. Louis* in 1957, and The *Flight of the Phoenix* in 1965. He also appeared in the lead role in *The Glenn Miller Story* in 1953. He will perhaps best be remembered as the drawling, friendly-faced cowboy in westerns such as *Winchester 73*, *The Man from Laramie*, and *The Man Who Shot Liberty Valance*. For a star used to the highest accolades, he was given top billing in the Air Force Reserve on 23 July 1959 when he was promoted to Brigadier General. Truly a great finale for a fine actor, pilot and leader of men.

Stewart often starred on stage and in June 1975 while he was performing *Harvey* in London he took the opportunity to visit Norfolk and in particular, his old haunts at Tibenham and Old Buckenham. During a visit to Norwich in 1983 for the 2nd Air Division Reunion he attended the 30 May Memorial Day at Cambridge, as

Technical Sergeant Forrest S. Clark, a B-24 gunner in the 44th Bomb Group, recalls.

'We were on a bus riding through the English countryside headed for an American Cemetery near Cambridge. We had a special passenger that day on the bus, one whom I had seen many times before, but not in this environment. That passenger was Jimmy Stewart, who was sitting with his lovely wife up front. I was seated about ten rows back. I had seen Stewart years before in *Mr. Smith Goes to Washington* and others of his famous films, but I had only heard of his wartime experience. Here on this bus on a cold damp English day I got a real close-up of him. We talked briefly and he asked me what group I was in during the war. When I said the 44th Bomb Group he replied:

"Oh, you mean the Eightballs."

'He knew that much about my group and I admired him for remembering.

'As we got off the bus at Madingley Cemetery we walked toward the memorial flagpole area where a great many memorial wreaths and various 8th Air Force Groups including Stewart's group had placed tributes. What I recall most about Stewart was his tall, angular frame and his kindly face, but even more impressive was the manner in which he spoke. It appeared to be at that time a soft American voice shadowed by the most peaceful kind of intonations. He spoke like a kindly uncle would to everyone. He walked tall and straight with the particular gait and posture so familiar to moviegoers the world over. I remember how he stood with his head bared to the cool English breeze from the nearby fens. He stood before the memorial and spoke quietly yet eloquently about the sacrifices of the thousands of American men who lay at rest beneath the white crosses all about us. He spoke lovingly of past times and youth, when all of us were virile and passionate as he was in that time 50 years ago. He gave the memorial tribute that day. Later that night at a crowded reception in the Guildhall of that ancient medieval city of Norwich, Stewart could be picked out of the crowd, towering above all others amid the glitter of bedecked officials and veterans of the air war. Stewart told of one day when he and another command pilot decided to buzz the group commander's living quarters at their base. They tried to awaken the commander from his usual nap. Stewart still chuckled over that episode of youthful exuberance and joy. We all told our favourite war stories that day. I think Stewart proved once again how close he was and how close he remains to his comrades of WWII. It was like flying again in the same formation. All considered it to be an honour. Keep 'em Flying, Jimmy!'

James Stewart died in at his home in Beverly Hills on 2 July 1997. He was 89.

12

LADY JANE

Christmas Eve, 1944, B-24s taxi out at Horsham St Faith

Young Peter Bence perched in the roof of a bombed-out bank at the top of Earlham Road next door to the Grapes hotel in Norwich and trained his pair of broken German binoculars on the drizzling sky. Like a lot of the city's schoolboys, he often watched the coming and going of Consolidated B-24 Liberators of the 458th Bomb Group from nearby Horsham St. Faith. Friday afternoon, Thanksgiving Day, 24 November 1944 was no different.

Nine-year-old Michael Flood, one of a group of young lads playing in trees nearby, looked up as a Liberator flew low over the city, just above the rooftops.

Another who peered skywards was 16-year-old Les Huckle, who was walking up Grapes Hill on his way home after calling at Williments model shop in St. Benedicts, an old part of the city, which had been badly bombed by the *Luftwaffe*. He had almost reached the top when he heard the 'deafening roar' of Liberator engines.

The pilot, Ralph J. Dooley, was only three years older than Huckle. Dooley had left school in his home town of Philadelphia, Pennsylvania in 1942 and for nine months worked for a railroad company before joining the United States Army Air Force in February 1943. He was commissioned a 2nd Lieutenant in February 1944, about the same time that the 458th Bomb Group landed in Norfolk to take part in 8th Air Force missions against Germany. The 458th's debut came on 24 February, when they made a diversionary sweep over the North Sea for heavies attacking enemy targets. On 2 March, the Group flew its first bombing mission, with an attack on Frankfurt. Missions followed thick and fast and losses mounted. Twelve Liberators were lost during March, while in April nine more were destroyed.

In the States, meanwhile, in May 1944, the crew that would be led by Ralph J. Dooley came together for training at Biggs Air Force Base at El Paso, Texas. John Kowalczuk, who joined the crew as the bombardier, first flew with Dooley on 13 May 1944. He recalls,

'I was aware that Dooley and Arthur Akin [the co-pilot] knew each other before they showed up at Biggs. Dooley was a freckle-faced kid of 19. He was very pleasant with the crew in conversation and passed out compliments at the right moment. An intelligent young man, who knew how to handle an emergency, he enjoyed smiling with the fellows and those around him. I was the only married person and, at the age of 26, was the oldest on the crew.'

The Dooley crew at Lille, 24 September 1944. L to r: S/Sgt Oscar B. Nelson, waist gunner; Burton Wheeler, co-pilot; Paul Wadsworth, radio operator; 2nd Lt Paul E. Gorman, navigator; S/Sgt Don P. Quick; S/Sgt John J. Jones, engineer; top turret gunner, 2nd Lt Ralph J. Dooley

On 26 August, they were assigned to the 753rd Bomb Squadron, 458th Bomb Group in the 96th Bomb Wing, 2nd Bomb Division, at Horsham St. Faith. Dooley and his crew perfected their navigation on cross-country flights and made practice bomb runs on ranges using explosive white powder bombs. In September, the B-24s were modified to haul fuel to France for Patton's armour. On the 19th the 458th Bomb Group carried 38,016 gallons of fuel to France (they delivered 727,160 gallons in 13 days of 'Trucking' missions, as the flights were called). Akin flew five trucking missions while Dooley had to wait until 25 September, when he and six crewmembers carried fuel to Lille. With him went co-pilot Burton Wheeler, gunners John J. Jones, Don P. Quirk and Ralph Von Bergen, radio operator Paul A. Wadsworth, navigator Paul E. Gorman, and John Kowalzcuk.

The trucking mission was uneventful but the next one, the following day, was not. Kowalzcuk recalls:

Barracks at Horsham St Faith

Removing a wounded gunner, 25 August 1944

Lady Jane

Horsham St Faith

Thanksgiving, Horsham St Faith

'Operations did think of cancelling the trip, but we were game and took off late afternoon. We had to maintain an altitude of 3,000–4,000 ft to avoid radar detection. It was getting dark as we approached the coast of France. We got too close to Calais where the Germans still formed a pocket of resistance. They started firing machine guns and we could make out the tracers heading towards us. Dooley used evasive action and flew in an easterly direction towards friendly territory. Darkness began to creep upon us.

'Minutes later we could just see the runway of an airfield near what we thought was Brussels. As Dooley headed into the landing approach, it became dark. As he was descending, a few hooded strip lights came on, thus making it possible to land. The surface was rough with bomb craters on both sides and there was only a 3000-ft runway normally used for fighter aircraft, but we were down safely and damn glad to find out where we were (Evere, occupied by 83 Group).

'British forces were in control of the airfield and we created a lot of excitement with our arrival. Ours was the first B-24 loaded with gasoline to land on such a treacherous strip.'

The fuel load was eventually unloaded and, after a short stay in Brussels, they returned to Horsham St. Faith on 28 September. They were glad to be back.

On 2 October 1944 the 458th was stood down. Akin and his crew took part in a practice mission, flying the Group assembly ship *Spotted Ape*. For the mission Akin and his co-pilot, Al Chaney, swapped places. On takeoff the No. 1 engine caught fire, burning a hole in the retracted tyre. After one circuit of the field they landed. However, the tyre burst immediately on contact. Dean Ballou, the tail gunner, was injured in the crash, but not seriously.

On 7 September, Dooley and Akin flew their first combat missions when the 458th bombed the Rothensee oil refinery at Magdeburg. Burt Wheeler recalls:

'Dooley had to use near takeoff power while climbing to altitude over the North Sea. Realizing the fuel would not last to complete the mission, he aborted.'

Akin and his crew also aborted, after the navigator had oxygen problems. Dooley's next mission was on 9 October, when the Liberators headed for the marshalling yards at Koblenz. The 458th encountered some light *flak* but Dooley's crew came through unscathed. On 12 October, they took part in a mission to Osnabruck and on the 14th Dooley's and Akin's crews were part of a 33-ship formation for the mission to Cologne.

Dooley taxied 42-45133 'K' off dispersal No. 40 and Akin, opposite at No. 47, followed. When they arrived over the target, clouds covered it. The cold was

B-24 Liberators of the 458th Bomb Group, Dooley's aircraft (J) is in the middle

intense. *Flak* was accurate and Dooley's ship suffered minor damage. Akin was forced to abort when one of his gunners developed stomach pains.

On 26 October the 458th bombed the Mittelland Canal. Bombs were released from 19,2000 ft through thick cloud. A later reconnaissance showed an 85-ft breach in the canal.

On 9 November, in support of the US 5th Division near Metz a bombardier in the 753rd Squadron made an early release of the bomb load and other aircraft made their release at the same time. Bombs erupted among the US troops on the ground. One result of the debacle was that crews were denied a credit for the mission and the Distinguished Unit Citation awarded to the Group in September was revoked.

John Kowalczuk, Dooley's bombardier, had been a member of the 10th Infantry, 5th Division, before transferring to the Air Force. He recalls:

'I was taken off the crew at my own request. I wanted to perform as a real bombardier and not as a toggle switch operator. I did that on four or five missions with Dooley, who did not want to take up the lead position. He wanted to go home as soon as possible by flying off the wing tips. "Get 35 in and you're on your way," he would say.

'I made a strong remark to the head man by stating that either he let me fly as a lead bombardier or send me back to the infantry "to do a man's job."'[1]

On 21 November 1944 Dooley's crew, in *Table Stuff*, was among 28 Liberators which set out for an oil refinery at Harburg. They returned safely. Then the Group stood down for three days because of poor weather over the Continent. On Friday 24 November, the weather was still far from good. Local ceiling was about 500 ft with visibility 2½ miles with intermittent drizzle. Akin's crew was off duty and Alex Shanoski, Akin's flight engineer, decided to spend the day playing cards, catching up with letter writing and doing his laundry. Burt Wheeler, Dooley's co-pilot, was away visiting another base seeking information about the death of his brother, who had been killed on a mission over Germany on 7 October. So when a practice mission was called, the purpose of which was for pilots to gain more experience in instrument flying, Dooley, who had logged just ten hours on instruments, was short of a co-pilot. When Arthur Akin checked in at operations, he volunteered to take Wheeler's place in the co-pilot's seat next to Dooley in 42-45133 *Lady Jane*. As Shanoski recalls, "Akin didn't have to fly that day, he just loved to fly."

The B-24s took off, Dooley and Akin in the cockpit of *Lady Jane* with seven other men aboard. Paul Gorman settled into his navigator's position and gunners John Jones, Oscar B. Nelson, John A. Phillips, Ralph Von Bergen and Don P. Quirk took up their positions. There would be no guns carried, so the gunners were just along for the ride as was Paul A. Wadsworth, the radio operator. Policy dictated that all fuel tanks were filled on takeoff. Dooley and Akin taxied out and climbed into the heavy sky. When they returned and lined up on Runway 35 – the shortest but the one equipped for instrument landings – the weather had closed in and soon became a question of whether crews would get down safely.

Alex Shanoski was in the barracks when the practice mission came in.

'It was a real mess,' he remembers, 'the planes had all their lights on and were just overhead – missing the rooftops. They couldn't find the end of the runway. We could hear the planes and briefly see them as they disappeared into the low clouds.'

The field personnel were certainly sweating the bombers down. Liberators were flying at almost building level in a somewhat broken pattern. It was eerie for the ground crew to look up and see a black shape and landing lights so near the ground. They felt they could almost stand on the roof of one of the buildings and touch the planes as they went by. Without let-up, flares were fired into the sky to help the

---

[1] Kowalczuk became a lead bombardier and completed 18 missions, his last on 18 April 1945.

crews locate the runways. One-by-one, the bombers landed and soon there were only a few still flying in the muck.

Dooley made his approach to Runway 35. He slowed to just above stall speed, then decided to abort. Those on the ground could hear the deepened pitch of the props as he applied power and overshot the field. Dooley decided against climbing back into the cloud and making an instrument approach for the second landing – it would be visual. Dooley circled Norwich, remaining below the cloud in order to keep the field in sight and keep the landing procedure short.

Les Huckle had just reached the top of Grapes Hill when *Lady Jane* appeared overhead: 'I looked up and the huge shape of a Liberator appeared over the top of St. John's Catholic Church. The plane was so low it almost touched the tower and seemed as big as the church itself. I could see that one of the engines had stopped as its propeller was stationary.'

John Southgate was on his cycle and had stopped at the traffic lights at the top of Grapes Hill. 'I could clearly see the port inner engine was smoking and on fire' he recalls.

Both he and Les Huckle would go on to join the Norwich City Police Force and retire at the same time. However, during their careers, neither ever mentioned the aircraft to each other.

In the bombed-out bank on Earlham Road, Peter Bence continued to train his German binoculars on the Liberator.

'I noticed that it was unusually low, slightly to my left and trailing smoke. A few seconds later I could clearly see fire around a port engine and a crewmember leaning out of the port side waist window. He appeared to be looking at the fire or getting air. I seemed to be looking down into the aircraft.'

Police Constable John Fletcher had just come off duty and was walking home down Earlham Road. As he reached the junction with Heigham Grove, he heard the roar of engines too. He saw the plane disappear over the treetops, then re-appear, 'gaining altitude and banking over the City Station goods yard.' Norwich citizens, used to German bombing raids and the horrors of war, feared for their lives as the Liberator flew low over their rooftops. Twelve-year-old Shirley Crocker and her mother, standing talking in the hall of their house in Earlham Grove, had their conversation halted by 'the loudest noise overhead that we had ever experienced. So much so that we both put our hands over our ears and cowered in fright. We were quite convinced that the plane was going to take our roof off; it was so close.'

Mrs Ward was walking home after attending the clinic on Earlham Road and was passing St. Phillip's Church when, suddenly, *Lady Jane* struck the top of the tower. She recalls,

'Pieces fell all around me but I didn't get hit. There was only one other woman there and she went hysterical'.[1]

Gladys Woodhouse, a member of the Royal Observer Corps, in her house on Derby Street knew the B-24 was in trouble 'because of the noise it was making.'

'I was with my neighbour at the time so we both ran out into our back yard. It was then that we heard the crash as the plane hit the church. We stood and watched the Liberator fly almost on its side towards the City Station. We felt so helpless just watching as the crew struggled with the aircraft.'

Michael Flood and his pals playing in the trees had lost sight of the Liberator but, a short while later; they heard a 'bang.'

'We all thought the plane had come down in the cemetery so we went to have a look. Down Heigham Road, we noticed the wing tip against the church tower. Me being small, it seemed like the whole wing stood there.'

Hazel Dade was playing in her garden at 55 Clifton Street, with some younger friends when she heard the noise.

'I looked up and there it was just above rooftop height. We all threw ourselves to the ground as the bomber went over us. It had a piece of the tail hanging on about 10 ft of wire that hit our chimney and broke the pot. The plane then swerved around Harmer's shoe factory and appeared to turn over. After the crash we all ran over to the building site but were stopped going into Barker Street by the vicar, Reverend Lanchester.'

Vera Read, working on the third floor of the Harmer's factory, was facing the window and saw the aircraft plunge by.

'How the pilot missed the tall building, I don't know. I heard a muffled crash above the noise of the machinery. It all happened so quickly.'

Ray Fisher, standing outside Southgate's grocery store on the corner of Golding Street and Dereham Road, first saw the B-24 immediately after it hit the church.

'It was facing up Dereham Road towards Bowthorpe Road in a very high nose up attitude with about 12 ft of the right wing and most of the aileron missing. The engines were on full power but the aircraft was flying sideways across Dereham Road towards Heigham Street. The aircraft stalled, the right wing dropped and the plane rolled over onto its back. The total time between hitting the tower and the crash was no more than 20 seconds.'

---

[1] St. Phillips, built in the 1870s, was demolished in November 1977 despite moves by the Norwich Society and the Norwich Preservation Trust to save the structure.

Peter Bence, who had jumped down from his perch into the loft and scrambled out of the bank, ran down Grapes Hill into Barn Road. 'At the Heigham St junction I saw people running towards Old Palace Road. I could see lots of smoke and could hear the sound of ammunition exploding. As I ran along Heigham Street, a fire engine passed me. I reached the site of the crash and squeezed through the crowd. As I did so, I heard a police officer or air raid warden shouting to us to keep back. The last sight I had of the aircraft was an engine with the landing gear sticking out.'

One of the first on the scene was Ken Yaxley. He first saw the aircraft when he was cycling down Heigham Road.

'I had just turned in from Earlham Road when the aircraft came over the Black Horse pub. It was very low. I saw the plane hit the church – it seemed only a glancing blow. I raced along Heigham Road and Old Palace Road. As I turned into Barker Street I saw a US serviceman arguing with the yard's gatekeeper, who was not going to let him in the corporation yard. Well, the American hit the keeper and ran to see if there was anything he could do. The aircraft was a mass of flames.'

Thirteen-year-old Olive Hutson was shopping at Dashwood's shop in West End Street when it careened over the top 'making a horrible noise.' She feared for her two sets of aunts and uncles who lived in Barker Street.

'The police were stopping people going into the street,' she remembers, 'so I explained to them that my grandparents lived there. They let me go. It was a terrible sight, just a ball of fire. Lots of men ran into the yard to see if they could help, but they couldn't get near. It was a miracle how the plane missed the houses.'

Ernest Pratt was just leaving his butcher's shop on the corner of Railway Street. He remembers the heat from the fire overhead was frightening. Michael Yallop had just walked out of the sweet shop on the corner of Sayer Street and Heigham Street when a man, cycling past, jumped off his bike and threw himself up against a wall for protection, fracturing his arm in the process. Brian Coleman and Peter Yardy were working at Soman Wherry Press in Heigham Street. Their workshop was lit by a red glow and rocked by the explosion. Tom Bany, the manager, whose son was in the Royal Air Force, ran in and asked the two men to go and help. They ran out the back of the printing works, along the side of a dyke and into the City Station yard, along the rails and through the coal yard. They saw two or three of the crew lying in the centre of a large spillage of fuel that was burning fiercely. In a desperate bid to answer their screams for help, they crawled to within 40-50 ft but, because of the intense heat and many explosions, were unable to reach them.

About this time, the National Fire Service arrived. The crew was also unable to aid the airmen. Bill Batson, a member of the fire crew, recalled the sight as his most horrific of the war and remembers the three men. They had perished by the time the fire was brought under control. Four US ambulances and fire trucks, which raced from Horsham St. Faith, took a wrong turn, which placed them on the other side of the River Wensum, separating them from the crash.

Eleven-year-old Brian Clayton remembers that one of the group of boys he was playing with in an alleyway between Wingfield Road and Baker Road, jumped onto the running board of one of the trucks. Grabbing the wing mirror, he redirected the convoy around by Oak Street, City Station Bridge and down Heigham Street. Mr. Wortley, a member of the City's Civil Defence and Rescue Service, had responded with a rescue party from a depot at the Eagle Baths in Helford Street and arrived on the scene at 1706, but there was nothing they could do and at 1735 they returned to their depot.

News of the crash was broken to John Kowalczuk by Burt Wheeler that evening at St. Faith. The funeral took place at the US Cemetery at Madingley in Cambridge on Wednesday, 28 November. After the war most of the crew were returned to the USA for private family burials. Today, only Donald Quirk and Ralph Von Bergen lie in the Cambridge Military Cemetery. Akin's crew was assigned a replacement pilot, Lieutenant Robert Eidelsberg, and they completed their final mission on 30 March 1945. John Kowalczuk became a reservist after the war and was recalled to service in 1951 until October 1953 for the Korean War. He retired as a Lieutenant Colonel and is now living in Ohio. Burt Wheeler lives in Boston, Massachusetts.

Residents of the Heigham Street area provided a plaque in memory of the crew, which was unveiled on 6 November 1945 by the Lord Mayor of Norwich, Mr. E. F. Williamson, in the presence of Brigadier General E. C. Kiel. In 1972, the plaque was moved, because of redevelopment, to a wall on a block of flats in Freeman Square on the other side of the road. On 24 November 1994 more than 300

Major General Bill Kepner, US Eighth Air Force receiving the Freedom of the City of Norwich from the Lord Mayor, Mr E. F. Williamson

people gathered there in the sunshine to remember the nine young men. The Reverend Michael Jones, vicar of St. Barnabas, Heigham, conducted the service. Michael Quirk and his wife Cindy came from Indiana to honour Michael's brother, Don, the tail gunner. Michael was 13 when his brother was killed. Christine Armes, long-time resident in America and frequent visitor to her home city of Norwich, who traced relatives and helped Roy Durrant, City Councillor for Heigham Ward organize the service, read the names of the men who died. A reading by the Sheriff of Norwich, Bill Carpenter, from the book of John, had a line, which summed up the feeling of the occasion.

'Greater love hath no man than this, that a man lay down his life for his friends.'

Just how much control Dooley and Akin had over the aircraft will never be known, but there are people who maintain that their actions saved the lives of many.

Olive Ashford, née Hutson:

'The crew gave their lives but they saved lots of others. Their families can be really proud of them all.'

13

WE WISH YOU A MERRY CHRISTMAS

Christmas 1942 was the United States Army Air Force Fortress Groups' first in the ETO (European Theatre of Operations). In an attempt to integrate the English and American communities General Dwight D. Eisenhower instructed all units that, where possible, they should have Christmas dinner in English homes.

Charles H. Mills, 458th Bomb Group:

'I was on my first visit to Norwich, I was there with my buddy Fred Bumch when we were walking through the market and a man approached us and asked us if we would like to share Christmas dinner with a British family.'

Sergeant Robert 'Bob' S. Cox, a mechanic in the 466th Bomb Group at Attlebridge, Norfolk:

'There was a farm off the base and a real nice old lady worked on the farm. She didn't have any sugar and we couldn't hardly ever get any fresh eggs so we'd trade her sugar for eggs. One Christmas her 14/15 year old boy brought us a cake. She'd saved her sugar and made us a cake.'

The Americans reciprocated. Many an American airbase opened its doors to the British public. Major Newton L. McLaughlin, Special Services Officer, 448th Bomb Group at Seething:

'On Christmas Day, our base served dinner to the London children billeted in our neighbourhood and many of our men were guests in English homes.'

On Christmas Eve 1943, 8th Air Force bombers were dispatched to attack V-1 flying bomb sites in France, which went under the code name, *Noball*. To Joe Wroblewski it seemed like 'every plane in Britain was up' on 24 December. Some 670 bombers hit 23 V-1 sites without loss. VIII Bomber Command was stood down from Christmas Day until 30 December, when 658 heavies bombed oil plants at Ludwigshaven.

Russ D. Hayes, 389th Bomb Group, *Little Gramper* crew 'took a happy but sad photo of Christmas Day' in his barracks at Hethel.

'We were to win a bottle of Scotch for the best decorated barracks. The Christmas tree was cut from the countryside, as was the holly to decorate it. Art Marsh picked up some of the tinsel on a two-day pass to London. Marsh also had an idea for the collared balls to hang on the tree. He rounded up all the condoms he could, got some multicoloured paints from the line, and recruited a few windy boys to blow them up and paint. It worked for about two of every five. By the time

Celebrations at Hethel

we had enough to decorate the tree we all had rainbow coloured spots on our faces caused by blowouts from rough brush bristles. I wonder how they "stood up" under their primary uses. All but five men (my crew) in the picture were lost in the next two missions. A very lonely place with so many empty beds to stare at.'

There were no empty beds in the burgeoning POW camps in Germany where thousands of 8th and 15th Air Force crewmen were languishing behind barbed wire. On Christmas Eve at *Stalag Luft III*, Sagan, heavy bombing could be heard in the distance. It proved a better Christmas present than the POWs could have hoped for. Although the war would not be over by Christmas the men believed that the end could not be long in coming. It led to even greater enjoyment among the prisoners, who attended carol services, saw a Christmas play and enjoyed meals of banquet proportions. At *Stalag XVIIB* the Germans entered the festive spirit by playing some music over the camp Tannoy system. One tune, which had a significant meaning for the prisoners, was Bing Crosby singing *I'll Be Home For Christmas, If Only In A Dream*. It was a dream and soon the prisoners were trying to settle down to a long, cruel winter.

At *Stalag Luft III* on Christmas Day there was even bacon, sausage and toasted bread for breakfast and the Germans waited until 1100 to hold *appell* (roll call). At night, celebrations got into full swing. Many different nationalities used the occasion to climb the wire fences into adjoining compounds and it became so bad that gunfire was heard. Next morning counts and recounts tried to establish the imbalance between British and Polish personnel in the American compound. Many prisoners were marched away to the cooler while others rapidly consumed the last of the homemade alcohol before it was confiscated.

By the afternoon of New Year's Day, snow began to fall and added to the post holiday gloom. *Appell* was held indoors and the lighting and water supplies were cut off. Hopes of a quick end to the war were rapidly diminishing. The Germans remained in good spirits and some guards joined in with British, American, Russian and other nationalities in a huge snowball battle. Meanwhile, the real battles continued.

William Y. 'Bill' Ligon Jr. a B-17 gunner in the 385th Bomb group at Great Ashfield, wrote in his diary on Sunday 13th August:

'...had a chicken dinner when we got back today. Ice cream too...Things look better every day, don't they? I don't think it will last too much longer. In fact, a lot of fellas expect to be home for Christmas...'

Bill sadly never made it. He was KIA on 6 October 1944 when he and the crew of *Dozy Doats*, flown by Lieutenant Everett L. 'Ike' Isaacson, was one of eleven Fortresses in the group that was shot down on a costly raid.

On the fighting fronts, Germany still felt secure behind the Atlantic Wall while in the POW camps throughout the *Reich*, the other battle – for survival – went on. Richard Olsen, a 19-year-old radio operator in the 451st Bomb Group of the 15th Air Force in Italy, was shot down on 11 December 1944 on his tenth mission, to the marshalling yards at Vienna. He was sent by train to *Stalag Luft I*, Barth on Christmas Day 1944. Passing through Vienna, Olsen noticed that chaff dropped from their bombers was used as a substitute for tinsel on Christmas trees in the streets!

Lieutenant Lawrence Jenkins, a co-pilot in the 2nd Bomb Group, 15th Air Force, who had been hospitalised at *Stalag Luft I7B* Krems, Austria, since being shot down and severely injured in both legs on a mission to Vienna on 16 July, recalled his first Christmas behind the wire.

Father Gerald Beck, Catholic Group Chaplain at Hethel. The father would often drive his jeep from Liberator to Liberator to make sure any one who wanted to could receive communion before take-off

'When Christmas 1944 came we wanted to get some of the spirit so my cook traded some cigarettes for a couple of eggs. He tried to make a pudding, which he invented with a bit of chocolate and the eggs. It was good because it was the most food we had had for some time. Once he tried for some beans but it was hard to do, as farm labour could not come into the hospital very often. We cut whatever wood we could from beds, floors, tables and building to make hot water for brews. We had to watch out for wood in the black bread because slivers didn't go well. Our barley soup was so full of weeds that when you cleaned it out there wasn't much left. The potatoes were so watered and full of dirt we would leave them all day to dry out.'

Lieutenant Loren E. Jackson, pilot of *Crash Wagon III* in the 551st Squadron, 385th Bomb Group, and a POW at *Stalag Luft III* since he was shot down on 12 June 1944, recalls:

'One of my most poignant memories is of Christmas Eve 1944. The Germans permitted us to be out until 9 o'clock that night (normally we were locked up in our blocks at 6 pm). We were visiting back and forth, greeting our friends and wishing each other a Merry Christmas. We expressed our strong conviction (and ardent hope) that the Germans just could not hold out much longer. One memory in camp during the Yuletide season is the *Kriegie* parody on the song *I'll Be Home For Christmas*:

> *We won't be home for Christmas,*
> *Don't depend on us.*
> *We'll have snow*
> *But no mistletoe*
> *Or presents on the tree.*
> *Christmas Eve will find us*
> *Standing at appell,*
> *We won't be home for Christmas,*
> *We know that very well.*

'After we were finally locked up at about ten o'clock, we heard music coming from the centre of the compound. It was an American brass quartet with a trumpet, alto, baritone and a trombone. The group played Silent Night. I will never forget that moment and how the strains of that beautiful carol permeated the cold, black chill of that winter night in the heart of Germany.'

Germany was still not beaten when December 1944 brought the worst winter weather in England for 54 years. Water froze in the pipes and a thin film of ice coated runways at bases throughout eastern England. The temperature dropped to as low as –18⁰C but the worst feature of the weather was lack of visibility during missions. On 16 December Field Marshal Karl von Rundstedt and his *Panzer* columns punched a hole in the American lines in the forests of the Ardennes. The operation was similar to his advance into France in 1940 and opened up a salient or 'bulge' in the Allied front lines. The bombing force in England was grounded by fog, just as Hitler had hoped, and was unable to intervene. It was not until 23 December, when traces of fog still shrouded the bases, that many groups managed to take off and offer some hope to the hard-pressed infantry divisions in the Bulge.

The heavies were dispatched to communication targets in an effort to stem the tide of troops and materials entering the salient. The 1st Bomb Division's attack on the marshalling yards at Ehrang, Germany, earned a commendation from Brigadier General Howard M. Turner.

'I wish to extend to you and all officers and men of the bombardment groups which participated in the mission of 23 December 1944 my congratulations for the excellent manner in which the mission was executed. Operating in extremely adverse weather conditions these units exhibited a high degree of determination and skill in clearing the Division area, attacking the marshalling yards at Ehrang and landing in weather conditions equally as adverse, without the loss of a single aircraft. Excellent bombing results were obtained. Convey to participating officers and men my appreciation of a job well done...'

On Christmas Eve 1944 the Field Order at all bases called for a maximum effort. General Doolittle wanted to hit German airfields hard to prevent the *Luftwaffe* supporting German land forces in the Ardennes. However, some Third Bomb Division bases were still congested with First Division Fortresses. Many had landed there after the mission of 23 December when their home bases had been 'socked in.' Visibility was still poor and led to many accidents during takeoff. At Podington Lieutenant Robert K. Seeber's Fortress crashed into a wood about 200 yards to the left of the runway. The wood had not been visible during takeoff because of the thick fog. About two minutes later, Seeber's B-17 exploded, killing six of the crew. At Glatton the 457th managed to get six aircraft off in reduced visibility but the seventh crashed at the end of the runway and operations were brought to a halt for a time.

Despite these crashes, the Eighth mounted its largest single attack in history with a record 2,034 heavies, including war-weary hacks and even unarmed assembly ships. At Rackheath a record 61 Liberators, including the assembly ship *Pete The POM Inspector*, were airborne in only 30 minutes. Lieutenant Charles McMahon, a 'Happy Warrior' pilot now on the Group Operations' staff who decided to risk one last mission, flew *Pete*. He came through safely armed only with carbines in the waist positions. In addition, 500 RAF and Ninth Air Force bombers participated in this, the greatest single aerial armada the world has ever seen. The First Division would be involved in a direct tactical assault on airfields in the Frankfurt area and on lines of communication immediately behind the German 'bulge.' Crews were told that their route was planned on purpose to go over the ground troops' positions for morale purposes.

Overall, the Christmas Eve raids were effective and severely hampered von Rundstedt's lines of communication. The cost though was high. Among the losses caused by enemy action was a Fortress with Brigadier General Fred Castle, CO, 4th Wing aboard.

Castle had led the 3rd BD on his 30th mission in *Treble Four*, a 487th Bomb Group Fortress, with Lieutenant Robert W. Harriman's crew. All went well until 23,000 feet over Belgium, about 35 miles from Liege, his right outboard engine burst into flame and the propeller had to be feathered. The deputy lead ship took over and Castle dropped down to 20,000 feet. But at this height the aircraft began vibrating badly and he was forced to take it down another 3,000 feet before levelling out. The Fortress was now down to 180 mph indicated air speed and being pursued by seven Bf 109s of *IV./JG3*. They attacked and wounded the tail gunner and left the radar navigator nursing bad wounds in his neck and shoulders. Castle could not carry out any evasive manoeuvres with the full bomb load still aboard and he could not salvo them for fear of hitting Allied troops on the ground. Successive attacks by the fighters put another two engines out of action and the B-17 lost altitude. To reduce airspeed the wheels of the Fortress were lowered and the crew ordered to bail out with the terse intercom message, 'This is it boys.'

Castle managed to level out long enough for six of the crew to bale out but at 12,000 ft the bomber was hit in the right wing fuel tank, which exploded, sending the B-17 into a plunging final spiral to the ground. Castle was posthumously awarded the Medal of Honor, the highest ranking officer in the 8th AF to receive the award. Harriman and Castle were buried in the American cemetery at Henri-Chattel.

Many aircraft crashed during their return over England as drizzle and overcast played havoc with landing patterns. Tired crews put down where they could. They joined in the festive spirit as best they could knowing that another strike would be ordered for Christmas Day. Two Norwich girls remember Christmas Eve 1944 fondly – 22-year-old Sheila Peal recalls:

'...snow on the ground, frosty, and we all walked down Thunder Lane to midnight service at Thorpe St. Andrew. Two of the GIs were of Welsh extraction and had wonderful singing voices, and we all sang carols all the way down and back, finishing up with *The Old Rugged Cross.*'

Ann K. Spredbury:

'The US chaplain from Horsham St. Faith brought a group of incredibly handsome young men to sing at Silver Road Baptist Church. I still remember the face of the one who sang the solo *The Old Rugged Cross*. After the service, we had a cup of tea with the airmen and I learned one was called Spain. Because I didn't understand his accent, I never found out why! But Chappie told my mother, a young widow then, that he would arrange for me and my sister to spend Christmas Day at the airbase, while she relaxed at a friend's house.

'It was a very cold morning when the jeep arrived, and the ice crunched under our feet. How smart Chappie's uniform seemed, with its brilliant badges and bars. He took us to his office on camp and let us play with the typewriter and the kittens which slept in a box under his desk. Later, we saw a Disney film and walked along endless corridors of glittering Christmas cards and lifesaver sweets that hung as trimmings over our heads. Chappie cut strings of them down to give to us. The long lunch tables set for crowds of children were decorated with foil-wrapped chocolate bars laid end to end down the centre. A GI scooped some up and put them in my lap. We were served with turkey and cranberry sauce ("they put jam on their meat," I told my mother that night).

'Then there was pumpkin pie – a marvellous new taste.'

Derek Daniels was one of the local children who were entertained at a Christmas party in the Red Cross clubhouse at the 231st Base Hospital, Morley, near Wymondham, Norfolk, on 23 December 1944.

'They came and collected us from our homes in ambulances and took us back to the Hospital where we had a great time. We saw a film show and were given toys and sweets galore (for in Morley as elsewhere we were only allowed two ounces a week, we were rationed) But not here! There was candy as the Yanks called it and gum by the yard, The toys were fun – some having been made by the wounded men, while they were convalescing. Then we had an enormous feed to end the party. We had fish, chips, meat, pickles, mince pies, Christmas pudding, crackers, and for drink it was either Coca-Cola (American only in those days) or cocoa. We

Wymondham, 1944

Southern Comfort, a 'snow-covered' scene at Shipdham, which was created for a Christmas card in 1944

were on rations at home. We thought we were in Canaan as it were, for it was certainly a place which flowed with milk and honey.'

'Christmas Eve 1944 finally arrived,' recalls General Andrew S. Low:[1] 'dressed in white. Even as the 453rd was going all out against Hitler's Fortress through the medium of the air, those who had remained at home were going out in a different manner. The 453rd played host to more than 1,250 British children ranging in age from four to 14. They were gathered from the neighbouring villages and towns. Many were orphans or evacuees from the London Blitz.'

The party had been in the making since 1 November. Some of the personnel conceived the idea of making toys for the children of Paris, so many of whom had never experienced the spirit and thrills of a child's Christmas. The idea spread like wildfire to and among the neighbouring children who began to donate their own toys or make new ones. Rag dolls, wooden toys and myriads of Christmas cards were enthusiastically donated by these youngsters for their small French allies.

Wheels began to grind. The American Red Cross chose more than 300 French

[1] *The Story of the 453rd Bombardment Group (Heavy)*

A show organised by Major Newton McLaughlin at Seething

children to receive the gifts on Christmas Day at the ARC Club at Rainbow Corner in Paris. The Group received permission to fly the gifts to Paris. An all-French speaking crew was chosen to ferry them over. Technical Sergeant Reuben Brockway was picked to portray Santa Claus, uniform and all, but minus the paunch.

A nameless Liberator, veteran of 74 missions without an abort, was chosen to act as Santa's reindeer and sleigh. Personnel on the base contributed their PX rations to fill the stockings of the little guests. The Aero Club was all bedecked, even to the Christmas tree. Decorations consisted of silver cones and balls made of *chaff*. Coloured chains were made of red and silver strips of paper. Lights were added. Everything was set.

The children began to arrive in GI trucks and were placed in three groups according to age. Those from four to seven gathered at the Aero Club where they were entertained. Here, too, they received their stockings filled with candies and toys from Santa himself and were served ice cream and coke to their heart's content. Those aged seven to eleven were taken out to the perimeter and shown through the planes. Then came the big show.

The procession walked to the hardstand where a huge platform had been erected alongside one of the ships. It was this ship that was to carry the gifts of these young-sters to their little French friends. With Sergeant Al Klauber of the 734th Squadron acting as 'emcee' and Santa receiving the gifts, Judith McDavid, eleven-year-old orphan of the Blitz, christened the ship *Liberty Run.*

Fully loaded, the ship attempted to take off but slipped off the runway as the engines were revved up. Fortunately, the Liberator was not damaged but takeoff was postponed 'till morning. Meanwhile, those aged eleven to fourteen had been taken to the base theatre where they were entertained by Corporal Sissenstein of Special Services who was quite an amateur magician. He kept them laughing and held their interest with his feats of magic and sleight of hand. Joined later by those who had witnessed the christening of the plane, the entire group was shown animated cartoons and a comic feature. Then they returned to the Aero Club where they, too, received gifts and filled themselves with candy, ice cream and cakes. After the last child had been fed, they were returned to their homes. It is safe to say that many will long member the Yankee hospitality shown them on this Christmas Eve by the personnel of the 453rd Bomb Group.

As night fell, the Aero Club was thrown open to all regardless of rank. Officers and GIs celebrated Christmas Eve in true American style. At the base chapel, Chaplain Healy led the Midnight Mass as many observed Christmas Eve in the ETO as they had observed it at home. Still others celebrated by drowning their sorrows, if they had any, in mild and bitter plus a surprising amount of wine, Scotch and rye.

After a final checkup, *Liberty Run* was ready. At 1015 the engines were revved up and the ship raced down the runway and into the air. Two hours and 15 minutes later, at 1230, the plane touched down. The precious boxes were eagerly unloaded and disbursed by the Red Cross hostesses and Field Attendants. At Rainbow Corner in Paris, Santa handed the gifts to the children.

Without a doubt *Liberty Run's* mission was a grand success. The French children who received the gifts experienced something new even as had those who had given them and ferried them across the Channel.

Back at Old Buck, the Group was stood down. Needless to say, the Officers' Club and Non-Com Club did a bang-up business as practically everyone took advantage of the situation. The traditional turkey was served for Christmas dinner with all the trimmings. Many of the personnel invited their lady friends to a real Yankee dinner which consisted of tomato juice, fresh fruit, turkey, giblet dressing, and vegetables, hot parker house rolls and butter. However, all good things must come to an end and so did Christmas. Fortunately, for many who had taken their celebrating a bit too seriously, 26 December saw the group stood down.

Technical Sergeant Forrest S. Clark at Shipdham recalls two very different Christmases in the ETO.

'I was in a base hospital for Christmas 1943. I had narrowly escaped with my life in a crash of a B-24 a few days before and had an injured back and legs. The crash left me in a blur but I recall Christmas because of two or three odd things that happened. There was a makeshift Christmas tree in the hospital and I could see it from my bed. Also, we had male nurses or hospital aides and I do not recall seeing or hearing any women nurses in the hospital. One of the odd things that happened

Liberty Run

WAACs celebrate Christmas at Shipdham

had to do with a so-called secret cache of alcohol in one of the hospital cabinets. We were all supposed to be injured combat crew men but somebody, I think one of the male nurse aides, got the idea to open that cabinet and pass around some unadulterated alcohol for a little Christmas holiday cheer. The stuff was so potent that after a snifter or two all the patients and the hospital aides were getting high on it. It was decided that this was the best way to celebrate and combined with the contents of some Christmas gift packages of goodies we were having a high old time. We were all in this elevated state when one of the officers from the Wing decided to make a little holiday visit. We could hardly restrain our glee as the officer and aides passed around the row of beds wishing each of us a happy holiday. We had a happy holiday all right but it wasn't from the official visitors. The Christmas card that year on the base was a picture of a Flying 8 Ball and wishes for a Victorious New Year with the Morse code signal of the victory sign on it.

'A few days after Christmas 1944 I returned to England[1] after escaping from

---

[1] Flying in Lieutenant Rockford C. Griffith's crew, Forrest and everyone aboard their Liberator were interned in Switzerland following the mission to Lechfeld on 12 April 1944.

Switzerland through France with the aid of American and French underground agents. I was in what I thought was the relative safety of London. Despite the war and the intense bombing of the city, a gay holiday mood appeared to prevail. I had checked into a Red Cross club where British and American servicemen and women could find lodging and was catching up on many hours of lost sleep. London did show many scars of the German bombing and it was impossible not to be reminded of the damage done and lives lost in the Blitz. People were going about their business as usual, taxis were running, stores were open, and everything was going according to routine. However, I looked down the street and two or three buildings from where I was standing I could see that an entire block of houses had been levelled, smoke was rising from the rubble and rescue crews were pulling people out of the wreckage. Parts of the buildings were still burning.

"'We've been hit by one of those German V2 rockets," said a British bobby standing nearby when he saw my surprise and shock. "They come over every day now, little gifts from Hitler.'"

Meanwhile, missions continued.

Bomb damage behind St Paul's Cathedral

Piccadilly Circus, 1944

Max Stout, co-pilot, 453rd Bomb Group, Old Buckenham:
'On 27 December 1944 we were to be the first plane off. It was an instrument takeoff. We were late to taxi and when we arrived, a new crew was lined up ready to go. Being a new crew in the 733rd I suppose they were eager to show their mettle. The order of takeoff wasn't all that important.'

The plane hurtled down the salt strewn, slippery runway. The B-24 refused to rise more than a few feet and crashed near the edge of the field. Three gunners scrambled clear before the bomb load exploded in three terrific explosions. The mission was scrubbed with no more planes taking off.

Captain Ralph H. Elliott, pilot, 467th Bomb Group wrote a letter to his wife Vonnie in the States on 31 December 1944.

'...New Year's Eve and still in England, Honey. I had hoped by now to be nearly through and on the way home to you, but it looks like luck's against it. It's hard to realize that 1945 is nearly here and that time has passed so rapidly – and yet so slowly. Looking back, a lot has happened, hasn't it? Just a year ago tonight we went to a show after getting out of a very crowded officer's club, and at midnight I kissed my wife and we wished each other the best. I'd give everything to be able to do that again this evening, but I'll do the next best thing and say, Happy

New Year, Sweetheart. If only you could enjoy London with me...not much fun alone.'

Andy Low concludes:

'New Year's Eve found the Group doing business with Hitler, the only kind of business he knew. Nevertheless once the day's business was over, the personnel turned to ringing out the old and bringing in the new in true American style. With a dance at the Aero Club, open house at the Non Com Club and plenty to cheer with at the Officers' Club's new Snack Bar and bar, the men soon got into the proper spirits. As many rang in their second New Year in the ETO, there was a fervent toast that there would be no more.'

American serviceman Robert Arbib, author of *Here We Are Together*, writing in the *Daily Express* in January 1945, said:

...we shall remember, too, our Christmas parties for the orphans and evacuee children. No one could ever forget those parties, with the kids yelling and gobbling ice cream, sitting on our shoulders and singing for us.... going home along the lane clutching armfuls of toys and candy, chewing gum and biscuits. Fifteen hundred we had at one party.

MOONLIGHT MEMORIES

*W*hen *I was young there were big bands. And a song called 'Moonlight Serenade.' We listened on the radio to the music of the big dance bands broadcasting from faraway romantic places like Frank Dailey's Meadowbrook, the College Inn in Chicago, and the Glen Island Casino 'just off the Shore Road in New Rochelle, New York,' as the radio announcer used to say.*

Moonlight Serenade. The theme song, the song that identified Glenn Miller's big band in the late 30s and early 40s. Willie Schwartz, a clarinetist in the Miller band, once said in an interview,

'I don't know why, but to me there was always something sad about that song.'

Sad? Yes. And to my generation and me Moonlight Serenade meant much, much more. Moonlight Serenade. A whole world to discover out there to high school students studying homework while glued to the radio.

'How can you study and listen to the radio at the same time?', our parents would ask. High school swing bands copied Miller while we learned to dance, awkwardly, at proms in the high school gym.

Moonlight Serenade. A vague longing. College dances, the sweet perfume of gardenia corsages, dancing so close that you caught the fragrance of your girl's freshly washed hair.

Moonlight Serenade was the last dance, cheek to cheek.

Moonlight Serenade was young love, found love, lost love, young love.

It was Peggy and Cathy and Jean and Denise and Pat. Malt shops and juke boxes, record machines that played one record for a nickel, and a quarter bought five plays.

Saddle shoes, blue jeans, and Ford V-8s. Sitting at a desk overlooking a tree-shaded campus, studying for final exams and listening to music coming from the Cafe Rouge in the Hotel Pennsylvania in New York. It was a handsome young saxophone player named Tex who played haunting solos.

Moonlight Serenade. It sang of going off to war and the goodbye kisses. It was a Quonset hut in England, writing home and tuning in to the Glenn Miller 8th Air Force Band on Armed Forces radio. It was the Miller band filling hangers at U.S. air bases in England, galvanizing the troops. It was returning from a combat mission in the skies over Nazi Germany, reaching the English Channel, the radio operator finding Moonlight Serenade on the BBC and the pilot linking it into the airplane's intercom so the bomber crew could hear it too.

Moonlight Serenade. Emptiness. Loss. The BBC news broadcast announcing that Major Glenn Miller was gone, missing from a flight over the English Channel. Later, at the Rainbow Corner in Paris, after a parachute jump and a journey across France, listening to the great AEF band without Major Glenn Miller, we heard Moonlight Serenade *as a requiem to a man and his music and as a goodbye to our youth.*

Moonlight Serenade. Sad? Yes. And much, much more.

When I was young, there were big bands. And a song called Moonlight Serenade.

Keith Roberts, Navigator,
578th Vickers Crew

14

MOONLIGHT SERENADE

Glenn Miller and singer and actress Irene Manning at a 'Music for the Wehrmacht'
broadcast, November 1944

The Glenn Miller orchestra was famous in pre-war America for its distinctive sound, arrived at by mixing some jazz and a large element of swing, and unabashed showmanship characterized by the flapping of their mutes, standing for solos and the choreographed pumping of trombone slides. Miller pursued musical supremacy, demanded perfection and drove his musicians hard. In March 1939 the band was contracted to play for the summer season at the celebrated Glen Island Casino in New Rochelle, New York. They broadcast from the Casino ten times a week, thousands of listeners tuned in and soon the band was a household name. One hit record after another followed, including *Little Brown Jug, In the Mood, Chattanooga Choo Choo, Serenade in Blue, I Got a Gal in Kalamazoo* and of course *Moonlight Serenade*, which became Miller's theme song.

When the band went on the road, each live venue became a sellout. In Hershey, Pennsylvania, the band broke the attendance record set by the Guy Lombardo Orchestra eight years earlier and in Syracuse, New York, it played for the biggest dance audience ever. In December 1939 the band was hired for a three times weekly CBS national radio programme sponsored by Chesterfield cigarettes. In the summer of 1940 the results of a poll made the Glenn Miller orchestra the top band in the country with almost double the number of votes of its nearest rival, Tommy Dorsey. Appearances in two Hollywood movies followed. In 1941 the Glenn Miller band featured in *Sun Valley Serenade* and a year later they appeared in *Orchestra Wives.*

By this time the United States was at war and the draft deprived Miller of most of his established musicians. At age 38 Miller was spared the call up but if he enlisted he could perhaps help the war effort in a musical capacity, possibly by updating military music for the troops. Miller first offered his services to the US Navy but was turned down so he tried the Army. On 12 August 1942 Miller wrote to Brigadier General Charles D. Young, outlining a desire to enable music to reach servicemen at home and overseas on a fairly regular basis. He argued that this would considerably ease some of the 'difficulties of army life'. Miller's desire to join the armed forces may not have been driven by patriotic reasons entirely. In August 1942 a strike by the musicians' union against the record companies began and it was to last until September 1943, effectively keeping the bands out of the recording studios for a whole year. Although the record companies eventually capitulated, the strike was a severe blow for the Big Bands. Where once Benny Goodman was guaranteed $3,000 a night and Tommy Dorsey was getting $4,000, suddenly one night, the total take was just $700. A wartime 20% amusement tax on nightclub receipts (which continued into peacetime) did not help. Tastes too began to change towards romantic singers who were much in demand for radio performances. In 1943 Frank Sinatra left the Tommy Dorsey band and other vocalists like Perry Como and Eddie Fisher followed. By the end of 1946 eight of the top US bands had disbanded.

Miller reported for induction on 7 October 1942. Eventually, he was named Director of Bands Training for the Army Air Forces Technical Training Command and authorized to organize a band at Yale University, which had become a training area for cadets. The outfit, officially known as the 418th Army Air Forces Band, was activated on 20 March 1943 with permanent station at Yale University.

Yale was not just a training area for cadets. It had links with counter-espionage going back to the days of the War of Independence when three members of the Culpepper spy ring, who graduated in the class of 1773, were established there secretly by George Washington to gather intelligence on the British. Unlike the British, the US had no independent intelligence agency for most of its history. Spying was a rather informal affair, confined to the wartime military. With the outbreak of WWII it became clear that the US needed a large-scale operation, and quickly. What better place than academe? Especially since Yale was a hot bed of intrigue with unique secret societies such as the exclusive and infamous 'Skull and Bones' society, whose members are sworn to secrecy for life about the club's activities. The society's origins can be traced back to 1832, when William Russell founded it as retribution for a classmate's having been passed over by Phi Beta Kappa. The Skull and Bones cryptic iconography is derived from German University societies. Henry Lewis Stimson, President Theodore Roosevelt's Secretary of War, and Averell Harriman, American Ambassador to Moscow were members.

Many of the leading agents in the OSS (Office of Strategic Services), which was founded in 1942 for the acquisition and analysis of intelligence, were provided by Yale. Henry Luce, owner of Time-Life, and his wife Marjorie, Henry Stanley founder of Morgan Stanley, and Captain Charles Black (who later married Shirley Temple) were 'bonesmen' too. In fact so many 'Yalies' joined the OSS that the university's drinking tune, the 'Whiffenpuff Song' became the secret organisation's unofficial song. At the heart of OSS and home to most of Yale's academics was the Research and Analysis branch (R&A) where social scientists, historians, linguists and even literary critics studied friends and enemies, real and potential, present and future. By the end of the war, R&A had gathered 3 million index cards, 300,000 photographs, a million maps, 350,000 foreign serials, 50,000 books, thousands of loose postcards – all indexed and cross-indexed, many of these gathered under the cover of the Yale library.

Walter L. Pforzheimer, who helped found the CIA, was educated at Yale, entering in 1931, then joining the army. Shortly after graduating from Officers Candidate School he was approached by a young officer who asked if he was interested in working in the intelligence community. 'Beats digging ditches,' he thought and became part of the OSS. After the war he became the OSS's Legislative Counsel for liaison with Congress and played a major part in writing the bill that brought the CIA into existence in 1947. His father made his fortune in oil but became a significant book collector. For Walter's 21st birthday, he gave him a library. It was, said Walter, a shock that shaped his life. He went on to collate a huge selection of intelligence material. When he gave the works to Yale University in 2002, they included more than 15,000 books.

Apart from R&A, OSS comprised four other major categories: Secret Intelligence (SI) was responsible for intelligence gathering. Secret Operations (SO) parachuted agents into the occupied countries; Morale Operations (MO) was involved with propaganda broadcasts to the enemy to undermine his morale and lastly X-2, the counter-intelligence service. X-2 also handled the German Ultra intelligence deciphered at Bletchley Park in Bedfordshire and was dominated by Yale students and Yale alumni such as English Literature Professor Norman Holmes Pearson and James Jesus Angleton, who went on to a legendary career as director of the CIA's counterintelligence staff. Both belonged to the 'Skull & Bones' and myth says that the society's members form a clique that rules the world. They have promoted one another in enormously successful political and business careers and presided over the creation of the atomic bomb as well as the CIA. Even today, there is reportedly a 'Bones club' within the CIA, which helps promote the intelligence careers of members of the Yale secret society. A statue of Nathan Hale, which stands in front of the headquarters of the Central Intelligence Agency in Langley, Virginia, is a replica of one on the campus of Yale University.

On 28 July 1943 Glenn Miller's new swinging military band made its debut in the Yale Bowl to a rapturous reception from the cadets. The Miller band continued to play at retreat parades and at review formations on the Yale Green but really let their hair down performing at dances, open houses, parties and luncheons. On radio Miller's musicians broadcast *I Sustain the Wings*, a series designed to boost Air Force recruitment. The band was such a hit and its appearances at bond drives so successful that Miller began to fear that they might be held stateside instead of being sent overseas to boost troop morale.

He need not have concerned himself for the band would go to England. But was there an ulterior motive? While at Yale was Miller recruited for OSS propaganda activities and morale operations and even psychological warfare? It would not have been out of the question. OSS operatives included the cream of Hollywood: actors Sterling Hayden (John Hamilton), William Holden, Broderick Crawford, Julia Child, Charlotte Gower and Hollywood directors such as John Ford. After the war Ford produced two movies about the OSS called *13 Rue Madeleine* with James Cagney and *Operation Secret* with Cornel Wilde. They were based in part on the exploits of Colonel Peter Ortiz, one of the most decorated Marine officers of World War II, who had been a member of OSS since 1943.

OSS and the US intelligence services reportedly stopped at nothing that might help the US war effort. It has been suggested that they rigged the Norwegian stock exchange and even enlisted the help of the Mafia and German organizations. In 1941, the security of the port of New York was a matter of great concern, not only to the Third Naval District, but also to the Secretary of the Navy and the President of the United States. Everyone knew that the Mafia controlled the waterfront and Charlie 'Lucky' Luciano, who was serving 30 years for running New York prostitution, was obviously an important man in the underworld. Naval Intelligence was extremely concerned about sabotage and espionage on the New York waterfront. They were alarmed also at the shipping losses. Between 7 December 1941 and February 1942 the US and its allies had lost 71 merchant ships to *U-boats* and by May 1942 272 ships had been sunk along the Eastern Seaboard Frontier. To secure the New York waterfront a Navy-Mafia alliance was concluded and Operation *Underworld* was born. As part of the deal, on 12 May 1942 Lucky Luciano was moved from the bleak Clinton Prison at Dannemora near the Canadian border to the more comfortable Great Meadow Prison in New York State.

By December 1942 Lieutenant Commander Charles Radcliffe 'Red' Haffenden and his staff of 50 officers and 81 EM and civilian men were working closely with their mob connections. Early in 1943 the Office of Naval Intelligence (ONI) set up a new department called F-Section to collect strategic information which would assist *Husky*, the allied invasion of Sicily. The mob co-operated and the greater part of the intelligence developed in the Sicilian campaign came from a number of Sicilians associated with Luciano. Haffenden was delighted and even went as far as proposing that Luciano be released. The mobster remained in prison however, but in February 1946, he was given passage to Italy to spend the rest of his life in exile. He died of a heart attack at Naples airport on 26 January 1962.

Officially, Operation *Underworld* never happened. On 17 May 1946 in an inter-office memorandum, J. Edgar Hoover, the chief of the FBI, wrote on the report,

This is an amazing and fantastic case. We should get all the facts for it looks rotten to me from several angles… a shocking example of misuse of Naval authority in the interests of a hoodlum. It surprises me that they didn't give Luciano the Navy Cross.

On 24 May 1946, after just four months as Commissioner of Marine and Aviation for the city of New York, Haffenden was dismissed.

Towards the end of the war in Operation *Sunrise* John Foster Dulles negotiated a separate peace with the German army in Northern Italy. Six days before *VE Day*, Operation *Sunrise* succeeded. Dulles recruited SS General Reinhard Gehlen, head of military intelligence for German forces in the Soviet Union. Gehlen's information was of substantial interest to those planning the cold war, so he and his organization were enlisted in the 'good fight' against the Soviets. Gehlen became director of the West German intelligence agency on its establishment in 1955. According to an article by John Loftus in the *Boston Globe* (29 May, 1984) Dulles, with the assistance of the Vatican, engineered the escape of thousands of *Gestapo* and *SS* officers. Among these, it now seems likely, were Josef Mengele, Klaus Barbie and possibly Adolf Eichmann. Exfiltrated Nazis were free to offer their services to Latin American dictators and drug traffickers as well as the CIA. As Dulles said, 'For us there are two sorts of people in the world: there are those who are Christians and support free enterprise and there are the others.'

Meanwhile, in the spring of 1944 the AAF orchestra was finally ordered to England. Miller's arrival there can be attributed to General Dwight D. Eisenhower, the Supreme Allied Commander, who wanted Miller and his band for his brain-child, the AEF (Allied Expeditionary Forces) programme. Ike wanted the programme put out on air to the Allied troops who were taking part in the invasion of France and subsequent campaigns. Despite difficulties, Eisenhower's persistence, backed by support from Winston Churchill, finally ensured that the AEF programme reached the airwaves and the new programme was inaugurated in March 1944. It went out for the first time over the BBC transmitter at Start Point, Devon the day after the successful allied landings in Normandy, 7 June 1944. Miller and the band, which was now known as the American Band of the Supreme Allied Command, arrived at Gourock, Scotland on 28 June and entrained for London where they were immediately caught up in the V-1 flying-bomb blitz on the capital. Almost five thousand people were killed. Miller persuaded the top brass to move his

Glenn Miller in concert in an 8th Air Force hangar

unit and on 2 July they left their billet at Sloane Court and travelled to Bedford, fifty miles north of London and safe from flying bombs. On the day after the men had vacated Sloane Court, a buzz bomb fell a few feet from the building, blowing away its entire front and leaving the place in ruins.[1]

At first Miller and his executive officer, Lieutenant Don Haynes, were billeted at the American Red Cross Officers' Club in Bedford but later Miller was given a flat in Waterloo Road and the band was billeted in two large detached houses in Ashburnham Road. VIIIth Air Force Service Command Headquarters at Milton Ernest Hall on the banks of the Ouse River about ten miles north of Bedford carried out the day to day administration of the band. In between broadcasts and rehearsals at the Co-Partners Hall the band was taken to the headquarters in trucks for its meals. Captain Bob Seymour, in the Communication Section, recalls:

'It was about the most pleasant place to be during wartime that one can imagine. Our little post, being the closest military establishment, was designated as the payroll location for Glenn and the band. Some of the band members would hang around our place on days off, play poker or softball. Once in a while we'd have parties and invite the local gentry and some of the lonesome girls from Bedford or Cambridge. Captain Miller usually obliged by bringing out a small all-star band to play for dancing, featuring such renowned sidemen as Peanuts Hucko on woodwinds. One night Glenn goosed my hutmate's girlfriend on the dance floor resulting in a minor squabble. Probably too much Scotch from our regular RAF ration. A hard life, indeed! But aside from those times we worked hard and did a good job. We kept them flying.'

A small detachment from Miller's AEF band performed for the first time on Saturday evening, 8 July, at a dance for officers of VIIIth Air Force Service Command headquarters at Milton Ernest Hall. On 9 July the Miller band assembled in the Corn Exchange in Bedford for a rehearsal for their first programme, due to be broadcast that night, live on the American Armed Forces (AEF) network. That evening the Corn Exchange was filled to overflowing. Among the audience were some of the biggest names in showbusiness in America, including Humphrey Bogart and Lieutenant Colonel David Niven, Associate Director of Broadcasting services. Niven reported to Colonel Ed Kirby who had been appointed by SHAEF as Director of Broadcasting services with responsibility for liaison with the BBC. This magical opening performance was followed by hundreds more in England, many of them for

[1] Ever since 1940 Bedford had played host to major recording and broadcasting departments of the BBC and the Music Department and the BBC Symphony Orchestra, among others, had been moved to the comparative safety of Bedford.

troops at American bases throughout East Anglia. The band was so much in demand, especially for radio work, that it became impractical to take the whole unit to every venue. Miller formed sub-sections of the full band to perform different types of music on four radio series. *Strings With Wings* featured a full string section headed by George Ockner; *The Swing Shift* had a seventeen-piece dance band led by Ray McKinley; *Uptown Hall*, with a seven-piece jazz ensemble under Mel Powell; and *A Soldier and a Song*, boasted crooner Johnny Desmond accompanied by the full band.

MILLER PLAYS IT HOT AND SWEET
by Peter Lisagor

A Liberator Base, Aug. 20 – Major Glenn Miller, still scorching his trombone with sweet breaks, has brought his magical arrangements and a 45-man band of GI's to the swing-hungry ETO, and if his luck holds, he hopes to offer two Continental concerts for an all-soldier show audience in Paris and Berlin.

In a room marked "Gentlemen" – the only place he could be separated from throngs of idolators and autograph seekers (it was crowded but the jostling was more purposeful) – Miller told how thrilled he was by his present mission.

"Gen. Doolittle put it best," Miller said, "when he told us that every soldier is bucking for one thing – to get home. He can't do that until the job's done, so the next best thing is to bring a little bit of home to him. That's our mission."

By way of fulfilling it, Miller confines his concerts to the old familiar tunes, each with their thousands of memories for the soldier.

"They haven't heard the new tunes," he explained. "But 'String of Pearls,' 'In The Mood,' 'Cow-Cow Boogie,' 'Moonlight Serenade' and 'Chattanooga Choo-Choo' remind them of the days and nights they treasured." And the lads "eat it up."

Miller, whose band was tops in the U.S. for three years before he volunteered for the Army used to count the house in civilian life. "Every head meant about 60 cents to me." Now, he says, his reward comes from the eager faces, alive and thankful for the memories.

"The best night's pay I ever got was watching those faces light up when we played," he said. "I feel now as though I'm doing something really worthwhile."

He wants no controversy with Sigmund Romberg and other long-haired musicians back home who claim the GI will want musical sedatives other than jive after the war. His answer is simply, "Let them bring that kind of music over here and see for themselves."

Miller thinks his GI band is better than the one that brought him fame in the States. He has a string section of 20 men — drawn from the Cleveland, Boston and New York Philharmonic orchestras –

so-called "long hairs," who, as one of them put it, "are delighted because Miller's a real musician and he knows what those boys out there want."

Five members of his band played with Miller as civilians, among them S/Sgt. Jimmy Priddy on the trombone, M/Sgt. Zeke Zarchy on the trumpet and S/Sgt. "Trigger" Alpert on the bass. Pianist Mel Powell was with Benny Goodman, S/Sgt. Hank Freeman was first sax with Artie Shaw, Sgt. Bobby Nichols was a trumpeter with Vaughan Monroe, Sgt. Bernie Privin played trumpet with Charlie Barnett, Goodman and Shaw, and Sgt. Carmen Mastren was a guitarist with Tommy Dorsey.

One of them, T/Sgt. Ray McKinley, led a well-known band of his own after years on the drums with the Dorsey Bros., and later, with Jimmy Dorsey's crew, and his drum solo is a highlight of the Miller program. Also in the organization, which is really a complete radio production outfit, are T/Sgt. Jerry Gray, an arranger with both Miller and Shaw in civilian life, who wrote "String of Pearls" and "Here We Go Again," and made the famous arrangements of "Chattanooga Choo-Choo" for Miller and "Begin the Beguine" for Shaw; arrangers Sgt. Jimmy Jackson, S/Sgt. Ralph Wilkinson, with Raymond Paige and Kostelanetz, and the music for Moss Hart's "Winged Victory." Lt. Don Haynes, Miller's civilian manager, is his Army "booking agent."

At this base, the heavy-bomber group under Col. Luther J. Fairbanks, of Burt, Iowa, celebrated its 100th mission and Miller's band was the big event. In a giant hangar more than 3,000 GI's and their gals weaved and writhed like an agitated sea as Miller and his boys went "In the Mood." This was a Saturday night in Duluth, Atlanta, Portland, Punxutawney, Pa., and 3,000 other places in America, and one look at the sea of faces explained Miller's "It's the best night's pay I ever got."

Stars and Stripes. **21 August 1944. The dateline should be 18 August, not 20 August as shown. The 100-mission party for the 466th Bomb Group was held at Attlebridge on 18 August 1944.**

Miller and the band were also in great demand for propaganda work at the American Broadcasting Station in Europe (ABSIE) in London. ABSIE was controlled by the Overseas Branch of the Office of War Information, a civilian propaganda outlet for the American Government. ABSIE seduced its overseas listeners with musical programmes and many of the announcements and some of the vocals were in German. Bing Crosby and Dinah Shore, who read from phonetic German scripts, were among the American stars who broadcast. The first recording session was held at the HMV studio, Abbey Road, St. John's Wood in London on 30 October 1944. Following its success Glenn Miller and his band recorded a series of transcriptions for half hour weekly broadcasts beamed at the German Army on the 'Wehrmacht Hour'. The first programme was aired on 8 November 1944.

On the evening of 7 November Miller and the band broadcast from their Bedford studio at 1830 hours. Next day he was booked on a C-47 shuttle flight from Bovingdon airfield, Hertfordshire to Orly airport in Paris. Miller had orders to attend a conference in Paris with Lieutenant Colonel David Niven and General Ray W. Barker, SHAEF G-1. SHAEF wanted the band, beginning on or about 15 December, to make a six-week tour of American bases and field hospitals in France, which would include entertaining the troops on leave in Paris on Christmas Eve and New Year's Eve.

Glenn Miller and John H. Woolnough, 18 August 1944 at the 100th Mission Party of the 466th Bomb Group at Attlebridge

Although the conference was scheduled for 15 November, Miller had apparently decided to leave a week early so he could enjoy the delights of Paris first.

At Milton Ernest Hall he had become friendly with Lieutenant-Colonel Norman Baessell, who was responsible for establishing advanced air deports on the continent. Baessell made frequent flights to France and Belgium and was notorious in Paris for spending money like water, buying drinks all round in restaurants and bars. It was rumoured that he was involved in the Black Market. Baessell had promised to show Miller 'the town' when they were in Paris. The morning of 8 November was cold and frosty. Bovingdon was a tiring 50 mile drive from Bedford so Baessell, who was also leaving for Orly from RAF Twinwoods nearby, offered Miller a 'lift' as far as Bovingdon in his UC-64A Norseman. Miller accepted. Baessell had counted on George Ferguson in Belgium being able to fly a Norseman to Twinwoods but Ferguson's commander had refused him permission.

Undeterred, Baessell contacted Flight Officer John Morgan, a pilot in 8th AFSC, at Honington and instructed him to fly his Norseman to Twinwood Farm airfield to pick them up. Morgan did not obtain flight clearance until noon. While they waited, Miller, Baessell and Haynes had lunch at Milton Ernest Hall. When the three officers arrived at Twinwoods Morgan and the Norseman were waiting. Morgan took off and headed for Bovingdon where Miller left to board the C-47 for Paris. The Norseman continued on to Orly, returning to England on the 18th when Morgan dropped Baessell off at Abbotts Ripton. That same day Miller returned to Bovingdon on the SHAEF shuttle from Paris.

On 25 November Lieutenant Don Haynes flew to Paris to make all the arrangements for the band's visit to the French capital. On Tuesday 12 December 1944 Miller and the band made their last live broadcast in the UK from the Queensbury All Services Club in Old Compton Street in London. That same day an order issued by SHEAF signed 'By command of General Eisenhower' instructed Major Glenn Miller to '…proceed by military aircraft (ATC) on or about 16 December 1944…to…Supreme HQ, Army AG-TM on the Continent'. The order does not say why Miller needed to proceed to the Continent but it seems that Haynes, on his trip to France on 25 November, had overlooked how the band would be transported from Orly airfield to Paris. Depending on which account you read, Miller is supposed to have told him that he would fly to France instead of Haynes, who had orders to fly to Paris 'on or about 14 December', and sort this out personally! Miller is reputed to have told Haynes to, 'Uncut the orders and have them changed.' In a Haynes diary[1] account for 13 December the 'diarist' says that he 'got Glenn's orders cut to fly to Paris tomorrow.' Why? Even if he had cut the orders afresh they could not have been issued until 16 December and in any event, Eisenhower's order dated 12 December already allowed for any changes to be made!

Miller never showed up in Paris and it was assumed that he and his plane had 'disappeared over the Channel'. Officially, on 15 December Miller and Norman Baessell had left Twinwoods in a UC-64 Norseman piloted by John Morgan and it had gone down in the sea off France en route to Villacoublay, south of Paris. Miller's orders were to 'travel by military aircraft' and Orly could be reached directly, and relatively more safely, by C-47 from Bovingdon. In fact on Wednesday 13 December Haynes had booked Miller on a flight from Bovingdon to Orly the next day. It therefore begs the question, why board a single engined aircraft a day later, on Friday 15 December, and on a plane which was going to the 'wrong' airfield? The simple answer could be that Miller never did and that the events of 8 November,

---

[1] A diary which appeared in the early 1950s, seems to be genuine and a factual account. A second which, surfaced after Haynes's death in 1971, appears to be a work of fiction.

where he was booked on the C-47 shuttle flight to Orly, were used to explain away the events of 15 December 1944.

According to diaries in the name of Don Haynes, on Tuesday 12 December Haynes walked back to the Mount Royal Hotel with Miller after the Queensbury concert and on the Wednesday evening took Miller's bags to the Old Quebec Street Air Terminal. Then he and John Morgan, who had come down to see the final concert, went to the Milroy Club in Stratton Street, Mayfair, with a girl singer. There they met Sqn Ldr Tony Bartley DFC and Lieutenant Tony Pulitzer and they partied until the early hours. But before midnight Haynes and Morgan left to drive back to Bedford in thick fog. Soon after, Glenn Miller said goodbye to the others and walked away in the fog early Thursday morning towards the Mount Royal Hotel in Marble Arch. In words which could have been written by a Hollywood scriptwriter, 'He was never seen alive again'.

The AEF band played their first concert in France at the Palais de Glace on 21 December but no announcement was made about Glenn Miller being missing. The next two concerts were cancelled but the Christmas Eve broadcast obviously would have to go ahead. The Non-Battle Casualty Report stating that Glenn Miller was 'missing' was released on 22 December and in New Jersey Mrs Helen Miller, Glenn's wife, was notified by telegram the following day. No mention was made in either document as to the type of aircraft, departure airfield and destination. The Haynes' diaries give two different airfields Morgan is supposed to have flown from to Twinwoods and neither ties up with Morgan's Form 5 Record of Flight Times. An amended Casualty Report, issued in March 1948, stated that the aircraft 'crashed somewhere in the English Channel while on a mission from Twinwood Field, England to Paris, France…' The original Casualty Report included the words, 'Was taken to airfield by off. of AAF Band who witnessed takeoff' In the second version of his diaries Haynes is said to be that officer, having driven Miller and Baessell to Twinwoods to wait for Morgan to arrive! In the entry for 15 December Haynes is asked by Baessell to bring 'Glenn's baggage' — the very same baggage that Haynes had taken to the Old Quebec Street Air Terminal on 13 December!

At 1800 hours on Christmas Eve, an hour before the scheduled broadcast to America, the news was at last released. Miller's loss was a blow to civilian and troop morale, already low following news that on 16 December von Rundstedt's *Panzers* had cut through the American lines in the Ardennes and opened up a salient which became known as the 'Bulge'. Obviously the war would not now be over by Christmas.

A Beech C-43

That Miller disappeared there is no doubt. However, all the theories as to why and how may be way off course. Legend blurred the issue and was reinforced when in 1954 the Hollywood movie, *The Glenn Miller Story*, starring Jimmy Stewart and June Allyson, was released. While most cinemagoers believed the storyline totally and still do, others have their doubts. Brian C. McCulloch was six when he first saw it.

'My dad leaned over to my mother and said; "They don't have that quite right." He was referring to the scene where Glenn Miller leaves Twinwoods airfield in Bedfordshire. When we left the theater, I asked my father what he had meant with his comment. He told me that he was Glenn Miller's driver the day Miller disappeared. He added that the vehicle was a Dodge staff car, not a jeep and that he was a Staff Sergeant, not an officer. My mother said she was going to write to Hollywood to set the record straight. Forty-nine years would pass for my dad's role in the story of that day in December 1944, when the Miller legend was born, to become public. More interestingly, my dad remembers the plane that day to more closely resemble a Traveler, a biplane, than the currently credited Norseman, a high wing monoplane. As a flight cadet, he had trained in biplanes. Also, he does not remember a plane as large as the one used in the movie.[1]

'Several hours later, the military police and/or intelligence arrived at Milton

---

[1] The Beech C-43 Traveler served principally in the United States but a few reached the ETO in 1944. Thirty UC43s were supplied to Britain under Lend-Lease. Interestingly, the Air Attache operated one at the US Embassy in London!

Ernest Hall. Colonel Early later told my father that they had collected a footlocker and some other personal effects left behind by Major Miller. The Colonel ordered him not to mention Miller's most recent stay at Milton Ernest. He said nothing until he got home.'

Another theory that has been proposed is that Glenn Miller's Norseman aircraft was brought down by bombs jettisoned by an RAF Lancaster, which has prompted claims that it 'finally solves the mystery of his disappearance'. Could this have happened? To cross under the Lancasters the UC-64 Norseman would have had to fly west of London. We are led to believe that Morgan could not fly east of the capital because of a prohibited area in the Thames Estuary called the *'Diver* Gun Box', where anti-aircraft batteries were concentrated to shoot down flying-bombs heading for London. In fact Morgan did not need to 'avoid' the *Diver* box. It was inactive. The 137 Lancasters flew through the *Diver* box back to their base at Methwold! Morgan was not an instrument-rated pilot. He would hardly, therefore, choose to fly in bad weather along a longer route to Paris when he could more easily cross the Channel at its shortest point. No pilot, instrument rated or otherwise, would choose to take this route in winter.

Milton Ernest Hall

What evidence is there of Glenn Miller even being aboard the 'bombs theory' aircraft in the first place, especially if it did not 'stop off' at Twinwood Farm or Bovingdon en route to Paris? Morgan was cleared direct from Abbotts Ripton to France and he did not land at either Twinwoods or Bovingdon. No record was ever made in the log at the Flying Control at RAF Twinwoods of a Norseman having landed there that day. Lancaster navigator Fred Shaw's 'Norseman surrounded by bomb explosions' was almost certainly another UC-64, which left from Grove, near Wantage, Berkshire, and which was destroyed en route to Creil or Villacoublay, France. Miller's subsequent disappearance, or rather non-appearance – for whatever reason – had to be explained somehow. And the loss of an aircraft – any aircraft – over the Channel was convenient. The only snag in the 'cover plan' story is that on paper, Miller was 'put aboard' the wrong Norseman!

We may never know what became of Glenn Miller but in mid-1995 there were the first rumours that the OSS may possibly have been involved in his disappearance. An English OSS researcher in Northamptonshire received word that William E. Colby, a 'brave and resourceful OSS officer'[1] would be returning to the area where during the war several country estates were taken over by SOE (Special Operations Executive) and American OSS units as headquarters and as training facilities. Operatives such as Colby and agents and guerilla forces were flown out of airfields like Harrington, 9½ miles west of Kettering, in black painted Liberators operated by the American Carpetbagger group and parachuted into the occupied countries. There they linked up with underground organizations to help organize sabotage and the disruption of enemy supplies. Hundreds of *Jedburgh* teams, agents and guerrilla forces were dropped into France just prior to and after the Allied invasion of Normandy, 6 June 1944, to disrupt then harry the retreat of German troops. *Jedburgh* teams consisted of three members, usually English, French and American. On 14 August 1944 Colby was part of a *Jedburgh* team codenamed '*Bruce*' that took off from Harrington and was dropped near Montargis in France.[2] After the war OSS evolved into the Central Intelligence Agency (CIA) and in 1950 Colby joined the new organisation. During 1973–November 1975 he was Director of the CIA.[3]

---

[1] *CIA A History* John Ranelagh.

[2] See *The Bedford Triangle: US Undercover Operations From England in WWII* by Martin W. Bowman. PSL, 1989. Sutton 1996, 2003.

[3] In *CIA A History* John Ranelagh says that ... 'Apart from his temporary assignment *to* the Phoenix programme in Vietnam in the late 1960s, [Colby] had worked continuously on the clandestine side of the agency... Like many other people, Colby had been affected by the mood of disillusionment and dissent that developed as the Vietnam War progressed and, after the death of his daughter in April 1973 he was thought by colleagues to have become more religious (he was a Catholic) and reflective.'

Holmewood Hall

The place of execution?

When the English OSS researcher met his distinguished visitor he assumed that Colby would want to visit Harrington. Colby however expressed a wish to be taken to Holmewood Hall, a large red brick house on a vast estate north of Glatton (Conington) airfield. During the war Holmewood Hall was called Area 'H'. In woodland west of the hall behind high security fencing with triple bands of barbed wire a huge OSS Supply Depot comprising large double-walled brick structures with protective walls contained supplies, explosives and ammunition and weapons. These were loaded into canisters and transported to RAF Tempsford and Harrington in covered trucks either hired from or painted in the livery of the London Brick Company. Area 'H' was also a holding area for OSS agents and OGs (Operational Groups) from Area 'E' who were accommodated in the grounds under canvas. Area 'E' was the code name for Brock Hall at Weedon near Daventry, which had been used by the SOE until 1943 when it was turned over to OSS. The estate was put to use to train a Special Operations Group of Americans of Norwegian descent called NORSO in guerrilla tactics behind enemy lines in France in August 1944. After the liberation of France some NORSO personnel were returned to the USA for special training prior to working with OSS units in China. Those who remained in England came under the command of Major William E. Colby and they would be used behind enemy lines in Norway. They would have transited through Area 'H' at Holmewood Hall.[1]

As the English OSS researcher and former CIA director walked along the concrete roads winding through eerily quiet woodland in what was once Area 'H', Colby, a man of very few words, paused at the moss covered and overgrown firing range and soliloquized.

'This is where Glenn Miller was executed.'

It so stunned the English OSS researcher that he could not bring himself to ask why anyone would want to execute Glenn Miller or why Area 'H' was used. Finally, Colby broke the silence when he said that he would like to be taken to Gaynes Hall. In WWII Gaynes Hall was a highly secret, heavily guarded SOE facility near what are now Perry village and Littlehay Prison not far from Graffam Water (Diddington reservoir). When they arrived at Gaynes, Colby pointed to a field adjacent to the prison where clumps of trees were growing and chillingly told the bemused OSS researcher:

'This is where Glenn Miller is buried'.

---

[3] See *The Bedford Triangle: US Undercover Operations From England in WWII* by Martin W. Bowman. PSL, 1989. Sutton 1996, 2003.

Apparently, the trees were saplings that had been planted around the time of the burial to conceal several graves in the field. But whose bodies were they?

In 1944 *Nazis* and other identified individuals captured during the Allies' advance were reportedly flown to airfields like Tempsford and transported to a large PoW style camp in the grounds of Gaynes Hall for interrogation. Those that proved 'uncooperative' were apparently taken to a large walled 'courtyard' at the rear of the Hall, blindfolded and strapped to a chair and were executed by SOE operatives. (Bullet holes can still be seen in the wall). OSS personnel also reportedly executed uncooperative Nazis in the grounds of Area 'H'.

Colby gave no indication as to why Miller was shot at Holmewood and then buried at Gaynes.

A possible explanation is that Area 'H' was technically 'American soil' but it would revert to private residential use after the war. Gaynes Hall was a British Government establishment and post war it was a Borstal for young offenders. Though the hall later reverted to a private residence the field supposedly containing bodies became part of the prison complex.

Less than a year after his visit, William Colby went missing from his Washington home, in April 1996. Local authorities had little idea what happened to this seasoned sea-going man who lived his life on the ocean but he was found floating face up in a swamp on 6 May. The body was so decomposed that further analysis of what may have caused the former Director's death was deemed 'unlikely'.

A retired American officer, who at present remains unidentified, has provided a tenuous yet possible scenario for Glenn Miller's demise. The officer claims that he was stationed in England among other places during WW2 and had strong links with OSS. Remarkably, 'Officer X' as we shall call him, independently stated that Holmewood Hall and Gaynes Hall were the two locations involved in the execution although he has never met nor has any connection with the OSS researcher who was privy to Colby's assertion. 'Officer X' says that OSS shot Miller for refusing to go along with plans to smuggle some very important looted works of art to America via England. The pieces in question were wall tiles from a Russian palace that were stolen by the *SS* in 1941 and hidden somewhere in Germany until 1944 when they were moved due to the advancing allied troops. The location of the pieces were handed over to OSS operatives by a German officer who had been captured and saw this as a way to deal his way out of trouble.

'Apparently,' 'Officer X' claims, 'Miller was involved in this business from early on but it got out of control as soon as the Allies had access to Paris and certain key captured German officers. Up to December 1944 (and until well after the end of the war) a lot of *Nazi* loot made its way back to the States secretly via UK and USAAF airfields. In WW2 the smuggling of stolen *Nazi* loot was an excellent opportunity to make money. Many American officers were willing to take the chance.

'Officer X' goes on to claim that one of the 'arrangers' in the UK was Norman Baessell, the so-called passenger on the Miller flight. Also the profits from some of the loot made a good 'black budget' for the OSS to operate with. Miller wanted to back out because he thought that this particular shipment was too big in size to be able to move via the usual methods and that they might be caught. 'Officer X' says that Miller did not die in a plane but was shot by OSS and as far as he was aware much of the loot was hidden in stately homes until it could be moved stateside and that there are 'items' remaining at certain houses to this day.'

OSS and the Mafia apparently crossed swords over the recovery of European art treasures; upward of 20% of which was looted by the *Nazis*. During and after World War II the United States Government, in part through the *Safehaven Program*, sought to identify, recover and restitute *Nazi* looted assets, expending considerable resources trying to recover looted treasures. Some 823 American airmen in Troop Carrier Command were assigned to the Office of Strategic Services Art Looting Unit for flying this material back and forth. The American Commission for the Protection and Salvage of Artistic and Historic Monuments in War Areas (The Robert Commission), the US Army's intelligence units, and Monuments, Fine Arts, and Archives officers, and State Department Foreign Service officers, among others, were also engaged in efforts to identify, recover, and restitute looted art works. However, many thousands of pieces of art were never recovered by their rightful owners. As late as 1994, 16 of the 40 top paintings were still missing. In 2001 a Jewish family claimed that *Le Grand Pont*, a painting by Gustave Courbet at the Yale University Art Gallery, belonged to them and was acquired by a former *Nazi* Party member after the family fled Germany during World War II. The painting was one of 48 European artworks on long loan to Yale from Herbert Schaefer, a lawyer living in Spain who said he had bought the painting legally from a dealer in 1938. Eric Weinmann of Washington claimed his mother bought the painting in 1935 from another Jewish family at an auction in Berlin. The Weinmanns fled to England in August 1938, leaving all their possessions behind. In March 1997, Philip Saunders, editor of *Trace*, the stolen art register, stated that

There are at least 100,000 works of art still missing from the Nazi occupation.

15

SECONDS FROM SAFETY

By March 1945 the Third *Reich* was on the brink of defeat and the systematic destruction of German oil production plants, airfields and communications centres had virtually driven the *Luftwaffe* from German skies. Despite fuel and pilot shortages, Me 262 jet fighters could still be expected to put in rare attacks and during March the *Jagdevbande* made almost all enemy fighter interceptions of American heavy bombers. However, the German jets and rockets had arrived too late and in too few numbers to prevent the inevitable. On 2 March, when American bombers were dispatched to synthetic oil refineries at Leipzig, Me 262s attacked near Dresden.

On 3 March, the largest formation of German jets ever seen made attacks on the bomber formations heading for Dresden and oil targets at Ruhrland and shot down three bombers. The *Luftwaffe* seemed to have found a temporary new lease of life for that night thirty Me 410s attacked airfields in Norfolk and Suffolk. At Bury St. Edmunds at 2300 hours, the air raid warning siren was sounded. But the *Luftwaffe* had not dared to attack the bases for a year and no one took much notice. Six of the attackers were shot down, two of them by RAF Mosquitoes. The attack on Bury St. Edmunds damaged the control tower. Great Ashfield was bombed and strafed and Rattlesden, Lavenham, and Sudbury were also attacked. The intruders returned again on the night of 4 March but damage to the bases was insignificant.

The penetration by these German raiders went largely unnoticed by the inhabitants of the Suffolk coastal towns as the enemy aircraft crossed the beaches, skimming over the steep cliffs and headed inland. Ever since 1943, Fortresses and Liberators, P-47 Thunderbolts, and P-51 Mustangs of the 8th Air Force based in East Anglia had become an increasingly common sight and sound as they returned from the often costly daylight raids on the European continent. At night, sharp-eyed and attentive listeners could distinguish the unmistakable shapes and sounds of a Lancaster or Halifax.

Lowestoft, a popular seaside resort and a busy fishing port, which marks the northern end of the Suffolk Coast Path running south for 50 miles to Felixstowe, was often the gateway for these Allied and *Luftwaffe* aircraft. Lowestoft Ness has the distinction of being Britain's easternmost point. The town's prosperity began in the mid-1800s with the exploitation of the Dogger Bank and North Sea fishing grounds. The main catch was herring, which were cured in the town and sent to

London, the Midlands, and as far afield as Australia. The height of the herring boom came just before the First World War when more than 700 steam powered drifters regularly sailed from Lowestoft.[1]

B-24 Liberator and B-17 Fortress crews in the Second and Third Air Division wings in Norfolk and Suffolk well remember Lowestoft. Navigators spotted the sea-going trawlers and identified the local landmarks – the old lighthouse, the South and Claremont Piers, the sandy south beach, and the mouth of the River Waveney at Lake Lothing. Then they followed the snaking waterway feeding them into their home bases in the Waveney Valley.

Vere A. McCarty, a bombardier in the 446th Bomb Group at Bungay (Flixton), one of three groups in the 20th Combat Wing recalls:

'From the air Lowestoft was a very welcome view to see, coming home across the North Sea from its not so welcome side.'

On 14 March 1945 the bravery of a young American pilot saved Lowestoft from a tragedy of immeasurable proportions. 2/Lieutenant Robert H. Portsch, 24, from Bloomfield, New Jersey, a B-17G pilot in the 836th Bomb Squadron at Lavenham in west Suffolk was on his 14th mission. With the end of the war only weeks away, a vast armada of 1,188 B-17s and B-24s, escorted by 13 fighter groups, attacked three tank and armoured vehicle plants, two oil refineries, seven railroad marshalling yards and other targets, throughout the shrinking *Reich*. The target for the 487th Bomb Group was the marshalling yards at Hanover, Germany, and 36 Fortresses took off from Lavenham.

En route to the target Portsch's No.2 (port inner) engine began to lose power. Unable to hold position in the formation, he was forced to abort the mission while over Belgium. Eventually, when smoke began to appear, the No.2 engine had to be shut down and the propeller feathered. Portsch nursed the Fortress back across the North Sea and as he crossed Lowestoft at 1450 hours, observers on the ground saw the troublesome engine suddenly explode into flames. The burning bomber, loaded with eight 500-lb high explosive bombs and two incendiary containers, began a wide circle to the left, back toward the open sea. Parachutes were seen descending as the crew began to abandon the aircraft. The tail gunner finished up hanging

---

[1] The fishing fleet today consists of fewer than 50 motor trawlers. In World War Two, Lowestoft old town was badly damaged by German bombs. South of the bascule bridge, which spans Lake Lothing, a narrow strip of water which bisects the town in two, is the resort half of the town which was largely laid out in the 19th century by Sir Samuel Morton Peto. This builder's firm built Nelson's Column and the Houses of Parliament in London in the 1840s. Peto had built a railway so that fish could be delivered fresh from the market to Manchester.

from a lamppost in Victoria Road, Oulton Broad. The last crewman jumped safely. He related how, when last seen, his pilot had been calmly going through the procedure to set the autopilot, so that he too could bail out. The flaming bomber was by now heading for the coast, where it was hoped that it would crash harmlessly into the sea. It never made it. Instead, the Fortress rolled over and dived into a row of anti-tank blocks near Grove Farm, Carlton Colville, where it exploded into a blazing fireball. Unexploded bombs, bullets and wreckage, were strewn all around the farm, and although buildings were damaged and cattle killed, no one on the ground was injured, If the fuel and bomb-laden Fortress had crashed on the town itself, the outcome might have been completely different. Betty Larkin, 72 of Lowestoft Road, witnessed the crash.

'It just missed the houses, which was miraculous. That is why we are so thankful'

The body of Robert Portsch was found in a tree near the wreckage. He had managed to jump at the last moment, but was too low for his parachute to save him. His radio operator, S/Sergeant Douglas Seavert, also lost his life. As he jumped from the stricken B-17, he hit the tail unit and fell to earth in Dell Road without his parachute opening.

In 1986 workmen laying the footings for houses on what has since become Saxon Fields Estate, unearthed the wreckage of the wartime bomber from its resting place in a filled-in anti-tank trench. Numerous items, including a complete engine and propeller blades, were recovered and these are now displayed at the Norfolk and Suffolk Aviation Museum at Flixton, near Bungay.

To perpetuate a sense of history, and remember the men who died, five roads on the Saxon Fields Estate have been named in honour of Portsch's crew on this fateful day. They include 'Fortress Road' and 'Portsch Close.' In December 1992 Colonel Walter Berg USAF of the 81st Tactical Wing RAF Bentwaters, and his wife unveiled a memorial at the site. The memorial plaque was the brainchild of Betty Larkin's husband Cyril, and his twin brother, Claude, erected the plinth. At the ceremony Colonel Berg said:

'On 14 March 1945, two men gave their lives in the service of freedom, their country and our common cause.'

Aviation historian Bob Collis, who has pieced together the full story of the bomber and its crew, said later:

'The Carlton Colville memorial is a reminder of the price the Allied air forces paid for their victory over Nazi Germany. It is fitting that at a place, which was, in 1945, a scene of devastation after the bomber crash, a monument has been erected to honour the men who died, within what is now a new community. This memorial plaque, together with the road signs nearby, will hopefully perpetuate the memory of the loss of this Flying Fortress, and the sacrifice made by two young Americans in the cause of world freedom.'

A moving tribute to the crew who died in the B-17 crash was paid during the Lowestoft Air Show in August 1998. While thousands watched the aerial display from the seafront, Bob Collis maintained vigil at the memorial which records details of the crash in Ribbelsdale. He saw the B-17 *Sally B*, piloted by Squadron Leader Jimmy Jewell, turn inland after completing her appearance, join the display and come in to execute a banking left turn to salute 700-ft above the memorial site. With him to capture the moment on film was cameraman Bill Hansford.

Airshow controller Bernard Bagg was on the transatlantic telephone while the B-17 flew overhead to describe the scene to Dolores F. Moore of Mesa, Arizona, the sister of one of the American crewmen who lost their lives in the crash. Dolores was a child of 14 when her brother, Sergeant Douglas Seavert, fell to his death. In a poignant letter addressed to the people of Carlton Colville and Lowestoft, she had spoken of her heartfelt gratitude and sent her warm and loving thoughts.

'My brother Douglas Seavert was a quiet, sensitive young man, a quick thinker, dependable and thoughtful. I think it was because of all of these qualities he would have appreciated your remembering him and the others as you are doing today. I do. I was an immature 14-year-old when my brother died but I remember reading about the bombing of London and how sad we all felt at the suffering you endured. I know Doug would have felt that way too – he would also have been very angry.

Because of that, he would have done all he could to help end the war and being on board that B-17 was the way he chose.'

Dolores added.

'Thank you. I want you to know that we Yanks are deeply appreciative that you remember that we gave our fathers, sons and brothers in war, too. You've touched my heart with this observance.'

16

ZURICH NIGHTS

Forrest S. Clark

Forrest Clark (kneeling, left) and crew at Shipdham

'We had all nearly finished our missions and had some rough ones. The pilot, Lieutenant Rockford C. Griffith, had a particularly rough time in combat. By the time we went on the 12 April 1944 mission to Lechfeld we had cut in the roughest and most dangerous period of the 8th Air Force combat missions, the time when the *Luftwaffe* was very strong, the flak was heaviest and the losses were highest. By April-May the 8th was preparing for the invasion which was to come in June. However, when our crew was flying, the chances of surviving 25 or 20 missions were indeed slim. We had seen many of our friends go down over Germany. We lost our bombardier, Lieutenant Dave Edmonds and Sergeant Abe Sofferman, our first radio operator. Several crews we started with were gone by April 1944, victims of German fighters and *flak*. Neutral territory represented a last resort for crippled battle damaged bombers and crews. Saving aircraft was important also. Crashing in enemy territory or exploding in the air was not a way to salvage aircraft. Switzerland and Sweden always represented last resorts for first we would try to bring our planes back to our home bases.

'I had suffered frostbite, sinusitis, combat stress, and injuries to my back and legs in combat flying. But I was determined to go on. I had crashed, parachuted and narrowly missed being hit by enemy fighter fire. But to try to make it over 600 miles of enemy territory in a shot up bomber losing fuel by the gallons would have been foolhardy and costly in manpower and in equipment. There is no question that we would not have made it and would have crashed or exploded in mid-air. I fired off distress flares to alert the Swiss Air Force but we had to make an emergency landing at Dubendorf near Zürich. Our plane received four bursts of *flak* as we passed over the German-Swiss border. One of these *flak* bursts wounded Sergeant Harold Harmon, one of our waist gunners. As soon as we got down armed soldiers surrounded our plane, one pointing a gun at my head. I thought we had come down in Germany.

'Examples of American planes being shot at by the Swiss were commonplace. On 13 April a Swiss fighter shot down a B-17G of the 447th Bomb Group. The crew bailed out. On 24 April three Swiss fighters attacked a B-17G in the 384th Bomb Group. The bomber was set on fire and two crewmen killed. Perhaps the most famous of all these cases was that of a 389th Bomb Group B-24H on 5 September 1944. P-51s managed to shoot down Swiss fighters after they appeared to be attacking the bomber. Strange things happened in the stress and confusion of combat. In the months following the airwar in Europe General Hap Arnold investigated every US aircraft that went into Swiss territory and could not find one instance where a bomber or fighter diverted to Switzerland without just and compelling cause. I saw several battle-damaged B-17s and B-24s at Dubendorf so I know it was true.

T.Sgt Forrest Clark

'Zürich was an international crossroads of spies, intrigue and danger for all. One never knew who one was talking to or if they were carrying information for one side or the other in the conflict. One can imagine American airmen dressed in civilian clothes sitting at cafes, many accompanied by Swiss or German girls, while across the floor sat German officers, Swiss military and diplomatic officials and couriers for most of the Allied and Axis powers. To complicate matters we had no status as American airmen in Zürich and if caught we would be turned in to the proper Swiss authorities for discipline or jail. Information could be sold or bartered for any price on which depended human lives and perhaps the destruction of armies and cities. For me Zürich represents a deadly, yet enchanting interlude in World War II.

'Zürich had a huge railroad station, an ornate beaux-arts type architectural structure, fronted by a vast plaza, the *Bahnhofplatz*. From this hub point several avenues extended outward in all directions. Of course the most famous of these was the very chic shopping avenue, the *Bahnhofstrasse*, running from the platz to the *Zurichsee*. Brightly coloured tramcars ran down the middle of this avenue. At the dock at the far end there were gaily-flagged excursion boats ready to take people out on the lake. In the distance, at the far end of the lake, one could see the lofty snow-capped peaks of the Swiss Alps, a dramatic backdrop to the city of Zürich.

'There were quite a few pro-Germans in Switzerland, some even openly vocal. In the *bahnhof* (railway station) at Zürich where we caught a train for Adelboden with our Swiss guards a woman shouted, "You American gangsters."

'We had two commanders in each camp. One was the American commander, usually a major or a captain of an aircrew. But he was subservient to the Swiss Commandant who had to approve all orders. And the American commander had to go to the Swiss to get final approvals of policies. The Swiss never gave up their control and were paid per diem for each internee by the American government. So they were cleaning up on the Americans.

'We were billeted in the best hotels, while the British had other and the Italians inferior quarters. The Germans were in a barn. The Italians became the barbers of the camps and the Germans the most neglected. Many Italians were deserters from the Italian army and lived in a camp in Mürren while the South Africans and Aussies were mostly from the battles in North Africa who had escaped and made their way into Switzerland.

'During the time I was in Swiss camps I always wanted to get out because I realized what a great country the US was and how different living in an enforced isolation was. It was a kind of splendid isolation or enforced paradise.

'Another American airman, Carl (not his real name), spoke German well and looked like a German or Swiss. He was a good one to escape with. We met in Zürich posing as Swiss students. Carl and I, Louise and her girlfriend, Inga, two girls we had met, enjoyed the sights of the city, the nightclubs, and the opulent casinos, kursaals and the Corso as well as the numerous smokey cafes. Although known as a quite conservative city, home to Europe's banking interests and laced with a historic undercurrent of orthodox religion, Zürich had its underbelly, its underworld. It was into this underworld that we delved in the winter of 1944.

'Some days Louise and I split off from Carl and went our own romantic way. We used to ride the trains, kissing each other in embraces that attracted the attentions of the staid and reserved Swiss. On other days we were passengers on the lake steamers where the invigorating air and intoxicating motion of the water enhanced our romantic tendencies and we often spent the entire cruise locked in each other's arms. We passed the famous Baur au Lac Hotel, one of the world's outstanding hotels, founded in 1844. It faces the lakefront with its gaily-lighted façade sending streamers of coloured lights across the water.

'Most of the time Carl and I were on the loose in the city dressed as Swiss and dodging the Swiss authorities so it was a question of hiding our American airmen identities. We each carried phoney Swiss ID cards and passports, made out in German. Actually, the gaiety of the city masked extreme dangers. We frequented many of the student cafes, the small patisseries, the piano bars and hotel lounges of the city, drinking the middle European wines, the heady cognac, the schnapps, the beer, and trying our luck at the lakefront casinos. I remember the delicious Swiss minced veal and roast potatoes served steaming hot. It was here one night a particularly frightening episode occurred that remains burned in memory.

'There was a huge and Baroque casino on the *Zurichsee* not far from the tram lines where the elite of Zürich, the bankers, the brokers, the intelligentsia, the spies, counter spies and officialdom gathered. This particular night I recall there were several tables of Swiss and German officials, *Nazi* officers and diplomats sitting in one section of the nightclub. On a raised stage at one end overlooking the lake through huge glass windows, a troupe of dancers was performing. Some of the dancers, young Swiss and German girls were nearly nude. At the opposite end of the hall near the dressing room for the dancers, a line of officers awaited the girls as they came off their performances. Many were there to ask favours of the girls, to ask them to accompany them after the show. There was a larger spiral stairway leading up to the dressing rooms.

'I had left Louise at one of the tables and was ascending this stairway when a black man blocked my way momentarily. Recognizing me for one of the internees he clapped me on my back, raised his hand to grasp mine in a handshake and said too loudly, "What are you doing here? Don't you know it's past curfew?"

'I was taken back and could not reply at first. I realized in a flash that his greeting of recognition and welcome had signalled to all about that I was an American internee. I tried to dispel this by replying in French but it was no good. He still recognized me. I recognized him as an American from one of the internment camps in the Bernese Oberland. To make things worse, standing nearby well within hearing was a group of ranking Swiss or German officers. I could see from their uniforms the bulge where I was sure a German Luger was holstered. Just as I reached forward to grasp the hand of my fellow GI, a pack of American *Lucky Strikes* popped out of my coat pocket. Immediately I knew the officers recognized me as an American. One of them I remember wore the wings of a *Luftwaffe* officer on his grey tunic.

'We stared at each other for a very long time, a flicker of fear from my side and what I detected as a brief flame of hatred from him, passed between us. For one long painful moment I relived all those aerial battles, the sights and sounds of flaming aircraft spiralling down, the smells of gunfire, and the rattle and crack of flak against our bomber. Here was the enemy staring at me on a crowded stairway in an entertainment palace far from the bloody skies over *Nazi* Germany. For one second I imagined he would reach for his side arm and I would be looking down at a very lethal Luger pointed at my head. I didn't want to create an international incident.

'Then he turned away toward the others and engaged them in conversation. I am sure to this day that he knew who I was and where I came from. I did not wait for another such encounter but grabbed Louise and left the casino. As we did so the band struck up a German dance tune, which, as all such tunes, evoked a sense of military precision. I caught a glimpse of the dance floor and saw the officer with his fellows dancing with the Swiss *frauleins*.

'It was the habit of the time for the orchestras to play patriotic theme songs identified with certain national states. Strangely enough the *Beer Barrel Polka* was associated with the Germans. One tune that has haunted me all the intervening years was a French tune, *J'Attendrai*, meaning "I shall wait for you". Months later I stood in the doorway of a small bistro in Lyons and heard this song while French resistance fighters sat nearby. It may have been sung by that legendary chanteuse of the wartime years, Edith Piaf. This tune comes drifting across the years and space from the war to me yet. The casino has vanished, even the *Zurichsee* is not the same, the tram cars have changed, the sparkling air from the mountain passes has faded, but "*J"Attendrai*" remains as fresh and evocative as ever. Such is the magic and power, the cloying haunting erotic beauty of that time that it is preserved in a kind of memory aspic for eternity.

'I stayed with a few American internees in Zürich at a small *pension* in the suburban town of Baden, noted for its ancient baths. Under many of the hotels, medicinal spring baths provided a resort diversion as they have since Roman times. I recall staying in one such hotel and taking the train into Zürich's *Hauptbahnhof*, a trip of about 35 minutes, several times coming home in the early morning hours, crossing the ancient town square and circling the large ornate stone fountain in the centre, drunkenly singing "Deep in the Heart of Texas".

'One of my friends, after a particularly wild weekend in Zürich and too much schnapps, tried walking across a glass roof over a solarium to reach his hotel room. He fell through the glass to the consternation of the Swiss concierge and hotel guests. Next morning the offending American was taken away by two Swiss guards and thrown in the local jail.

'Baden was much as it had been for centuries, a small resort or spa town. It is not far distant from the German border and there were many German partisans in the vicinity. We also went to Winterthur for a tour of a local steel foundry, part of the Brown Boveri Works.

'However, it was Zürich, which held the festive spotlight for many reasons, not the least of which was the eligible Swiss females seeking adventure. At one party, there were five to six girls and just two or three Americans. This meant that there were two girls for each of us or perhaps three who could be passed around amongst us. We had two girls in each room of a rather large apartment in the city. The party night was long and drunken. Someone must have laced the drinks with narcotics because all of us fell asleep and when we woke, found that our Swiss francs were missing along with our American cigarettes. I remember being in one room alone but when I awoke there were two girls on either side of me in the bed; they too must have passed out. However, the rest were gone along with the Swiss money. It is surprising that so much decadence existed side by side with mass murders, destruction of cities and the holocaust.

'As darkness alongside light makes the light appear even more brilliant, so the horrors of war existing close by so much gaiety and abandon enhanced the latter in our youthful minds. Added to this was the fact that we were evading our guards, our keepers in the alleys, the avenues and vastness of the city. Often we would have to make a very hasty retreat from some cafe when we spied Swiss guards entering. We would go out a back door and run down darkened streets until we were sure they were lost behind us. This merely added to the zest of the incident.

'The Swiss had set up disciplinary camps for internees who tried to escape and whom border guards caught. These were harsh camps, approximating prisoner of war compounds, complete with barbed wire, guard towers and dogs. We had all heard stories about the living conditions in these camps and it was common knowledge that armed guards patrolled the borders. We knew our best hope of escape was through underground channels developed by the American embassy and the French *Maquis*, aided by a few Swiss sympathetic to internees. In Zürich, there was a little talk about these escape routes but the average Swiss citizen knew nothing of this and was largely unaware of the internees. Zürich was a forbidden paradise to us, a place where being anonymous gave us the only small chance for release of our tensions, fears and passions.

'The Swiss retained their banking interests as the world's bankers. It was here that many feared the loot of many nations was banked. Also it was in Zürich that spies and operatives of the Allies and the *Axis* powers planned the capitulation of Fascist Italy and the overthrow of Mussolini. However, Zürich had a past of intrigue and revolution as well as art and culture. It was in Zürich that Lenin started his long journey back to Russia to install the Russian Communist state after the Czars, and it was in Zürich that the Dada Movement in art and literature began as well as many of the works of James Joyce. Klee and Giacometti, and a host of other artists, used it as a base. Expatriate artists and writers walked its streets, and perhaps dreamed of their works, sitting at outdoor cafes on springtime days and evenings.

'My most vivid memories of the city are of the tramcars sweeping down the

Bahnhofstrasse, to the *Burkliplatz*, and the *Quai* of the *Zurichsee* where boats rode at anchor. Across the square flowers decked the outdoor terraces where diners took in the view across the lake to the distant Alps. It was all so very bright and light after the darkness of the British countryside and the blacked-out cities. Carl and I acquired the habit of knowing where the gayest afternoon cafe concerts were held and of mixing with the crowds of shop girls, students, office clerks and shoppers. It was at one of these concerts that we encountered for the first time another fantasy, the mysterious "coyotes" who bartered with the enemy in human lives. It was another example of the dark side of Zürich hidden beneath the brilliance of the surface gloss.

'While seated at a table a cab-driver approached and said in nearly perfect English that he would be willing to tell us how to escape from Switzerland if we would buy him a couple of drinks. After a considerable time bantering back and forth, he said that he was prepared to give us a guarantee of safe conduct but it would cost us a fee of 100 Swiss francs. We listened intently to him and gave him no indication of disbelief. Carl and I knew he was a "coyote" but we said nothing to make him believe we knew his scheme. We should have reported him but we did not as we were more intent that day on getting on with our girls. Romance and love, sex and desire filled us and we had no thoughts of escape at that time. After hearing his story in full, we told him we were not interested. However, it was not to be our last encounter with the coyotes. Fate had other surprises in store for us in this foreign city by the lake.

'Europe was occupied almost completely by the *Nazi* armies. Switzerland was an island within a continent of cruelty and hate. One had to cross several hundred miles of enemy-occupied territory to reach freedom. Yet the resolves of some of the internees, coupled with the powerful pull of home and the USA was so strong they overcame these hardships. Through their resolve and dedication to honour many returned. It was the patriotic thing to do to escape as a gesture of devotion to country and our cause against the enemy. Waiting out the war was difficult for many youthful internees therefore they risked their lives to get out. Sam Woods, an official of the American embassy in Switzerland based in the Zürich area, managed to help some internees escape through an open pipeline that led into liberated France with the aid of French underground operatives. His is a little known story of the heroism of the period, the heroism of internees, officials of the Allies and the daring and ingenuity of resistance forces. We knew of a case where internees dressed as women evaded the border guards and got across.

'One of the stranger episodes was told by Sergeant Krajewski a Polish American who was interned with us at Adelboden. He volunteered to work at burial details for some of the 62 Americans killed on Swiss soil. One day he noted that a certain convoy truck arrived at the burial site and he asked about it only to be informed in private that it was taking internees to the border under the pretence of delivering burial supplies, coffins, etc. Krawjeski hopped on the truck one day and found himself dropped on the shore of Lake Geneva. There he met a group of Polish troops escaping to France and was put in charge of them because he spoke Polish. Under cover of darkness they rowed across the lake to the French side only to find the boats had sprung a leak and were sinking. They had to swim to save their lives.

'We had many Americans try to ski out over the Alps but the Swiss had such trained ski troops that they caught 99 percent of them. We also had cases where airmen paid informers or contacts large sums of Swiss francs to get them out only to find the contacts were phoney ones and they never saw them again.

'One British Army man I met in Adelboden told me of a scheme he had to escape posing as a Swiss postal worker on the little postal bus that went from village to village and into Fruitigen and the rail line into Berne. I liked his idea but it has one hitch – we had to speak Swiss-German well and I did not. This British soldier had fought at El Alamein and in the desert but he knew little or nothing about hiking over the Alps. He was a good drinking companion but not much of an escape artist. I remember one who always wore the British army khakis who wanted to take a uniform with him in a knapsack to France. I am sure the Swiss put secret plain clothes men in our camp posing as friendly civilians to discover our escape plans.

'One of my crew, Sergeant Earl Parrish, paid a Swiss to get him out but the Swiss took his money and never showed up. Jack Harmon made friends with a Swiss girl and was called in before the commandant and told she was a German informer and he must break off from her. At that point he said he wanted to escape. Even more dramatically, Sergeant Warren Shattuck and I plotted an escape route one night in the hotel but unknown to us a Swiss informant must have discovered our plan and two days later some internees who tried the same route were captured. So there were spies and informants listening. You could trust no one.

'Early on the morning of 6 June 1944 I was rousing myself from sleep in a hotel high up in the Alps. We had to fall out for a roll call at the command of our officers and the Swiss commandant. It was a warm spring day and the alpine flowers were blooming on the mountain passes and meadows. Later I went into the village of Adelboden to check on some of my fellow internees who used to gather at the favourite village coffee house on the main street. It was about 11 am when one of my fellow internees flicked on a radio as we sat in the outdoor cafe. We began to hear reports of some kind of a military action in western France but it was not clear what it was. One had to tune to the Yugoslav free radio at that time to get the most accurate war reports because the German radio, Radio Berlin, could certainly not be relied on. For hours we listened to these reports but could not make much of them. This went on for two days and nights until finally on the third day it became apparent that this was no minor military action and indeed, it was the long sought invasion of Europe itself.

'"Can it really be true?" one of my friends said. Then something wonderful happened that I shall never forget. When this news had gained recognition, the bells of our small stone church in the middle of the village began to ring across the peaceful alpine meadows and kept on ringing for hours. Americans, British, and many other allied national internees came from all directions heading for the small village church summoned by the bells. It was quite an impressive sight to see these men, many of them battle hardened veterans of the North African and Italian campaigns, coming together. Others had been in the airwar over Germany and many had lost comrades to *flak* and enemy fighters. Once inside the church the Swiss pastor gave prayers for the men who were at that very moment facing the beachheads and the deadly fire of the enemy. He also prayed for the success of the offensive and for the leaders of the allied nations. This did not meet with favour by the village and canton authorities who maintained a strict neutrality. The German radio continued to minimize the military assault on Normandy and in the initial days of the attack broadcast reports that the invaders had been thrown back into the sea and defeated.

The Germans were giving exaggerated numbers for Allied losses and minimal losses for the defending German armies. Apparently the civil authorities in Berne and elsewhere had decreed there was to be a neutral posture by the civilian government to the invasion although many Swiss welcomed and supported it. However, the church was a different matter, and in some cases the clergy made little effort to hide its support for the invasion and the prospect it might bring an end to the war and following that, peace. I am sure many Swiss joined us in prayers. To hear the bells and to remember that they rang for one of the great military assaults in history that was taking place in that spring time was one of the most inspiring experiences of my young life.

'Most of us had to wait until Allied troops reached the French-Swiss border before getting out. However, D-Day gave us the hope that we would survive the war, the hope that we would make it home and back to our units. When the first news of the invasion was confirmed and appeared to be a success, Americans and

British internees started taking off to try to escape across the border of Switzerland and France. Many were captured and sent to harsh discipline camps for the rest of the war.

'In mid August 1944 the Americans got news that the Swiss were going to divide the group, sending the officers to Davos and the enlisted men to Wengen. I fell into the group to Wengen, which turned out to be even more escape proof than Adelboden. The reason given for this move was that the Americans were causing too much trouble in the village and the Swiss wanted to split up the crews.

'Wengen was a horrible place to get out of because there was only one way, a cog railway from Lauterbrunnen and Interlachen. It was a drop of several thousand feet down to Interlachen. All exit ways were guarded.

'In the winter of 1944, Carl and I became increasingly convinced that we should try to make it out by Christmas but we were too involved with the girls to make any definite plan and contacts. However one night in Zürich our romantic episode came to a dramatic and frightening halt.

'The Swiss Alps beguiled the poets of the Romantic Movement in Europe. The Bible speaks to us of the strength that comes to our souls from the eternal mountains. Shelley, Byron, Thomas Mann, and many others tell us in literature of the romantic power and mystic aura of these mountains. Hans Castrop in the *Magic Mountain* travelled the same route to Davos as that taken years later by the internees. We were all cast under the spell of the mountains: the effect of the womb-like enclosure of those mighty peaks shutting out the world of war and horror. The beauty inspired by the mountains uplifted many and seduced others.

'Carl and I were also under the spell of Switzerland, and its seductions and much of this was transferred to the girls of Zürich during those spell-bound nights in the city of Zwingli. Perhaps unknown to us we were drawing a kind of spiritual nourishment from nature's wonders. Despite the sex, the drinking, the seductions, the temptations, the parties, the escapades, the thrills of evasion, the atmosphere and scenery gave a spiritual dimension to the experience. Therefore, it was doubly difficult for us to turn away and to seek escape from these beguilements to both spirit and body.

'Whatever it is that makes wartime experiences enduring and redeeming, if they ever could possibly be, above all it is the sense of survival, a sense so strong that it approaches in intensity that of a religious conversion. To survive a war is like being born again, given a second chance, a chance at life over again. Out of this mélange of seduction and liberation came, slowly at first but more rapidly as time passed, the conviction in us to escape, to grasp the chance, perhaps our last chance.

Therefore, as the final weeks of 1944 passed into history, we decided to make the break. However, we had to have a plan. For a long time, we had none. Then one day I happened to be going through the pockets of my trousers and found, crumpled into a wad, the note with the address in Berne. It was in the note dropped in the cafe by an unknown person. That address was for the American Legation in Berne. That was when we decided to try to reach it.

'The final impetus came one night when Carl and I were in Louise and Inga's apartment sitting at the kitchen table having a few drinks when out of one bedroom a dishevelled figure ran, clutching his clothing. I saw at once that he held in his hand the bluish green tunic of a German officer. He uttered a few words in German and, putting on his pants, made it through the door to the corridor still half undressed. I knew immediately that the girls had been entertaining German and Swiss officers in the city. There was a knock on the door and a cry of *Polize*. Louise went to answer the door and I shouted to Carl,

"Let's get out of here".

'As we did I glanced down at the table and saw a German Army luger pistol. I knew at that moment that it was a matter of life and death to make a clean getaway from the apartment. We jumped out the bathroom window, down a narrow alley-way and into the street. We ran like we were pursued by the devil. I could hear the police whistle as it got nearer and nearer. We ran for several blocks until we thought we were far enough from the apartment.

"Wow, what do you think of that?" said Carl.

"I think it was a close call for us," I replied still breathless from the run.

"Not only for us but if we had been caught it would have meant a mass roundup of all internees in the city," said Carl.

"What did that German say?" I asked. I knew that Carl understood German.

"He said that he had been robbed and he was mad," said Carl. "That's as much as I could make out."

"Robbed" I said, "By the girls. Okay, that figures. We would have been next."

I remembered then that the night before I was in one bedroom and opened the door to see one of the girls make a dash for the bathroom.

"I'll bet they had the money stashed in that apartment somewhere and they also knew we had been paid the week before at camp.

"I think they were working for some coyotes," said Carl, "and splitting the bounty for each GI they turned over to the Germans."

"Should we report this to our officers?" I asked.

"The less said the better," Carl replied. "Besides I'm not reporting this to any chickenshit officer. We might get thrown in a Swiss jail or detention camp or worse."

'We jumped into a cab at the station. Off we went into the darkness: we did not know where. There was something suspicious about the cab driver and we didn't want to end up in a German stalag. We decided not to risk it and at a curve in the road where the cab had to slow down we opened the door and jumped out into a roadside ditch. The cab never returned for us. Luckily we were near the railway and walked back to the train and took it to our billet in Baden. That did it. It was certain now that we were getting out of Switzerland at any cost. We set our goal as freedom by Christmas 1944. We devised a daring plan of escape over the Alps but as in all of the best-laid plans of desperate men, they often go awry.

'We never went back to the girls' apartments but we did go to the little cafe where we had met many of the Swiss girls. A strange thing happened on our last night there. I think it was a little bar and lounge, which I shall call the Simplon, a few blocks from the Zürich Bahnhof. After we had taken a table near the dance floor with some other Americans, the small string orchestra that played for the afternoon and evening tea dances struck up the Swiss and American national anthems. That was most strange, we thought, because we were not supposed to be known there and had carefully concealed our identities. Just at that moment a Swiss civilian got up and in a drunken manner offered a toast pointing his wineglass at our table. It was a touchy and a touching moment. In all of WWII Europe at that time there probably was no stranger incident than a Swiss musical group of a neutral country serenading Americans with their national anthem while a mixed crowd of neutrals and likely some enemy officers and agents sat close by. We said nothing and acknowledged nothing but the point had been made and made forcefully to all present. We interpreted it as a tribute by the Swiss to the American and Allied cause in the war against *Nazi* Germany at that time. The Swiss were clever and mercenary enough to have realized that the Allies were winning the war by that time and yet a few years before it would have been a different situation. *C'est la guerre*, as the French say.

'I prefer to think that in some unspoken way that incident showed that the Swiss had already to a large extent placed their allegiances with the Allied cause against their neighbour *Nazi* Germany.

'We began to hear rumours of Americans and British getting out of Switzerland through Geneva but we were in Zürich in a very pro-German part of Switzerland. The area about Geneva was mostly pro-French. As the allied armies neared the Swiss border the rumours increased.

'We knew we had to cross some of the most impassable mountains in Europe, the Alps, and also that even when we got over the border there was an uncertain, dangerous and highly fluid situation with holdout German pockets of resistance, trigger-happy Maquis, communists, Vichy French and the advance of a victorious Allied army mopping up as it moved. Christmas in the USA looked too good to us and the decision was made. It was to be a daring plan to try to escape in the dead of an alpine winter. We did know one or two things. One was that the US Seventh Army had pushed the Germans up the Rhone valley as far as Lyons and near the Swiss-French border. The other fact was that we knew it would be only a matter of time before we would be picked up and sent to a disciplinary camp by the Swiss. We had no alternative but try to escape.

'We learned from a tip off that if we got to the American Legation we could get out of Switzerland. Sam Woods, the American consul, had got some American airmen out to France. We could not do it without the aid of the American legation staff. One of the unsolved mysteries of this period is that while General Legge was urging and actually ordering internees to stay in the camps, the legation staff in Berne were assisting them to get out. After the war there was an investigation and it was found that about half of the internees did escape before 8th May of 1945, the official V-E Day.

'We went by rail from Zürich to Berne under armed guard and at Berne we asked the guard commandant for a rest stop. Once outside the station we escaped and took a taxi to the American Legation. We were constantly in fear we would be discovered and turned back. I never could understand why the guards did not come back and search for us at the Berne railway station. Then when I saw that station years later I understood. Perhaps they did not notice our escape until the train started on its way to Adelboden. I remember how the guards would count off the internees by the numbers in German.

'I learned after the war that the girls from Zürich had gone to the internee camp, obviously to see what had happened to us, but were told we must have escaped.

'After four days we were placed in a sealed moving van and driven to the border near Geneva where we met our French underground guides for the trip across the mountains. The Swiss army guards were told to shoot at any escaping Americans and they were known to have done so. We walked for two days, hiding by day, and walking by night to the border where we crossed and hid in a French farmhouse. We were told to wait for our contact to pick us up. At dawn we started walking to the nearest town. There were snipers about and mine fields. We almost walked into a minefield. It was very cold and snowing. Finally, we were picked up by US 7th

Army patrols and taken to Annecy, in the Haute Savoie. From there we went by army convoys to Lyons and there we were debriefed. We were flown to Paris and on to Harrington where all POWs and Internees were sent. I was back at Shipdham in January 1945. I left Carl when we got back to the UK and never saw him again. I never found out who our guides were or exactly where the farmhouse was. Then it was off to Prestwick and return to the USA. I landed in New York around 15 January 1945.'

Epilogue

Four months later, the fighting in Europe ended and VE Day was 8 May. Some 55,500 aircrew in Bomber Command were killed in action or flying accidents, or died on the ground or while prisoners of war. Approximately 125,000 aircrew served in the front-line, OTU and OCUs of the Command and nearly 60 per cent of them became casualties. In addition, almost 9,900 more were shot down and made POWs to spend one, two or more years in squalid, desolate *oflags* and *stalags* in Axis held territory. Over 8,000 more were wounded aboard aircraft on operational sorties. The American air forces in the ETO December 1941-August 1945 suffered 63,410 casualties, or 52 per cent of the total air force losses in all theatres of war. This was the highest loss of any US theatre of operations. Of these, 19,876 men were killed and 35,121 MIA. 8,413 were wounded and 90,000 US airmen were taken prisoner of war by Germany.

VE Day